Baines's Baobabs – Kudiakau Pan   Paul Augustinus

DESERT ADVENTURE

IN SEARCH OF WILDERNESS IN
NAMIBIA AND BOTSWANA

Camping wild in Damaraland - Paul Augustinus

DESERT ADVENTURE

IN SEARCH OF WILDERNESS IN
NAMIBIA AND BOTSWANA

PAUL AUGUSTINUS

SWAN·HILL
PRESS

To Clarissa

Threebanded Plovers

Copyright © 1997 Paul Augustinus

First published in the UK in 1998
by Swan Hill Press, an imprint of Airlife Publishing Ltd

First published in South Africa by Acorn Books CC

British Library Cataloguing in Publication Data
A catalogue record for this book
is available from the British Library

ISBN 1 85310 981 9

Printed in Hong Kong

Swan Hill Press
an imprint of Airlife Publishing Ltd
101 Longden Road, Shrewsbury, SY3 9EB, England

CONTENTS

Desert lions on the Skeleton Coast at the Kunene mouth

FOREWORD

What makes a wildlife artist tick? Is it the desire to paint in a genre that has a huge potential market? Or is it perhaps the desire to be out and about in wild places – and art is simply the means of getting there? The fact is that today there are so many people who collect paintings of the natural world that this has attracted the attention of many artists who, although interested in wildlife, are certainly not passionate about it. These 'wannabes' crave the success, and prices, garnered by the really great wildlife artists, but have, however, no wish to spend ten years in some remote part of Africa. The result is that bad wildlife art has become a successful growth industry – harsh words but true.

Paul Augustinus's work is certainly not part of this wave of mediocre 'commercial' art; instead, he is an artist who has, above all else, loved travel and adventure. *Desert Adventure*, the artist's description of a year-long "journey through a wide cross-section of the African wildlife experience", is essentially about wilderness and, most importantly, what is happening to it. At face value, it is a comprehensive narrative, vividly illustrated with superb paintings, drawings and photographs of the fascinating places found in the desert country of the Namib and the Kalahari. There is, however, much more to the book, for it is also the story of an artist's love for a rapidly vanishing wilderness, which is here expressed in words and pictures to form a unique record of its beauty for posterity.

This love of wild places was born long before Paul Augustinus had developed his artistic talent for painting. He grew up in Kenya, Tanzania and Zimbabwe and, after working briefly as a geologist, was drawn to the wild northern reaches of Botswana to experience for himself what he was convinced were the last days of wilderness in Africa. He was not, as is the case with many artists nowadays, trained as a commercial artist who would then work in the advertising field before becoming qualified in 'fine' art. Instead, he graduated with a BSc. Degree in geology from the University of Natal before venturing to spend eight years under canvas in the wilds of Botswana, amid the splendours of the Linyanti, Chobe, Okavango and in the Ngwezumba Valley. Here his artistic talent was honed and heightened by the sights and sounds that surrounded him – the sights and sounds of a rapidly disappearing African wilderness. His first book, *Botswana, A Brush with the Wild*, tells a part of the story.

During all those years in Botswana, Paul constantly strove to develop his career as a credible wildlife artist – with the emphasis on the 'wild' in wildlife! In an effort to distance himself from the more clichéd aspects of the genre, Paul tells me that he has never considered himself to be a wildlife artist. Indeed, he exclaims: "Please don't call me a wildlife artist – I am a wilderness artist!"

In Paul's own words: "A love of Africa first and foremost, and then a BSc., have made me what I am today. At university, maths, chemistry, geology, and especially physics taught me to understand, rather than simply observe, the phenomena of nature. For example, an understanding of physics explains exactly how water refracts and reflects light. Now, with these principles in mind, I can paint almost anything – water of varying depths rippling over a sandy bed, or reflections on a calm surface – and get it looking just right. Although many artists would vehemently disagree, I am convinced that painting is essentially one of the sciences."

After a decade of camping under canvas, constantly surrounded by elephants and lions, 'wilderness artist' is a title he well deserves – he has earned it the hard way! In the course of his travels, he has been pursued and 'treed' by lions, charged by a leopard while on foot, and is one of the few people I know who has had his vehicle savaged by elephants not just once but twice – on both occasions in a remote area, a hundred kilometres from help.

I have known Paul for more than ten years, and have followed, with avid interest, his development and watched him mature into what he is today. He has always been willing to absorb the constructive criticism of his mentors and patrons – something which very few artists are prepared or able to do.

After a successful début auction at Christie's in London in 1994, Paul's paintings were again present at the second Wildlife Art Auction, in association with the World Wide Fund for Nature (WWF) in 1995. In his foreword to the catalogue for this sale, HRH Prince Philip, Duke of Edinburgh, President of WWF, writes: "In spite of the development of urban-industrial communities during the last two hundred years, many artists are still inspired by subjects from the world of nature and their work still strikes a chord with the discerning collector. This catalogue contains items created during the last two hundred years by successful wildlife artists and sculptors from around the world. . . . I am delighted to acknowledge that Christie's are making a donation of a proportion of the proceeds of this sale to WWF. I can only hope that the people who buy these works of art will be inspired to support the efforts that are being made to prevent any further extinction of wild species of plants and animals." These words undoubtedly sum up my personal feelings and those of many others who have a sincere concern for the preservation of what little is left unspoiled on this fragile globe we know as our 'world'.

Also in 1995 Paul Augustinus put together a solo exhibition at the Everard Read Gallery in Johannesburg which was a resounding success and completely sold out, only going to prove that all those years of painstaking dedication, together with the 'blood, sweat and tears', were worth it. Paul Augustinus has 'made it' in a manner which satisfies both his inner soul and that of the discerning art buyer.

In his continuing quest to see and experience the diminishing wildlife habitat, and in order to further consolidate his desire to be Africa's foremost adventurer/wilderness artist, Paul undertook, in December 1995 and January 1996, a five-week foot reconnaissance safari into the last undisturbed tracts of the Congo's rainforest with its pristine population of wildlife. These forests, vast and trackless, have remained in this state because of the hostile nature of the environment, which is

unhealthy for man and extremely humid. Only the forest fringes are inhabited by pygmies, and these hunter-gatherers were to be his guides. Paul and his wife Clarissa, along with twelve pygmies, spent five weeks roaming the dark primary forests in search of the lowland gorilla, forest elephant and bongo. Paul's goal was to complete paintings in oil on canvas of these secretive animals in situ. Eight-hour walks, often knee-deep in water or mud, were the norm every day. Parasites infested their legs and their bodies were covered with the stings and bites of tsetse flies, hippo flies, ants and hornets! However, as if sent to uplift this encounter with hell itself, many close sightings of gorillas, chimpanzees, bongo antelope and buffalo made the experience worthwhile. Their meagre food supplies were augmented by their guides, who hunted duikers, monkeys and bush pigs. The trip was a tremendous success and yielded the next generation of material in Paul's visual chronicle of an Africa that few artists have taken the time or trouble to experience at first hand. This journey was also the logical conclusion to their travels as told in *Desert Adventure*.

The results of this trip are four truly superb paintings, executed under conditions that defy description. When the painting of the forest elephant was complete, however, Paul had also achieved another long-standing goal: he had become the first artist actually to paint in the field, on canvas, finished paintings of savanna elephants, desert-dwelling elephants (as described in this book), and forest elephants.

Paul has also camped in the pristine wilderness of Alaska. Here he and Clarissa were flown in and left to walk across mountain ridges, snow-covered volcanoes and tundra plains where wolf packs roamed. Thus, grizzly bears, mountain sheep and caribou were added to his artistic repertoire.

Self-imposed goals are indeed what set Paul Augustinus apart from others, and that difference stands out in all his endeavours – whether it be film-making, photography, or painting, a sense of the thrill of travelling in special and unusual places comes through to captivate the reader or viewer. This book is not just about wild and wonderful places, it is also about adventure – a desert adventure.

It is my wish that all who hold this book will experience the magic that Paul has so evocatively created with his knowledgeable writing, superb paintings and

Porters fording a stream on a Congo rainforest foot-safari
P.A

ACKNOWLEDGEMENTS

Sketching Dall sheep in Alaska
P. A.

My thanks are due, first, to the Everard Read Gallery for bringing their demanding standards of excellence to bear on my work for all the years of our association.

Thanks, too, to Steve Bales of First National Bank for his insightful comments and advice, especially as my style has been changing over the last five years, and for his kindness in agreeing to write the foreword.

Many people have been involved in helping us in our travels and in the preparation of this book.

My thanks go to the Namibian Government for the permissions granted during our stay in that beautiful country.

To Rod and Sigi Braby, much appreciation is due for their hospitality at Möwe Bay and for letting us be a part of some of their adventures on the Skeleton Coast.

Much gratitude must also go to Garth Owen-Smith and Margaret Jacobsohn for their advice on the Kaokoveld and their introduction to the Brabys.

To Wilderness Safaris and Colin Bell, as well as Chris Kruger in Maun, many thanks for all the help in Ngamiland.

Special thanks to Chris and Karen MacIntyre for their hospitality in Maun and help over many years.

A heartfelt 'thank you' to Eleanor-Mary Cadell of Acorn Books for having skilfully steered me through the interminable and sometimes frustrating process that is called 'writing a book'!

Finally, I should like to thank all the people in Namibia and Botswana we met along the way, who made our 'desert adventure' such a memorable experience.

photography. I salute him for his forbearance, dedication to 'the cause', and his very real concern for the continued well-being of all those wonderful things which, it seems, humanity is so intent on eroding into oblivion through ignorance and greed.

May this *Desert Adventure* remind us all of our responsibility to preserve what is left for future generations to appreciate.

Steve Bales
Group Art Custodian
First National Bank Group
Johannesburg, February 1997

Paul Augustinus

AT THE EDGE OF THE WILDERNESS

"During the four months that I was absent from my men," wrote C. J. Andersson in the 1850s, "I travelled either alone or accompanied by a single native, sometimes on foot, and at others on horse-back or ox-back, over upwards of a thousand miles of country, parts of it emulating the Sahara in scarcity of water and general inhospitality. Tongue is too feeble to express what I suffered at times. To say nothing of narrow escapes from lions and other dangerous beasts, I was constantly enduring the cravings of hunger and the agonies of thirst." Another explorer of the same area that Andersson was describing put it more succinctly. "This", said Captain Messum, when he spoke of his own journeys in the barren wastes of the Namib's hinterland, "was the pleasure of travelling in Africa. It requires the endurance of a camel and the courage of a lion."

It is a sad fact that there is no place in Africa that is as wild as it was a hundred years ago. Consequently, when Andersson travelled through Damaraland or Ngamiland in the 1860s his definition of wilderness must have been very different from what we would now regard as wilderness, for no uncharted territory remains. Indeed, every single square metre of the continent has been mapped by the roving eyes of a hundred orbiting satellites. Even fifty years ago, colonial administrators, geologists and surveyors had

This forested valley, set amid the towering dunes of Sossusvlei in the Namib, is home to small numbers of springbok, ostrich and gemsbok.

tramped over the whole of Africa south of the Sahara and yet, half a century later, we are still searching for 'wilderness' as though it still really exists.

What is wilderness, anyway? For one thing, it is a definition that has been abused and appropriated by the tourist industry to describe places that ceased to be true wilderness half a century ago – the Kruger National Park, for example. Masai Mara is also a classic example of that promotional myth, as are a host of other places in Africa. These places are not wildernesses – rather, they are theme parks, biological funfairs, where modern explorers travelling in groups experience the wonders of the African bush through the window of a vehicle or from the balcony of a lodge.

Light years away from all these so-called wild places there are, however, still a few corners of southern Africa where the word 'wilderness' manages to retain just a little of its original meaning. The deserts and mountains of the world are always the last to be settled, so it is no surprise that nearly all of southern Africa's last wild places lie within the bounds of the Kalahari and the Namib deserts. Not for much longer though. At this very moment a tide of humanity is about to break over these last few hostile bastions of nature, and so the rush to experience the last taste of wilderness has now become a race against time. It will not be long now to the day when the tourist industry will have discovered all of the remaining corners and the alluring mystery of Africa will be a thing of the past.

When I arrived in Botswana in the late 70s, the tar road ended at Nata, wildlife literally abounded everywhere and the game areas were uncrowded. I spent several months at Kwekampa Pan, a place which boasted vast herds of buffalo, large numbers of lions and a fantastic elephant gathering in the late dry season. The roads were virtually non-existent and it was a lonely place which the Game Department largely ignored. Amazingly, I had it all to myself.

Oh, what a difference a decade can make! Ten short years later tourism had blossomed and transformed Maun into a tacky boom town, replete with video shops, supermarkets and shopping centres. At Ngwezumba, roads were graded, boreholes drilled, and campsites established. Rules and regulations began to be applied. And yet as this development took place, other more ominous things were happening. Poaching quickly decimated the herds of

buffalo, roan and zebra. Rhinos disappeared altogether. The social structure of every lion pride in Botswana was shattered as sport hunters eliminated all the big males. This overhunting, together with rampant poaching and mismanagement, has eliminated seventy-five per cent of the wildlife since 1980. It is truly a crying shame! But this is the way of the world.

If there is any wisdom that can be salvaged from all of this, it is that there is very little time left for adventure in Africa. Personally, I nursed a growing realization that if ever there was a time to do all the things that I had been putting off for the last decade, it was now. If I wanted to see the Skeleton Coast and the Kaokoveld before they were tamed by tourism and depleted by poaching or drought, well then – I had better get a move on and do it soon. Also, I wanted to explore, by dugout, the last wild places in the Okavango – the permanently flooded Jau flats. Gradually, the idea of a journey evolved and once the seed had been planted, it quickly germinated and flourished.

There were other reasons why I should make this journey – personal reasons relating to my profession. Originally, I had arrived in Ngamiland determined to make my name as a 'real' wildlife artist. From the very beginning I had struggled with the inconveniences of painting in a small tent. Flies, heat, wind, and dust were the bane of my painting endeavours, as were the marauding hyenas, baboons, and monkeys which passed through my little encampment. Yet what I produced in those halcyon years were truly paintings from the wilds. Consequently, my career had blossomed and all because of those many years of living in Botswana's finest game country. But the more I learned about other wildlife artists in general, the more I began to feel that I should distance myself from them. It seemed to me that wildlife art had become a genre for artists who shied away from getting their hands dirty. These other so-called 'wildlife' artists desired and depicted a natural world where there were no foul smells and where carnivores looked harmless, even 'cute'. They used photography to make up for their lack of wilderness experience and rarely did anything that could remotely be classified as dangerous.

In the United States a whole industry has evolved from this way of thinking. There are now many places where trained, tame animals, euphemistically referred to as

The Nata – Maun road in the late 1970s. P.A.

wildlife 'models', can be rented by the hour (with a handler, of course). Amazingly, this has become an acceptable method for many North American and European wildlife artists who are unwilling to spend time in the field to get their material. Instead they now 'travel' to one of many establishments where they can photograph a 'model' as it poses or performs to their requirements. Frankly, wildlife art was beginning to lose its authenticity and credibility. It was, therefore, time to extend my self-imposed brief and try to push that artistic mission ever higher by emulating the exploits of the great artist-travellers of the past – artists such as Thomas Baines and Wilhelm Kuhnert. The planned journey would thus also be my continuing homage to the field painters of a bygone era.

A few calculations showed that the journey I had in mind would be a long one: it would take ten months to complete. I then began to have doubts as to whether it was a sensible thing for me to put my hard-won career on hold for so long a period. Clarissa, at that time my fiancée, thought otherwise. "Hmm, I don't agree. If I heard you right, you will be painting when you can anyway. So all it means is that your output will be down a bit. Of course it means I'll have to resign my job." That thought brought a huge smile to her face. "And, hey, then I'll be able to work full-time on my thesis as well." And so the idea became a plan.

Clarissa handed in her notice and a departure date two months hence was marked on our calendar. When she had told her colleagues where she was going and that she was also going to be writing up her doctoral thesis at the same time, her peers were incredulous and not a little jealous. Rosemary, my mother, was also delighted to hear of our plans, and when I asked her whether she would be interested in going, she merely went to a cupboard and brought out a fully packed travel bag. This she placed at my feet, saying, "That's my reply! When do we leave?"

Early on Clarissa and I had decided that my old Land-cruiser was not up to the task. So, pooling our resources, we bought a brand new Hilux 4x4 for cash, and a week before we were due to leave we took delivery of a shiny, tan-coloured vehicle. What an occasion that was! Clarissa told me later that I drove the Hilux around with a silly grin on my face for the next two days, totally enraptured by the smell of the cab and the absence of rattles. A steel canopy was bought and fitted onto the back and, later, an

equipment rack of my own design was bolted in place on the roof. The addition of large steel bush bumpers was the final touch, and the total effect on me was such that I was unable to walk away from the vehicle without stopping at least twice to turn and admire its jaunty look.

When we had sorted out what we needed to take with us, the pile of equipment was a frightening sight. "We'll never get it all in", was my only comment when we had lined it up on the floor of the flat. There were Clarissa's research papers – 60 kilograms of them in a tin trunk. My art materials filled several boxes and the eight stretched canvases were inconveniently bulky, as were the photographic cases. There were our clothes and two tin trunks for the food. Also, there was a huge bulky tent that Clarissa and I would use for sleeping and as a work place. There were mattresses, sleeping bags, pillows, two camp tables and three folding chairs. Eight jerry cans, a high-lift jack, my tools and all the essential mechanical spares we might need completed the mountain of equipment. However, when we set about packing the vehicle on the

13

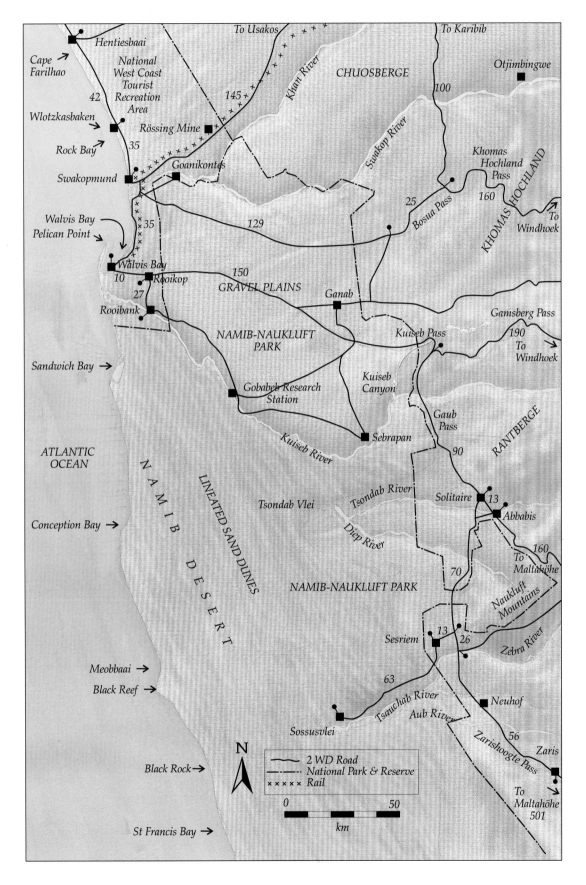

eve of our departure, a miracle happened – it all fitted in! Suddenly, there was nothing more to do but leave.

The great day dawned and even as the sun was rising, we were still adding items of equipment to our now heavily loaded vehicle. Rosemary, even at this early stage, had appropriated the back of the vehicle as her own, making a comfortable 'nest' among the trunks and bags. Indeed, for the rest of the year, this space was indisputably hers. In the front Clarissa and I stuffed last-minute items into the tiny spaces remaining behind the seats.

Our departure was from Durban, but the adventure really began only when we had crossed the border into Namibia. Unfortunately, I was burdened at this early stage of the journey with a bad case of 'Ngamiland snobbery'. It was a silly attitude, but I genuinely felt that, after all the good years of freedom in the wilds, Botswana would be a tough act to follow. Three days later, however, when we were past Maltahöhe and driving westwards along a dirt road towards the Namib, I began to feel rising excitement at the prospects for the coming months. Clarissa, who had previously been to Namibia, was positively bubbling with infectious enthusiasm. With her feet up on the dashboard and the road stretching away in front of her for a whole year, she was in high spirits. "Isn't this great?" she enthused as we sped along, delighting in the changing scenery around each and every bend in the road.

After Maltahöhe the road began to traverse vacant mountainous scenery and as we rattled along the corrugated road, there were many hints of the Namib's brooding presence. The vegetation thinned out and the mountains became more rugged. Then, here and there, small relict patches of dune sand began to appear in the lee of hills and scarps. We negotiated a long shallow pass and at the bottom of this we stopped to look at the distant outliers of the Namib's dunefields. Occasionally, a solitary gemsbok would canter off over the plains.

Finally, we arrived at Sesriem, where there is a small Parks office and a pleasant campground. Here, however 'officialdom' prevailed: there were declarations to be signed and permits stamped. After booking in we drove over to our allotted site where, under a vast acacia, we made our first 'desert' camp. The setting had an epic grandeur, the kind that only deserts are capable of evoking. Absolute silence reigned – in fact, after a whole day of driving the corrugated roads of the Namib, the silence was deafening! And to the uninitiated, this complete absence of noise and the wide open spaces brought with it a new understanding of the words 'infinity' and 'far'. For the first time I began to get a hint of what was waiting for us in the Skeleton Coast and the Kaokoveld. Inexorably, my 'Ngamiland snobbery' began to melt in the face of such raw beauty.

Meanwhile, we marvelled at what lay in front of us: a red sand desert stretched away into the distance, where shimmered a hazy mountain range. To the west, massive curling dunes crested the horizon. Nearby, a small herd of gemsbok stood huddled in the shade of another acacia.

Of course, Sesriem is really only the gateway to a far more special and spectacular somewhere – the dune scenery at the terminus of Sossusvlei. Early the next morning we set off down the track to this unique place. At the end of an hour's drive through a broad valley whose walls are the dunes of the Namib, the small track finally comes to the spot that has drawn photographers from all over the world. The high, sculpted faces of the dunes crowd in closer and at the point where the vlei disappears, there is an extensive area where acacia and other hardy trees flourish. Here, in the midst of the rolling red dunes, there is a veritable forest of green shady trees. Here, too, are springbok and gemsbok which can be seen in the distance picking their way among the trees and shrubs. Sossusvlei is the delight of photographers, professional and amateur alike, for Mother Nature has arranged the elements in such a way that every photograph is a guaranteed masterpiece. Indeed, the cracked mudflats, gnarled stumps and red, curving dunes all turn up regularly in the advertising content of foreign and local magazines – usually displaying some futuristic product in the suitably alien landscape that is Sossusvlei. For all its spectacular grandeur, Sossusvlei is not, therefore, a place to search for solitude. It is too beautiful and accessible for that to be possible, and so there are always people wandering about on some dune nearby.

The next day saw us on the road again, this time with Walvis Bay as our destination. The corrugated surface of the road became progressively worse and, half an hour later, the engine cut out and we glided to a halt. I was not to know it then, but this was the first manifestation of a mysterious problem with the engine that was to plague us for the rest of the year. Two frustrating hours later, I was still struggling to find the fault and the engine steadfastly

refused to start. Every cable and wire was painstakingly checked – but to no avail. Almost in desperation, I dismantled the carburettor and, finding no dirt there, put it all back together again. Miraculously, the engine burst into life, and with a collective sigh of relief we all got back in the car and resumed our journey.

By now it was midday and the sun burned down mercilessly as we continued onwards through the rocky desert. Soon we were descending a narrow pass beyond which lay the immense plains of the Namib Desert. The air was cooler here, a legacy of the icy waters of the distant Atlantic Ocean. The cab became chilly and we rolled up the windows.

An hour later the engine sputtered and went silent and we found ourselves yet again coasting to a halt. With a cold wind whipping my hair I dismantled the carburettor and again was puzzled to find that the jets were clean. After forty-five minutes' work I tightened the last bolt and nervously tried the starter. The engine fired on the first turn of the ignition. "Bravo!" declared Rosemary. Clarissa slapped me on the back as I wiped my hands. "Not bad at all. I'm impressed." Unfortunately, I had not the faintest

Sesriem is set in a spectacular location: flanked by the low dunes of a sandy desert on one side, dark, jagged mountains rise on the other. Separating these two scenic extremes is a low undulating plain where, beneath large and shady acacia trees, the visitors' campsite is to be found. Also a haven for gemsbok, both during the day and at night, it is here that these animals often venture among the tents of visitors in search of fallen acacia seed-pods.

clue as to what it was that I was doing right. We all piled into the vehicle again, but fifty kilometres down the badly corrugated road, the motor began to falter suspiciously for the third time that day. With the engine protesting, no one said a single word when I suggested that we spend the night by the side of the road. A towering outcrop of granite lay nearby and by extraordinary coincidence a small signpost stated that camping was permitted there! My chronic aversion to signposts that tell me what I can or cannot do was overridden by the happy realization that the day's journey was finally over. I coaxed the vehicle the few extra yards to a spot in the lee of the granite hill where there were some curiously shaped sandblast caves.

"Well, that's that! I'll fix the car in the morning." There was nothing more to be said, but all of us were secretly disappointed that a new vehicle should have caused so much trouble on its first day of bad roads. There were few words either after we had opened the doors to encounter an icy wind that sent us scrambling for anoraks and jeans. Deciding against the bother of putting up a tent, Clarissa and I laid out our things inside one of the small caves and then retreated to the vehicle for our supper. In the back, and out of the wind, Rosemary was extremely comfortable. With the curtains drawn and the warm yellow glow of the lights visible within, we were rather envious of her cosy refuge. The night set in and the wind began to blow with increasing strength, carrying before it a stinging curtain of

a single gemsbok ran out from the rocks of the granite outcrop & crosses the gravel plain. P.A.

The granite outcrop provided splendid views of the barren Namib plains — P.A.

sand. With this gale buffeting the vehicle, we gulped down tea and biscuits and gazed out at the twilight scene.

There was no doubt about it, the place had a wild sort of grandeur. All around were the limitless gravel and sand plains of the Namib and in the distance, dim and mysterious in the fading light, tall mountains rose up from the horizon. In the blue-black sky above us, a million stars sparkled like diamonds in the freezing desert air. A spectacular setting indeed, but mostly lost on us for we were depressed by the events of the day.

After breakfast the following morning, I turned the key in the ignition without confidence, but the engine started with a roar, and with it safely running, we hastily packed

and departed. The vehicle behaved perfectly from then on and an hour later we were nearing the outskirts of Walvis.

The town of Walvis Bay is a rather ordinary place to look at on arrival, but its position on the Namib coastline endows it with an aura of frontier ruggedness, an aura that is enhanced by the belt of curling sand dunes that presses close against the outlying suburbs. This makes it truly a desert town, yet with its freezing temperatures and misty fogs, it has a setting unlike that of any other Namibian town. As the gravel road gave way to tar and we approached the outskirts of the town, an acrid smell reminiscent of burnt anchovies filled the cab, even though the windows were shut tight against the cold outside. "My

Twenty kilometres from Walvis Bay, a lone vehicle travels the gravel road between the coast and the town of Solitaire. This route traverses the same barren gravel plain between the Kuiseb and Swakop valleys that the earliest hunters and traders crossed on their way to the interior.

goodness," sniffed Clarissa, startled by the incongruous odour flooding into the cab from the windswept desert sands. "That smells disgusting!" A few seconds later we had solved the mystery, for there in the distance were smoke-stacks and factories.

Walvis Bay is the centre of the fishing industry in Namibia and because of that, its residents are perpetually aware of the prevailing wind direction. They have one answer, in the form of a question, when asked whether they like living here: "Which way is the wind blowing?"

The town is merely what it looks like – functional. There is absolutely nothing remarkable about it except its exotic location. Passing the busy shops of the town centre, we came to the harbour – Walvis Bay's *raison d'être*. Here there are rows of government-style cottages and beyond them the stark outlines of the gantries, cranes and warehouses of the harbour itself. Out of sight of this, south of the town, are the more affluent suburbs.

On the edge of a vast tidal inlet, we found the campsite – our home to be for the next couple of weeks. The vehicle

was unloaded, the tent put up and Clarissa and I made ourselves comfortable. In one corner of the tent I set up my easel and laid out my art materials. In the other, Clarissa placed her table and we lugged her massive trunk of papers in from the car. When the back of the vehicle was emptied of most of its load, Rosemary quickly spread out her things to fill the space, further establishing her claim there.

The campground's location is superb, only a few yards away from the Walvis Bay lagoon. The mouth of this huge tidal inlet is nearby and, when conditions are right, hosts huge gatherings of flamingos. One morning, just as the sun was rising, the din of flocking birds was such that we had to investigate. On the promenade nearby we were greeted by the sight of thousands of birds fishing in the waters of the in-rushing tide. In the yellow half-light of dawn, lesser and greater flamingos were flying in by the thousands to join flotillas of pelicans. A feeding frenzy was under way, and the lagoon mouth was a blur of diving, wheeling, squabbling birds. What a sight it was to see gulls, cormorants and curlew sandpipers mingling, in

below — The Welwitschia
mirabilis, one of the strangest of
the Namib plants, often lives
longer than a 1000 years.

above — a ground
squirrel, keeping a
lookout on some
rocks in the Namib

above — The stately gemsbok
on the vast gravel & sand
plains to the north of the
Kuiseb River. These same
plains caused the early travellers
considerable problems.

Namib and Walvis Sketchbook

right — A view of the Walvis
Bay lagoon from near the
campsite. The dunes of the
Namib press close in to
the houses that ring the
lagoon.
below right — Gulls feeding
in the shallows of the lagoon

above — Black-backed jackals are
frequently seen scavenging along
the beach, just above the surf line
right — The Cape fur seal occurs
in large numbers on the Namib
coastline.

glorious confusion, in the foaming waters of the sea. An hour later the tidal flow had abated and there was not a bird to be seen!

On the opposite side of the lagoon, a vast mudflat stretched away to the horizon, where the cold murky waters of the Atlantic Ocean could just be seen. This is fog country. It always hung low over the sea, just off shore, and in the mornings its damp embrace was total. We would awake to a murky gloom that could last till midday. Cars would be forced to creep along with their lights on, while people, wrapped up as if on an alpine skiing holiday, would flit about mysteriously in the swirling mists. It was all rather moody – vastly different from the clichéd image of a desert location.

A few days later we drove up the coast for a visit to Swakopmund. Nothing can prepare the psyche for that first visit to this bizarre and fascinating place. Having driven along a winding fog-bound road, flanked on one side by the storm-tossed Atlantic and on the other by the tan dunefields of the Namib, we arrived in a town which would not look out of place in the Bavarian Alps. With roots firmly set in the Germany of a different era – a fact of which its residents are still very proud – it is a very 'Continental' town. Cake and coffee shops line the main street and when we entered one of these, the hot, smoky atmosphere reeked of Europe. There were even shops that sold ski wear. Nearby were many *pensions*, all very typically European in their façades. The street names reinforce that image, names such as Bismarck Strasse and Kaiser Wilhelm Strasse. However, it is the early colonial architecture that gives this town its remarkable aspect, and somehow this character has been preserved through the seventy years since Germany lost its colony after the First World War.

In 1884 Germany declared that all the territory inland from the coast bounded by the Kunene and Orange rivers was henceforth under the Protectorate of the Second Reich. Prior to this, however, Walvis Bay, the only suitable harbour on the whole coast, had already been annexed by the English in 1878. Germany was nevertheless determined to overcome that difficulty, and it was decided that a new town and port would be developed at a suitable site just to the north of the mouth of the Swakop River. Here two beacons were established on a rocky headland and the town of Swakopmund was born. Later, a wooden jetty was built to improve the landing facilities, and

right – Swakopmund has many landmark historical buildings, most erected in the 1890's. Amazingly most have survived to the present day in good condition.
below – Rosemary walks along the platform of the Swakopmund railway station. P.A.

Opposite
Top: Our rented hut in the municipal camp in Swakopmund. Frequented by the many sport-fishermen that come to the Namibian coast on holiday, this camp provides convenient facilities for cleaning the catch, hence the lurking presence of many pelicans. A stay here involves getting used to the constant thumps and bumps on the roof as pelicans land and take off all day long.

Below: Adjacent to the campsite at Walvis Bay is a vast tidal lagoon, which is frequented by large flocks of flamingos, pelicans, and other marine birds. This lagoon, which is but a few metres away from the campground, is sandwiched between a suburb of Walvis and the mudflats leading out to Pelican Point.

above - Prinzessin Rupprecht Heim - built in 1902 to serve as a hospital for the troops.

left - an elegant home near the holiday bungalows.

above - M.C. Human building was built in 1902, and has an interesting corner window box. It has a wonderful view of the pier and beach.

Swakopmund Sketchbook

at left - A sleepy town for most of the year, Swakopmund is a fascinating blend of the old and the new

above - The Kaserne, built in 1905, was the living quarters of the engineer's regiment.

above - The Pier. World War I halted its construction when it was only ½ complete. It was completed in 1919 - and was recently renovated.

Below – The house occupied by Nature Conservation on the corner of Bismarck St. and Kaiser Wilhelm Street. The right hand building on the opposite side is the Fürst Bismarck.

above – Cape cormorants sunning themselves on the rocks of the Mole.

right – The Magistrate's Court or 'Altes Amtsgericht' was built in 1908. It was once used as a hostel and known as "The Castle for the Virgins".

Swakopmund Sketchbook

below right – Haus Hohenzollern, built in 1909, has a splendid statue of Atlas atop its roof.

below – A surfer braves the freezing Atlantic water at a surf break just south of the Mole.

Above – The railway station, built in the late 1890's, is built in a style known as "Wilhelminischer Stil."

23

Desert elephants crossing the dunes on their way to Auses. PA.

this hardy relic still stands today. Between 1892 and 1915 Swakopmund flourished and many permanent structures were built, and it is these quaint buildings which make the town a delight to visit. They have interesting names and interesting histories as well. The elegant Haus Hohenzollern on Moltke Street, built in 1909, was originally a hotel. Such were the revelries and rampant gambling here that its licence was revoked by the municipality in 1912. One can just imagine what went on! Prinzessin Rupprecht Heim, built in 1902, Kabelmesse, Woermannhaus, Villa Wille . . . the list goes on and on.

Two weeks later Clarissa and I found ourselves back in Swakopmund for a different reason altogether. We had decided to bring our engagement to an end – and finally to tie the knot. And so it was that we were married in a tiny Rhenish church by a bemused pastor, with witnesses recruited at short notice. Our 'reception' was but a cup of coffee and a cake in one of the hotel cafés, but to us it mattered not a jot, for it had been a momentous day. With Rosemary comfortably ensconced in the campsite at Walvis Bay, Clarissa and I moved into a bungalow in the Swakopmund municipal camp for our honeymoon.

As the time passed, I laboured on commissions that I had undertaken before leaving Durban while Clarissa worked on her thesis. During the evenings we pored over our maps of the Kaokoveld and the Skeleton Coast. Uppermost in my mind were the classic photographs I had seen of desert elephants padding over the dunes to the lake at Auses in the Skeleton Coast Park. I already knew that Auses was strictly off-limits to people such as myself, yet I still dreamed of going there.

Early on with this in mind, I had walked down to the house in Bismarck Strasse where the National Parks people had an office. In the parking lot were some Nissan 4x4s, one of which was being loaded with supplies. A well-used high-lift jack was bolted to the roof and to the sides were attached two plain planks of wood. (I would later discover that these latter items were invaluable when a vehicle became bogged in heavy sand.) "This is more like it", I thought to myself as I made my way up the creaking stairs of the old building. The smartly uniformed woman behind the counter had never even heard of Auses, but when I produced my map and pointed to where I was talking about, she directed me to the Nature Conservation section downstairs. So off I went back down the stairs into the courtyard and over to some offices in what might have once been stables in the Kaiser's day. Here the atmosphere was very different. In the background a two-way radio crackled, and the walls were covered by detailed maps. Two uniformed rangers sat at their desks, and one got up and approached me.

"Can I help you?" he asked.

I explained what I wanted to do, but his replies were not encouraging. Everything we had heard regarding access to these areas was turning out to be true. The ranger was sympathetic, but quite candid about the way the system operated.

"We all want to get to these areas," he said. "But look at me. I'm a ranger and I've got about as much chance as a snowball in hell."

Any ideas I had about asking permission from the H.Q. in Windhoek were dashed when he told me that the Bartletts, of National Geographic fame, were making a film of that area. The ranger's tone now acquired a conspiratorial edge. "The only way that you can get to these areas is if you know someone. Do you know any of the staff in the Skeleton Coast Park?"

I shook my head.

"Then it's all locked up, I'm afraid."

That seemed to be that and our hoped-for contacts seemed to recede even further away. We had come up against a solid wall.

Our honeymoon sped by and a month after we had been married, we found ourselves nearing a time when decisions would have to be made. We had been sitting in Swakopmund for long enough. My commissions were complete and there seemed little point in dallying any longer. Then we had one of those strokes of good fortune that always seem to come at the last moment. While walking to the shops, Clarissa saw a battered Landrover enter the municipal camp and drive over to one of the bungalows. Recognizing the driver from an article that was in one of my magazines, she rushed back to our bungalow to tell me her news.

"Guess who's staying in one of the A-frames? Garth Owen-Smith!"

Anyone interested in rhino conservation knows this name, for he and Blythe and Rudi Loutit have been responsible for the remarkable turnaround in the fortunes of the elephant and rhino of Damaraland. Their dedicated

work in setting up the Auxiliary Game Guards and the monitoring of the rhino has resulted in the cessation of poaching. Their crowning achievement is that Damaraland is the only place in Africa, outside a proclaimed sanctuary, where black rhinos are on the increase instead of in decline. In the months prior to our departure, I had approached the Endangered Wildlife Trust (which partially funded their work) for information about the Damaraland rhinos, and the Director of the Trust, Dr John Ledger, had been very helpful indeed. He suggested that I try and meet up with Owen-Smith when I was there and also that I write to them beforehand, to let them know what I was doing. With Clarissa's news, I knew that I now had a golden opportunity to get some concrete information on the Kaokoveld – especially advice on where I could find the elusive Damaraland rhinos.

That afternoon I walked over to his bungalow, oblivious to the freezing Swakopmund weather. "How will I do this," I thought to myself as I approached the door. Unexpectedly, a dark-haired woman answered my knock. I introduced myself and explained why I was there. There was a momentary silence.

"Sorry, what did you say your name was again?"

"Paul Augustinus. I wrote to Garth a couple of months ago."

A puzzled frown creased her brow, then she said, "Ah, I recollect your letter. Sorry, but Garth's not here."

"Oh! Could I come back later then? I would really like to talk to him."

She shook her head and explained that they were in town only for the night and were busy with a report that had to be ready by the next day. I sensed that a brush-off was imminent and so decided to try name dropping as a desperate measure.

"Hmm, that's a pity. John Ledger insisted that I should try and meet up with you when I was here."

She shook her head again and then, reconsidering, added, "How about drinks at Kücki's this evening? And by the way, I'm Margie Jacobsohn."

That evening Clarissa and I drove the short distance to Kücki's Pub, Swakopmund's premier watering hole. Leaving the gloomy, mist-swirled street outside, we were soon swallowed up by the noisy crowd that filled the bar to overflowing. This is an establishment that has a lot of atmosphere, for it is here that one rubs shoulders with

A Steenbok in the bed of the remote Hoanib valley in Damaraland   Paul Augustinus

hunters, geologists, conservationists and overland travellers in very convivial surroundings. Here the chatter is of adventures in the hinterland, outlandish fishing tales and the like. Kücki, the German-speaking proprietor, was wandering about, seeming to know everyone as he greeted people here and there by name. Sitting at the bar and looking very much at home in these surroundings, were Margaret Jacobsohn and a bearded man whom I knew must be Garth Owen-Smith. Threading a path through the revellers, we joined them and introduced ourselves. Predictably, the evening began a little stiffly, but by the time the second round of drinks was being ordered, much of that stiffness had begun to evaporate. In retrospect, I feel that we were very lucky to have managed to tie them down for the evening. After all, in the general scheme of things, we were really of no importance. Garth Owen-Smith must have been along this road many times before. We were but the latest in a long line of 'arrivals', seeking information and trying to get a foot in the door of opportunity, yet he and Margie gave us their valuable time.

The evening sped by and soon the conversation turned to what they were doing and after that was guided by me to what we hoped to do. I expressed my desire to see Auses, the Kunene mouth, the Hoarusib Valley, and, of course, the desert elephants and rhinos which inhabited those places. Sensing that the time was right, I produced my detailed topographic map of Damaraland with a flourish. Garth was momentarily nonplussed at the significance of this. I continued, however, and asked him where I would find desert rhinos.

"Here and here", he said after some thought, his finger describing the large swaths of country to the north-east of the Sesfontein road. I became puzzled, for I understood enough to know that the valleys indicated by him were far outside the areas they inhabited. So I dropped the subject of rhinos. Next I tried to pick his brain on desert elephants and places with spectacular scenery. Also, places where I would be able to camp and paint in peace. Here, too, he became very cagey. But still I pressed on regardless, almost cringing at my own cheek in the face of his obvious reluctance to part with any details.

"What about the Hoanib?"

"The Hoanib? No doubt about it, that's a spectacular

26

place. There are elephants there as well, but they're just recovering from decades of poaching."

I could perceive concern here and later on it became clear what they were worried about. It seemed that the desert elephants used the valley as a highway between two distant watering points. "Walk up to these elephants", he insisted. "Don't drive up to them. In the past they have been very badly harassed by people driving along the bed of the Hoanib. And also, now for the first time in years there are calves with them as well."

Finally, after much talk and many drinks, the interesting evening came to an end. Before parting, however, Margie, who shared the common field of anthropology with Clarissa, took out a note pad and scribbled something on it. Passing it to Clarissa, she said, "If you really want to get to Auses and places like the lower Hoarusib, you might try contacting these people at that number. They are Rod and Sigi Braby. Rod's in charge of the northern half of the Skeleton Coast Park. Tell them I gave you their number."

Miracle of miracles – we had a contact!

The next day saw us in the phone booth next to the camp gate as early as possible, but the woman who answered the telephone cheerily said that the Brabys were up at Möwe Bay (the headquarters of the northern part of the Skeleton

Coast) and probably would not be back for a couple of months. Suddenly, we were back where we had started, a door of opportunity having been slammed shut in our faces just as it seemed that it was opening a fraction.

We slowly walked back to our bungalow, opened the door and looked around the friendly place that had been our first real home together. All around the room were arranged the paraphernalia of adventure – jerry cans, high-lift jacks, water containers and photographic equipment. In the corner dominating the entrance was the huge trunk of research material for Clarissa's doctoral thesis. My commissions had been completed, packed and freighted off to the Everard Read Gallery in Johannesburg. But the dry season was here and there were places to see, and with this thought came the realization that there was no further reason for us to stay on in Swakopmund.

"Look, it's not the end of the world, we will try the Brabys again when we come back in a couple of months", consoled Clarissa, seeing my disappointment at the turn of events. "Meanwhile, let's get up to Damaraland – we were planning to go there at some stage anyway."

It was true, our stay in Swakopmund was now over. It was time to look northwards to the places where adventure was to be found. That evening we started to prepare for our departure and make plans for the coming months. The wilderness beckoned!

CHAPTER ONE

INTO THE KAOKOVELD

The Kaokoveld is a place well known to those who seek adventure. Its very name is synonymous with broken leaf-springs, rugged lonely scenery and wonderfully nostalgic memories of wild camping locations. Some wise person once wrote that "great journeys are not memorable for what you saw but for where you camped". This is especially true of the Kaokoveld because here, more than in any other place in southern Africa, there is the opportunity to travel in lonely scenery inhabited by big game and yet still have the freedom to camp wherever the heart desires.

What is the bait that lures one to those hazy mountain ranges, those dusty riverbeds and the empty plains, all so neatly shrugged off by a geographer's generalization as 'desert'? There is only one answer to that question: "Wilderness!" For many it is also the desire to go anywhere interesting which does not require one to pass through a gate and be handed a leaflet which reads: "Game Reserve – you may not alight from your vehicle, you may not camp outside the designated campsites, do not do this, do not do that" – and so on! For those adventurers, the kind seeking refuge from the rule-book bureaucrats, the Kaokoveld fits the bill admirably. The barren expanses of the marginal lands between the wetter, more inhabited areas above the escarpment and the sand desert of the Skeleton Coast,

In the bed of the Hoanib River, there is a little-used track which winds through epic scenery of the kind that stirs the landscape artist's heart. The wilderness appeal of this atmospheric track to adventure is further heightened by the fact that at any point along its winding route, you may be stopped by elephants crossing your path.

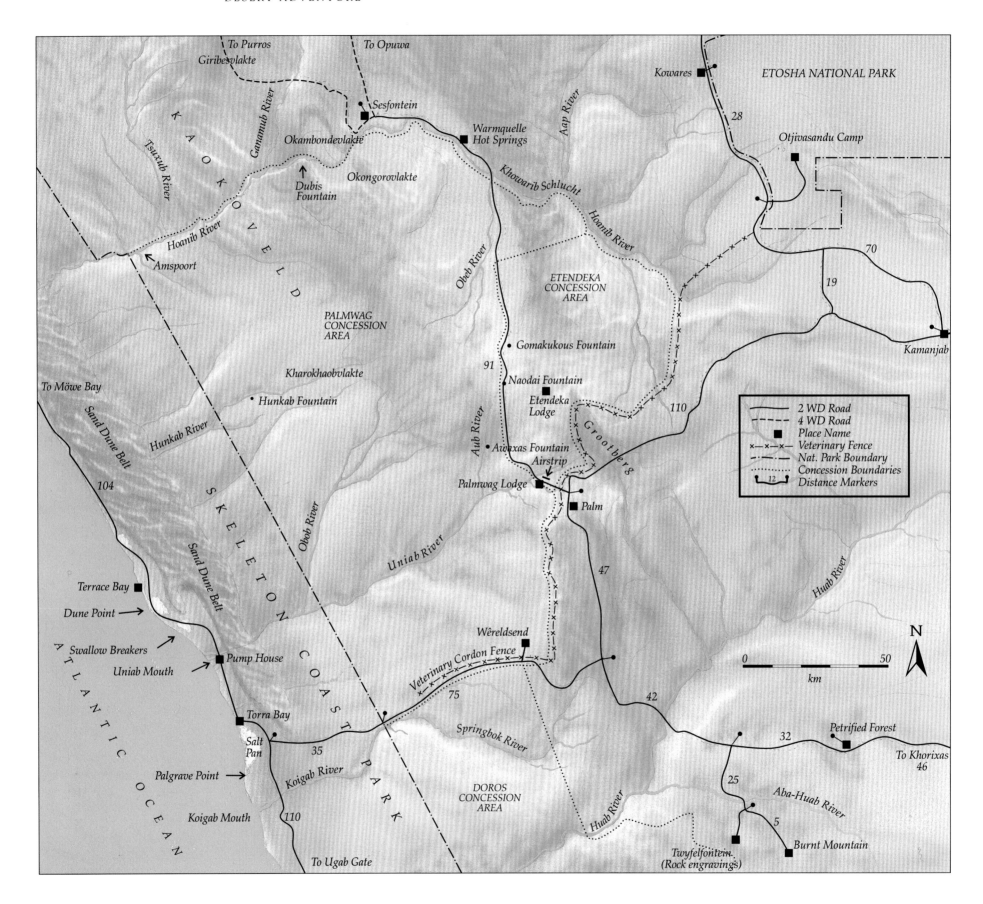

To Purros
Giribesvlakte
To Opuwa

Kowares
ETOSHA NATIONAL PARK

K A O K O V E L D

Ganamub River

Sesfontein

Okambondevlakte

Warmquelle
Hot Springs

Aap River

28

Otjivasandu Camp

Tsuxub River

Dubis
Fountain

Okongorovlakte

Khowarib Schlucht

Hoanib River

Amsploort

Hoanib River

Obeb River

ETENDEKA
CONCESSION
AREA

70

19

PALMWAG
CONCESSION
AREA

Gomakukous Fountain

91

Kamanjab

To Möwe Bay

Kharokhaobvlakte

Hunkab Fountain

Naodai Fountain

Etendeka
Lodge

110

2 WD Road

4 WD Road

Place Name

Veterinary Fence

Nat. Park Boundary

Concession Boundaries

12   Distance Markers

Hunkab River

Aub River

Awaxas Fountain
Airstrip

G r o o t b e r g

S K E L E T O N   C O A S T   P A R K

Sand Dune Belt

Palmwag Lodge

104

Obob River

Palm

Terrace Bay

Sand Dune Belt

Dune Point

Uniab River

N

Swallow Breakers

Pump House

0   50

km

Uniab Mouth

Wêreldsend

42

Torra Bay

Veterinary Cordon Fence

47

75

Salt
Pan

35

Springbok River

32

Petrified Forest

Palgrave Point

Koigab River

25

Aba-Huab River

Koigab Mouth

110

DOROS
CONCESSION
AREA

Huab River

Huab River

To Khorixas
46

5

To Ugab Gate

Twyfelfontein
(Rock engravings)

Burnt Mountain

A T L A N T I C   O C E A N

have everything that an adventurer could want: virtually no permanent inhabitants, spectacular scenery and in Damaraland, the portion of the Kaokoveld to the south of the Hoanib River, the presence of desert elephants, rhinos, lions and plains game.

The few rough tracks that thread the valleys and plains are not, however, for the fainthearted – especially the ones that ascend and descend steep slopes or mountain passes. Often, under a burning sun, backbreaking repairs have to be made to wash-aways that bar the route ahead. Also, a knowledge of how to repair a vehicle and read a topographical map are absolute necessities here. However, the rewards for travelling alone in this area are that you camp in splendid isolation amidst a vast wilderness of gravel plains, deep valleys and towering mountains.

The journey from Swakopmund to the wilds of Damaraland is one that starts in Europe and ends on a different continent. A few days after our evening out with Garth Owen-Smith and Margie Jacobsohn, we were ready to leave. The vehicle was loaded up and we were soon driving slowly through the fog-bound streets of Swakopmund, past the Prince Eugen Hof, Haus Hohenzollern and down the Kaiser Strasse. Once over the bridge and on the way to Walvis Bay the illusion of Europe faded a little as the coastal dunes became visible through the mist, but the car heater remained fully on and we were still cold.

At the Walvis Bay campground, Rosemary was pacing up and down, impatient to leave, her small airline bag packed and ready to go. Blowing clouds of condensation as she spoke, she said she was sorry to be leaving but glad to be on the move again. An hour later, with tent and camping equipment packed away, we were speeding back along the road, past Swakopmund and towards Hentiesbaai.

At Hentiesbaai we turned inland away from the grey, oily swells of the Atlantic. For a while the road in front of us disappeared in a swirl of mist which was broken with sudden bursts of sunlight. The road wound in and out of the foggy patches and then, abruptly, we emerged into bright sunshine. We were back in Africa and surrounded by the wide open plains. Far to the east and over one hundred kilometres distant, the Spitzkoppe massif could easily be seen, its solitary, distinctive peak jutting up from below the curve of the horizon.

An hour after we had turned inland away from the

coast, Clarissa leaned over and turned off the heater. The chill influence of the Atlantic was waning fast as we drove inland, and not long after that we tore off our anoraks and jerseys and wound down the windows. By the time we were approaching the small town of Uis, built around a now defunct mine, we felt the effects of a burning African day much in the same way as a tourist from Europe feels the heat when stepping off the plane at Nairobi. The transition was complete!

Another hour later and we were driving through Khorixas, the administrative capital of Damaraland. (Damaraland has since been incorporated with Kaokoland and the new entity renamed the Kunene Province. However, as the journey took place when it was still known as Damaraland, I will continue to refer to it as such for the sake of continuity.) This small, scruffy place (Khorixas) has little to tempt the traveller to stop. Beyond, however, the road at last became more interesting. Gone was the tarred surface and the country on either side lost the tidy, farmed look that it had assumed above the escarpment bordering the Namib Desert. Passing the first few homesteads, the impression of decay became more evident. The stock fences were in a state of complete disrepair and the homesteads themselves, so picturesque at a distance, revealed themselves as buildings that had seen better days.

Damaraland has a very strange and convoluted history. White colonial farmers were already settled here in the fifties and sixties, but the aridity dictated that this was always going to be very marginal sheep country. In addition, the Etosha National Park extended into the Kaokoveld and its presence described the limit of settlement for the white farms that abutted upon its border. Although that portion of Etosha was excised in the 1960s, modern Ordnance maps show that nothing much has changed on the ground since then. Even after the deproclamation of the Kaokoveld portions of Etosha, and the subsequent removal of the white farmers to make way for a displaced community from South Africa, the area that used to be part of Etosha was never subdivided into new farms. The land remained as undeveloped and as wild as it had been under the National Park system, yet it lingered on as a sort of grey area that abounded in rhino, elephant and plains game. This curious situation has had a great effect on the wildlife of Damaraland, but it is also part of

The patterns chipped into this flat rock surface at Twyfelfontein are thought to have been visualized by the artist while in a trance state. Increasingly, anthropologists are becoming more convinced that most rock art was done under trance conditions. Found at many rock-art sites around the world, these patterns are considered to be a possible proof of this, as recent scientific studies have shown that the first stage of 'trancing' brings with it visions of geometric of entoptic phenomena in the form of shapes.

another story, a story that started a thousand kilometres away in the Upington area of South Africa.

In the apartheid era, an area of land to the north of the Orange River, near the Augrabies Falls, was expropriated by the army for military purposes. The indigenous people of this area, known as the Riemvasmakers, were therefore removed. Confused and distressed, their headman would say, "The riem [or thong for tethering the animals] that was made fast sixty years ago was now being torn loose . . . I don't know why the Government wants us to tear the riem loose." The bureaucrats in Pretoria were now left with the problem of where to put these displaced people. They decided that the people most racially similar to the Riemvasmakers of the Augrabies, were those living to the west of the town of Welwitschia in north-eastern Namibia. As a homeland was needed for the Riemvasmakers, those white farmers who had settled to the west of Welwitschia,

including those ranching right up against the Kaokoveld portion of Etosha, were removed. The Kaokoveld portion of the Etosha National Park, situated to the south of the Hoanib, was then deproclaimed, and this, combined with the land vacated by the white farmers, created the homeland of Damaraland, with as its capital, the town of Khorixas (formerly Welwitschia). The unfortunate Riemvasmakers were resettled in their new homeland, but they found themselves in an unfamiliar environment and, unlike their previous home, here there were elephant and rhino to contend with. The destructive behaviour of the elephants on stock fences and water pumps, as well as the depredations of marauding lions, was not to their liking, and in the subsequent years they dreamed of returning to their real homeland near Augrabies.

In the areas that had been part of that very much larger Etosha, elephant, rhino and plains game were plentiful, but in the era that followed the proclamation of the Kaokoland and Damaraland homelands, the government washed its hands of the wildlife. Thus, in the 1970s, army and government officials alike treated these areas as their own private hunting grounds and by the end of that decade, the great herds had been eliminated. Barely fifty black rhino remained, the desert elephants decimated to a fraction of their numbers in Damaraland and completely eliminated from the Kaokoland highlands. Between 1980 and 1983, 123 elephant carcasses were found. Of these, 107 bore bullet wounds, or had had their tusks removed. It was only in 1983 that this terrible situation began to be reversed through the fine work of Garth Owen-Smith, the Endangered Wildlife Trust, Blythe Loutit, Save the Rhino Fund, and members of Namibia's Department of Nature Conservation. In that year the elephant and rhino populations stabilized and began increasing gradually to the present day. Such is the magnitude of the turnaround in the fortunes of the region's wildlife that the Kaokoveld is now one of Africa's conservation success stories – all the more amazing in view of the fact that none of it was land set aside for wildlife.

Seventy kilometres beyond Khorixas we came to the turn-off to Twyfelfontein, and were soon wending our way down a road that passed through some fascinating desert terrain.

Twyfelfontein will be found in every Namibian guide book and it is a place that must not be missed. Where else in southern Africa can one find an art gallery filled with thousands of masterpieces, most of them many thousands of years old, situated in a remote and uninhabited desert? Of course, when you finally arrive at this gallery you do not see a manmade construction like the Louvre. Instead, there is the vast sweep of an ochre-coloured valley wall. Here and there on this natural amphitheatre trees sprout and bushes flourish among the tumbled blocks of sedimentary rock. At the foot of this grand geological sweep is the spring that gave the locality its name. This 'fountain' is of course the reason for the existence of the rock engravings for which this locality is justifiably famous. I was later told that a black rhino from the nearby Doros Crater occasionally visited the spring. Now there is a pump over the spring and a small settlement of people have made this place their home. Damaraland Nature Conservation have also provided the basic necessities for visitors.

All of that is irrelevant, however, for up there on the slopes surrounding the spring is the greatest collection of San Bushman rock art in southern Africa. It is easy to read such a statement, but only when you see it for yourself can you understand how true the words are. So it was for us, and we quickly realized that this was a place that needed a whole month fully to appreciate its extent and not the few hours we had to spare.

Twyfelfontein is a place of superlatives. There are over 2500 different engravings here. The broad flat sheets of rock are often literally covered in depictions of animals. Interestingly, the spoor of both game and humans figures prominently in the murals and pavements that lie scattered about, while only 27 of the images are of people. There is also a small number of rock paintings. This mixing of mediums is very atypical for southern Africa and has confused the anthropologists studying the site.

Of course, because I was an artist on a mission, this place had an added significance for me. Not only were the images beautiful to look at and spectacular in their extent, but here was a vast statement from a vanished people who had been the ultimate field artists. So it was with professional and deeply sympathetic interest that I

Open to the elements and engraved into the flat surfaces of the many tumbled and fractured boulders of Twyfelfontein, the works of enigmatic and long-departed artists crowd together in a seemingly hodge-podge fashion. There are over 2500 of these images, only 27 of which depict humans.

viewed the works of my fellow artists.

There are three ways in which the rock engravings were executed by the artists. The first was by 'pecking' with stone on stone; the second, cutting the image with a sharp stone; and lastly, simply scraping with stone. Yet with these crude tools they created images that are elegant and profound and have withstood the ravages of time better than any Rembrandt or Van Gogh painting. Selection of the surface for the depiction was of crucial importance to the artist. What was needed was a flat-surfaced rock that had weathered, forming a skin of a different colour from the unexposed rock beneath. All rocks develop this weathered surface skin, known by geologists as its 'patina'. When the skin, or patina, was removed by one of the methods described above, the freshly exposed rock stood out in strong contrast to the surrounding weathered rock. These were the artists' materials and techniques.

The age of the engravings can be roughly determined by the 'repatination' of the engraving, for the rock exposed by the artist is subjected from the very first day to the elements of weathering and so repatination inevitably takes place. By comparing the patination of the engravings, the age of the oldest of most of the pecked and scraped engravings in southern Africa seems to correspond with the advent of pottery, about 2000 years before the present. These types of engraving were, however, still being executed much more recently. In 1870, Sir George Grey's librarian in the Cape, the German philologist, Wilhelm Heinrich Immanuel Bleek, and his sister-in-law, Lucy Catherine Lloyd, began interviewing /Xam Bushmen

at their Mowbray home in Cape Town. One of them told Lloyd that his father had chipped images of gemsbok, quagga, ostrich and other animals, only one hundred and fifty years ago, at a place where they used to drink before the arrival of the Boers.

It is in the interpretation of rock art that objectivity becomes blurred and muddied with the subjective influences of our present day. Indeed, my first introduction to Twyfelfontein was an article in a magazine which suggested that the galleries of engravings were a form of schoolroom for young hunters and that the spoor so liberally depicted, performed the same function as a guidebook to mammals, that is to say, purely instructional. The modern interpretation of rock art is not so simplistic, and the current belief by most (but not all) anthropologists is that these images were 'symbolic' representations, usually visualized under a trance state or performance. Trance performance plays an important role in the religious activities of many societies. Special techniques are used to enter a trance, and religions that employ these methods are known as 'shamanistic'. Regarded by his people as the go-between for the material and spiritual worlds, this 'shaman' was mainly a healer, rite specialist, and political leader. Often, he was also an artist.

One of the characteristics of the trance state is the experience of hallucinations that provided the shaman with experiences and visions that were extraordinary. His surroundings would be visually distorted and accompanied by an increasing sensitivity of the body's senses. The images that were subsequently drawn would thus be very hard to interpret without an understanding of the nature of the hallucinations and the society that generated them.

Modern researchers have carefully experimented with and examined visual experiences perceived under altered states of consciousness with the above in mind, and it is interesting to note that all people from all societies are affected in the same way because of the make-up of our nervous system. All share the same sequence of visions which proceeds in three stages. The first is the experiencing of visions of geometric shapes, known as 'entoptic phenomena'. These usually take the form of chevrons, zigzags, dots, flecks, and grids, sometimes seen as moving or enlarging patterns. The second stage usually involves an attempt to interpret the entoptic shapes by elaborating them into something familiar, and here the

Opposite
Giraffe are particularly common in the array of wildlife depicted at Twyfelfontein. This is thought to be because, in the area between the Kalahari and the Namib, the giraffe was a 'powerful' animal in spiritual terms. Further eastward of this site, in the Kalahari itself, where the Bushman regarded the eland as the most 'powerful' animal spiritually, the eland is the animal most commonly depicted at rock-art sites.

Right
The elegant images of wildlife and their spoor are created by chipping or cutting away the weathered surface of the rock. This weathered 'skin' is known as the 'patina'. Scientists have worked out the rate of repatination of the exposed rock, and so can roughly estimate the age of the engravings – 2000 years being the oldest at Twyfelfontein.

culture of the person starts to influence the hallucinations. The third stage is a radical transformation where the trancer becomes part of the imagery.

Armed with this knowledge, Twyfelfontein becomes a much more interesting place. Yet it must be remembered that even the experts can only, at best, make rough speculations on the 'meaning' of the assemblages, for we lack hard evidence of many important aspects of the social make-up of the society that produced them.

At Twyfelfontein there are, however, some things that are definite and interpretable. There are several assemblages of entoptic images, although these are very few in comparison to the vast number of engravings at the site. Modern theorists would regard this as hard evidence of the first stage of hallucinations experienced by a trancer. There is also much evidence of symbolism and this itself is a complex subject. Rock engravings in southern Africa are noted for the wide diversity of the animals they depict, whereas paintings are much more restricted in their subject matter. Why this is so is not known. However, the most commonly depicted animal in both mediums is the eland. Symbolically, the eland was the most important and powerful animal to the San Bushman. Indeed, they say that all animals are subservient to it. It features in boys' first-kill rituals, which mark the transition to manhood. It features also in their marriage rituals and is indicative of the transition from the single to the married state. Their shamans use 'eland-power' to pass from the material world to the spirit world. In all these cases the eland symbolizes a transition.

Locally, however, other animals attained a 'powerful' status in preference to the eland, and the variety of animals engraved at a site demonstrates the sources of 'potency' for the various shamans that used the site as a 'powerful place'. At Twyfelfontein many eland are depicted, but the giraffe is the most common, with 315 specimens. This ties in very neatly with the fact that the Bushmen of this whole region, stretching right to Botswana, believe the giraffe to be very potent supernaturally. Even today, the remaining Bushmen of the subregion still sing and dance 'giraffe medicine'. This song and dance was given to them by their god, and the song quickly spread from Namibia to nearby Botswana where it replaced the older 'gemsbok medicine' of that region.

As you look down at the many engravings of giraffe

with this background knowledge in mind, you start to get a different feeling about this wonderful place. It is not a straightforward collection of art: instead, it is a book of the minds of a people who lived in a world so completely alien to our present existence that they might have lived on another planet. Here, laid out in such artistic splendour, are the imaginings and fears of a society just as preoccupied as we are with the before and after of our mortal lives.

Three hours at Twyfelfontein were far too short fully to experience the magic of the place, but as we drove away, I was aware that we were not leaving a magnificent art gallery but rather a sacred place, more akin in spirit to the Vatican or Stonehenge.

Beyond Twyfelfontein and its ghosts of the past, we were brought back to the present with a vengeance. Our vehicle, which had behaved flawlessly for the weeks we had been in Walvis Bay and Swakopmund, now, as we encountered bad corrugations, began to falter in the same way as it had en route from Sossusvlei. Finally, the engine died and, with a sinking heart, I guided the vehicle to a halt on the rocky edge of the road.

What galled me most was the fact that I had been diligent in Walvis about the mysterious ailment afflicting the engine. After fruitlessly trying to find the cause of the problem, I had innocently taken it in to a garage. Two days later and several hundred Rands poorer, I reclaimed my vehicle and was assured that the problem had been rectified. "Ach, it was just the electronic choke", the mechanic had assured me. "I replaced it with a new one."

In the blistering heat of the midday sun, bending over a red-hot engine and scalding my arms on the radiator hoses, I searched for the problem while Clarissa and Rosemary did their best to placate my rising temper. Again the carburettor was dismantled and all the lines checked for dirt, but there was nothing to be found. Then, after all my efforts, the engine mysteriously started and ran as though nothing untoward had happened. Hot and sweaty, we continued the journey, my own mind racing with images of what I would like to do to the mechanic when I returned to Walvis. More importantly, there was the disturbing thought that our brand-new vehicle was unreliable. Worse still was the fact that we were heading for a place where most people go with two reliable vehicles as a minimum. As the hours passed, however, and the engine continued to behave, I convinced myself that maybe I had indeed,

somehow, fixed the problem. Ah, such is the capacity of the mind to delude itself! It was just as well though, for had I known what surprises the vehicle had in store for us, I would have turned back then and there.

Since leaving Twyfelfontein the road had become progressively more interesting with every passing bend and rise. Mountain ranges shimmered in the distance. All around were the weird hills and valleys of a landscape sculpted by the desert's erosive power. We were literally driving on the bare surface of the planet's crust, folded and faulted in such a manner that to even the most blasé, it brought new meaning to the word 'geology'.

Increasingly as we progressed down this road, the scenery became wilder, the fences more dilapidated, and there were occasional glimpses of animals. The strange paradox about this part of Damaraland is that, although it is far from being uninhabited, it has the feeling of wilderness about it. This is because of the presence of large wild animals in an area that has long been formally settled and demarcated. Even more paradoxical in this developing world of ours, is the distinct feeling that nature is trying, and succeeding, to reclaim land that only a few decades before had been neat farms. When the white farmers had been replaced by the Riemvasmakers, who were unfamiliar and unhappy with the Kaokoveld, a decline had set in. Now, the fences are dilapidated and full of gaps, the windmill pumps broken, and the farmsteads unpainted and decayed. Elephants wander freely, knocking down what fencing remains and frequently competing with stock at dams and watering places. The final, cruel (for the human inhabitants) consequence of all of this is that Damaraland has become a much more intriguing place – and all as a result of the South African army wanting a piece of land near Augrabies!

By mid-afternoon the road began to descend into a broad and rocky basin and, fortuitously, a tree appeared around the next bend, signalling that it was time to halt for lunch. In its meagre shade we ate biscuits and cheese while water was boiled for some tea. With the vehicle clicking as it cooled and the air shimmering above the hot bonnet, the surrounding splendour was taken in as we regained our land legs. In the valley around us, small relict dunes of red sand nestled in the lee of protective gullies, their surfaces brushed smooth by the winds. Low, leafless bushes struggled for survival in the hollows and rock

Rosemary wanders off down the Huab valley floor

crevasses, and a light desert wind whistled through the branches of the tree above us, a noise so evocative that it accentuated the emptiness of the desert. Later, as we prepared to leave, an ostrich, briefly transfixed by our presence, bolted from a nearby gully and galloped up the side of the dune and over the hill. Far away in the direction it had taken and dancing in the heat haze, blue mountains beckoned. The Kaokoveld was not far now.

On the road again we continued down into a deep valley, the corrugations becoming worse by the minute. The jolts to the suspension became progressively more violent as the road snaked its way downwards. I hardly dared to think of the motor and its foibles, but my doubts hovered, unvocalized, just on the tip of my tongue. All thoughts of breakdowns were soon forgotten, however, as we bounced down the road to the floor of the valley, for this was the Huab Valley – and in the Huab there were elephants. For me, the Kaokoveld proper, would begin on the other side of the riverbed. I drove slowly across to the opposite bank and stopped. Here, before us at last, was the Kaokoveld of my dreams: we were on the threshold of an

Previous pages:
When the eye roves over the ramparts of tumbled blocks at the Twyfelfontein amphitheatre, there are constant surprises. Where, at one moment, there appears to be nothing amidst a wilderness of rock and mountain, in the next, you glimpse a recognizable shape. Here, the lone engraving of a single giraffe graces the side of a mountain in much the same way as the same, but living, animal can be found in other parts of Damaraland. Giraffe still roam the rocky hill slopes and valleys of present-day Damaraland. Keeping mainly the Uniab and Hoanib catchment areas, they use precipitous, treacherous paths to cross the high mountain ridges which separate the numerous valleys of the region.

Africa where adventure could still be found if we looked hard enough.

Years of dreaming of this moment had raised my expectations of the Kaokoveld impossibly high. My mind had created a certain image of the Kaokoveld and it simply never occurred to me that I might not see the elephants or rhinos of my imaginings. Of course I would find them. Looking around, I almost expected to see desert elephants looming behind every bush, but the valley floor was silent and empty. Heat shimmers danced above the sandy bed and a lone crow glided over to where we were parked. Small, stunted acacias colonized the sandy course and flash flooding had created braided streambeds around these hardy trees. Yet nowhere were there any signs of snapped branches, peeled bark, or telltale ochre-coloured piles of droppings. "Hm", I thought to myself as my image of the Kaokoveld came slightly down to earth.

Looking at our map, Clarissa and I could see that we were now only about forty kilometres from our destination, Palmwag camp. After a shout to Rosemary, who had wandered off down the streambed, we moved on, slowly rattling and bumping our way up the other side of the valley.

At the top of the pass we saw our first pile of Kaokoveld elephant droppings. Suddenly, the atmosphere of the boulder-strewn landscape was charged with a whiff of wildness – a magical transformation effected by the sight of those yellow piles of dung. Beyond, the road wound a sinuous route straddled by a range of high red mountains and, as the kilometres passed, more signs of elephant activity became obvious. On both sides of the road the dilapidated stock fences were flattened in many places and the round spoor of elephant pads was everywhere.

After passing the turn-off to the Skeleton Coast Park on our left, my trusty map showed that we were now travelling through some of the farms that had been settled against that old Etosha boundary – Driefontein, Spaarwater, and Bergsig. One after the other we passed the original homesteads of these farms. At a distance they appeared attractive, but on closer inspection their poverty became obvious. Not a blade of grass or leaf on a bush remained in the vicinity of the buildings. Goats, the cause of this blight, huddled in groups under scrawny mopane trees near drinking troughs. Tattered remnants of corrugated iron sheeting were scattered everywhere, along with

rusted implements and machinery. Fences lay broken and sagging. In the heat of the afternoon, there was no sign of the human occupants, and their absence added to the eerie, post-apocalyptic atmosphere which hung low over all of these places.

As we were passing 'Palm', the last of the homesteads before reaching the turn-off to Palmwag camp, fresh elephant tracks appeared in the road. Interestingly, I noted that they had joined the road along the track from Palm's farmyard, which had a large water-tank and trough. On down the road they wandered, the round spoor obviously very fresh and weaving a path from side to side in the same direction we were travelling. Also, alongside the larger round pads of the elephant, there were the tracks of a man and a dog.

Speeding now that our destination was near, we presently came upon the man striding down the road, his dog snuffling at the spoor of the elephant. As we slowed down to pass him, he turned to watch us. His skin was black from a life in the desert sun, his face half-hidden in the dark shade of a tattered bush hat. Poker-faced, he did not return our wave. Not much further on was the elephant. Having flattened one of the small remaining stretches of undamaged fencing, the animal was browsing among the scrubby bushes at the side of the road. As we ground to a halt on the gravelled road, our very first Kaokoveld elephant turned, spread its ears, and trumpeted at us. For an elephant that was living in an area of human occupation, it was quite brazen and showed no fear of the vehicle. Rather, it advanced towards us for a few steps,

A Damara elephant feeds off mopane scrub on the other side of the broken fence

stopped and then flung out its trunk at us again. The ears still outstretched, it listened intently for a while and then, losing interest, began to pluck at the bushes nearby. In the meantime, an inconvenient strand of the old fence was flung aside, almost defiantly. Finally, without the slightest concern, it dropped its trunk and turned to move off slowly down into a gully and out of sight.

I felt a lightening of my heart as we drove on. "Now, that's more like it", I thought to myself.

Soon we reached our turn-off, the Sesfontein road, and a few minutes down this smaller and less-used route we came to, of all things, a veterinary cordon fence. The sight of this fence threw me a little as I was unaware of its existence. It was not marked on my map and its presence was a forceful reminder of the nature of present-day wilderness. Fences such as these were not new to me – a similar one had been erected around the Okavango. Storms of controversy have raged around that fence, but whatever the disadvantages, it cannot be denied that the 'buffalo' fence around the Okavango, erected in the mid-1980s, has effectively halted the encroachment of stock and settlement into the enclosed area. I would later discover that the Damaraland fence functioned in much the same way. Erected in the mid-1970s by the Directorate of Veterinary Services, this huge double fence has been put up to comply with EEC requirements for the import of beef from Namibia. The directorate considered electrifying the fence but this was found to be too expensive. It roughly follows the boundary of the old Etosha Game Reserve, and veterinary regulations dictate that no meat or game products can be carried across it for fear of foot and mouth disease. There is thus no incentive to live to the west of it as livestock from that area can never be marketed to the east of the fence. Effectively, the area to the north and west of the fence has been made more secure for wildlife by default. The benefits of the fence notwithstanding, it is difficult to reconcile its presence with the concept of wilderness. It seems to shout 'authority' and, in my case, brings a sinking of the heart every time I see one.

Struggling to adapt to this unwelcome reminder of the real world, I coasted to a halt at the gate. Clarissa, seeing my frown, looked at the fence and shook her head. "You aren't going to let this fence get you down, are you?"

Parked near the gate was a game department vehicle and next to it a green-clad ranger was talking heatedly

with the khaki-clad gatekeeper. The latter gestured at a point on the fence on one of the nearby hills. "Ja meneer, die olifante . . ."

Looking over to where they were pointing, I could see the grey shapes of a herd of elephant moving slowly across the red boulders of the far hillside. Behind them the game fence lay flattened where they had crossed. Then the gatekeeper noticed us and he sidled over to our vehicle.

"Any meat or skins?" he asked, at the same time managing to look terribly officious. "Where are you going to?" Lifting the curtain, he peered through the back window and stared at the scene within. Lying among the bedding and tarpaulins, and semi-comatose from a combination of the jolting corrugations and the heat, Rosemary grinned back at him. The gatekeeper stared a while longer.

Eventually, the gate was opened and on we went. Soon we came to a sign that said 'Palmwag Lodge' with an arrow pointing down a small road to the left. Swinging the wheel, I accelerated along the bumpy road and presently came to the top of a small rise. There before us in the wide valley below was Palmwag. In the midst of a barren red rock desert, it was an island of green. Oasis would not be the wrong word to describe this idyllic spot. In the bed of the Uniab River, tall reeds and elegant palms rustled in the wind.

An emotion best described as *déjà vu* touched me then. In Swakopmund, while making plans after our evening at Kücki's, we had discovered that Desert Adventure Safaris (D.A.S.) had a lodge and campsite in the Kaokoveld. I had phoned their office in Swakopmund and had been told that, yes, we would be able to see desert elephant and possibly rhino if we were incredibly lucky. Encouraged, we decided to use Palmwag as a base for exploring the Kaokoveld. In addition, the locality of their camp 'Palmwag' rang a bell in my mind and I remembered something I had read many years before. It was 1980 and I was sitting in Houston, Texas, in the gallery of Vittorio Duina. This man, who had promoted my early career as an artist, had brought me to the USA to give me an opportunity to break into the international market. Sitting alone in his gallery over Christmas, surrounded by the classical, and often morbid Italian masterpieces, I had felt a need to read something about Africa. Duina, an avid hunter, kept a collection of books and magazines in the room I was using as a temporary studio. At random, I had

Only occasionally does rain fall on the very fringes of the Namib Desert, and then the rocky plains are transformed into seas of waving grass. Upstream of Palmwag campsite, Rosemary follows a path carved by elephants through fields of grass, a bountiful legacy from the good rains of the previous wet season.

picked up one of the magazines from the rack and found myself paging idly through a glossy hunting magazine. My interest was caught by an article on a hunting trip to the Kaokoveld. The author described flying from Swakopmund and landing at a hunting camp. "A true oasis of palms in the rocky desert – this was Palmwag." He went on to describe their hunt as fantastic. They had taken kudu, gemsbok and even black rhino. A photograph showed palms clustered together in a setting of desert grandeur. That image had stuck in my memory and now the very place lay before me, just as beautiful as I had imagined it would be.

The camp was a group of thatched buildings set in a semicircle and we drew to a halt in a gravelled yard. Even as we swung our doors open and stepped gratefully onto the still earth, a large, jovial-looking man came rushing from a door and beckoned urgently at us. "Kommen Sie hier, die elephanten drinken, kom."

We followed him wearily for it had been a long day, through the door past the bar and out onto the veranda. There below us in the reedbeds of the oasis was a group of elephants drinking from a pool. In the background the sun was low in the sky over a desert scene of magical beauty, perfectly framed by the namesakes of this unique oasis. Jurgen, as he introduced himself to us, was delighted we had seen the elephants. It seemed that we had been lucky and he was so proud to be able to show them to us, we had not the heart to tell him that we had already seen some just up the road.

Back in the bar after the elephant had moved off, Clarissa filled in the register that Jurgen produced. By necessity she was also our interpreter, for Jurgen spoke not a word of English and only a smattering of Afrikaans. When he saw Clarissa write 'four weeks' for the length of our stay, his eyebrows shot up noticeably and, looking over at me, he nodded slowly. "Vier Wochen, das ist gut, das ist

At Palmwag several springs come to the surface in the bed of the Uniab, both up and downstream of the camp. Here, amid the harsh, boulder-strewn hills of a barren desert, an oasis exists. Palms and tamarisk bushes flourish and green reeds sway in the dry breezes. Elephants often come to feed and drink at this oasis and, when night falls, they occasionally venture into the camp itself.

41

gut." We were later told by Jurgen that most visitors stayed two to three days at the most.

The sun was setting over the flat-topped mountains as we drove over to the campsite. There, on an island in the bed of the Uniab and beneath the rustling palms, we made our first camp in the Kaokoveld. I climbed up onto the roof-rack and soon was throwing down our camping equipment to Clarissa. Inevitably, Rosemary wandered off down the riverbed. A coolness descended over the desert's hot surface. It had been a very good day.

Later on that evening we wandered over to the bar. Here the atmosphere was indistinguishable from that of any similar camp in African game country. Be it Seronera, Chitengo, or Savuti, these cosy enclaves are part of the great wildlife experience. Small, cluttered and intimate, this is the place where stories of the day are swopped and many myths are created – exaggeration for effect is the norm in these intoxicating surroundings. "Exaggerate or die" is indeed the standard motto.

Behind the counter Jurgen welcomed us officially to Palmwag. Here, too, we were introduced to the other partner, Mr Gruttemeyer. What Mr Gruttemeyer's first name was I never found out, for he was outwardly a very stern-looking man. With Jurgen we were always on first name terms, but Mr Gruttemeyer would always be Mr Gruttemeyer, even when we came to know him better, for he was very helpful to us later on. Indeed, Gruttemeyer was the owner of the best poker face I had met in a long while.

The bar's decorations were uniquely Kaokoveld – dried bits of the Namib's outlandish flora and rusty fragments of old equipment from the turn of the century. An old German map of the area hung on the wall. As we sipped our iced gins and tonic, the tiny bar was full of chatter from the other guests. These were the clients of D.A.S., who had just returned from a trip overland to the Kunene. They had seen a rhino and were delighted with their luck. Jurgen reached under the counter, brought out some albums of photographs and slid them towards me. Page after page of visitors' photographs of desert game set fire to my enthusiasm. There were great shots of suspicious rhinos and elephant herds set against a background of epic desert scenery. There were also many photographs of 4x4 vehicles negotiating horrendous roads and gullies. Signalling to Gruttemeyer, I ordered ourselves another round, at the same time offering him a drink as well.

"Ja, thank you", he replied, with just a hint of a smile. "A scotch and water."

With this ceremonial ritual of politeness under way, I felt more confident introducing my next topic of conversation. So, after he had served the drinks and was pouring himself a scotch and water, I broached the subject of rhinos. More importantly, where we would be able to find them. Out came my topographical map of the area. For a moment Gruttemeyer was thrown by this visible declaration of my determination. Asking a question was one thing, but unfolding a detailed topographical map of the area at the same time was quite another.

"Some of our clients do see a rhino," he said indicating broadly at the whole map, "but it's impossible to say where you would see one definitely."

"O.K., that I understand, but where would I have the best chance of possibly seeing one?" I looked down questioningly at the map, but Gruttemeyer seemed reluctant or unable to give a specific answer. He pointed out of the door towards the Sesfontein road.

"If you go down that road for a little while, you will come to one of our concession signs next to a track. Take that track and you might be lucky." That was all he would say on the matter.

Soon after that we went back to our camp and fell into bed, suddenly very weary after the day's events. A cool breeze now flowed over the night landscape and stirred the canvas of the tent. Above us the fronds of the palms

A view from the bar at Palmwag Lodge   P.A.

rustled, reminding me of happy days under canvas in the wilds of the Makgadikgadi in Botswana. Looking through the gauze window at the stars, I felt very contented – and relieved! The events of the day augured well for the coming weeks we would spend in the Kaokoveld. Without a doubt, we would see more of the elephants, perhaps under more remote conditions, but there was also the possibility of rhino as well. In fact, all the possibilities looked good. A vast region of mountains and valleys was just waiting to be explored and secret camping places to be discovered. Additionally, and of great importance, there was the aesthetic beauty of the place: it was an artist's dream come true.

As my sleepy mind wandered out over the silent gravel plains, I caught a fleeting glimpse through the window of a meteorite streaking across the sky – a fitting end to our first day in the Kaokoveld.

At about midnight I awoke, blinking and confused to find Clarissa shaking me.

"Wake up, there are elephants outside!"

"Elephants?"

Outside the tent we could hear a crunching noise: a large animal was walking along the gravel path to our campsite. Then the footsteps halted and there was silence. A series of soft thuds were followed by a sound similar to that of a tap being turned on. With its ablutions over, the footsteps continued to come closer and closer. Gazing intently at the canvas walls, we followed its passage around the tent. Then the whole tent gave a shiver – the elephant had encountered one of the guy ropes stretched over the path between the tent and the riverbank. An exasperated exhalation was followed by more snuffling sounds as it explored the canvas flysheet with its trunk. On it moved, more carefully this time. Momentarily, the stars visible through the window were blacked out and then the elephant was past.

Even as it departed in the direction of the swimming-pool, we became aware that there were other elephants all around the island of palms on which the campsite was located. Quickly, we were up and out of the tent and standing next to the reassuring solidity of the vehicle. From above the bushes separating our site from the pool area, a trunk snaked into view, plucked delicately at some greenery and then sank back out of sight. Creeping to the

corner of the hedge for a better view, I beckoned to Clarissa, whispering, "Come, you've just got to see this."

There, in the clearing of lawn before us and beneath the stately palms that ringed the island, were several elephant. One was drinking from the swimming-pool. The others, keeping strictly to the edge of the lawn, plucked at the bushes and sniffed at the well-watered shrubbery. After Gruttemeyer's dog had discovered their presence, they moved reluctantly down to the river pool in front of the lodge where they dallied among the reeds and palms. In a short while they vanished into the night, the dog yapped a few more times, and then silence reigned once more.

The next day dawned hot and bright. Rosemary was very put out that she had not been woken for the elephants. In the solid confines of the vehicle canopy she had heard nothing. "You're pulling my leg", she had said, half-envious that she had missed the night's events. The

Our lean-to in the Palmwag campsite. Sometimes elephants would enter the campsite to feed on the watered shrubbery there, moving past our tent so closely that they touched the guy ropes.

fresh droppings right beside the canopy door were, however, eloquent proof of their presence and of the soundness of her sleep.

After breakfast, with a full fuel tank and plenty of water, we set off down the Sesfontein road, our eyes scanning to left and right for the rhinos that were undoubtedly there – somewhere. Thank goodness for our naïvety! Presently we came to the signboard that Gruttemeyer had mentioned the previous evening. The route whose entrance it guarded only barely qualified as a track. As I swung the vehicle off the road and on to this dubious route, I was soon to realize that all my years of experience with travel on bad roads in Botswana were to be of no help here. The wilds of northern Botswana have no rocks: it is all soft sand, and in the rainy season all that one really has to worry about is mud. Sandy Kalahari roads are no test of a vehicle's reliability, for even in the worst conditions, nothing is comparable to the rock and boulder-strewn tracks of the Kaokoveld.

For a while we jolted along on our chosen route. The track itself was only marginally flatter than the country it crossed, and here and there it followed the bed of a convenient watercourse. Our speed dropped to ten and then to five kilometres an hour as we slowly bumped along. There was no time to look around or search for elusive wildlife – driving here was a full-time job.

After an hour the road came to what appeared to be the end of its life at the top of a steep ravine of jumbled boulders which dropped away down the side of an escarpment. Walking to the edge of the escarpment, I was mortified to see the twin ruts of our track exiting from the base of the ravine. The implication was obvious: I would have to drive my brand-new vehicle down into that gully.

Walking around illuminated another aspect of the Kaokoveld – the clarity with which sounds carry over that rocky terrain. In the bush of the Okavango the calls of birds and insects form a continuous background hum. Here, there was silence and rocky country, which reflected noise with all the acoustic efficiency of the finest Roman amphitheatre. As Rosemary clambered over some rocks a hundred yards away, the metallic clinking sounds she was making were crystal-clear in the desert atmosphere. Idly, I tossed a stone down the gully and was startled by the loudness of the fist-sized rock's progress as it careened down the slope. I was even more startled when a kudu burst from behind a bush at the bottom and bounded across the plain below us, its clattering hooves still audible when it vanished into another gully a kilometre away. We pottered around a little longer, peering at the many strange plants that thrived miraculously on the rocky soil. Eventually, however, we were forced to bring our attention back to the obstacle in the way of our progress.

"That looks pretty steep, doesn't it?" noted Clarissa, echoing my own thoughts exactly.

We had no choice but to go forward, the bonnet of the vehicle dipping downwards at a remarkable angle as I guided it from boulder to boulder, the sides of the doors centimetres away from the walls of this little gorge. This was a new experience for me, particularly the sight of the contortions that the suspension was forced to assume as I inched my way down the ravine. I had visions of our Hilux striking poses similar to the ones depicted in those ridiculous advertisements in outdoor magazines – where the 4x4 clings to the side of a cliff like a mountain goat.

This and opposite pages. Hartmann's mountain zebras are often seen in the hills and valleys of the Kaokoveld. Most often they are glimpsed just as they halt on a mountain ridge to stare back at you for a moment. Then, amid the sound of distant clattering hooves and pebbles, they are gone. P.A

Finally, at the bottom of the defile, the track appeared again.

"Well!" declared Clarissa, opening her eyes and letting out a long breath. "That was interesting!"

By midday of that first day the surrounding landscape had ceased to be beautiful: it had become a vast oven. The pastel tones of the early morning landscape had evaporated into a glaring monochrome of washed-out reds as the sun rose higher in the sky. The coolness had faded in like fashion, replaced by a merciless heat as the sun shone ever brighter in the clear desert air, so that by midday, the rays, where they touched bare skin or the top of one's head, seemed to attain an almost physical pressure. The vehicle, normally our refuge in that shadeless desert, became instead an instrument of torture for all of us as we lurched along.

Six hours after leaving Palmwag we had travelled only forty kilometres. What with the jarring, the bumps, and the continuous gear changing, it did not seem possible that the odometer was right, but from our map I could see that this was so, for as the crow flies, Palmwag was only twenty kilometres distant.

As we drove into the campsite at Palmwag that evening, a more benign sun was already setting over the hazy skies of the western horizon. Weary and rattled in more ways than one, we returned much wiser than we had left. That first day had taught me a good deal about what Kaokoveld travel entailed. For a start, it was painfully obvious that travelling during the middle of the day was out. Secondly, the time had come to do a week-long foray into the remoter parts of the wilderness that lay at the doorstep of Palmwag. I could see that only in those places might we get lucky. That day, when the time had come to start homewards, we had had our lunch in a long and picturesque valley. It was here that Clarissa, wandering about among the small *Welwitschia* plants, had come across

In the first light of a cold Damaraland morning, the stark nature of the desert is softened by the pastel colours of sunrise. In the distance a giraffe lends perspective to the epic grandeur of the landscape.

a game trail with rhino spoor. The tracks were old and their outlines softened by the coastal winds, yet they were the first tangible evidence of the elusive animals we had seen. Even with this tantalizing clue before us, however, we had had to turn back.

"We should be camping out here", declared Rosemary when she saw the tracks. "This is the best place we have seen all day."

It was true. In the last hour before stopping for lunch, the country had taken on a very wild appearance and signs of game become more common. In the far west the horizon was topped by the first hints of the coastal fog belt and to the north, ranges of blue mountains shimmered in the heat haze. We were on the very edge of the Kaokoveld of my dreams, the place where there was freedom and mystery, the Kaokoveld where humans had never driven in fencing poles. It would have to wait a few more days, however, for I wanted to be sure that the fault in the engine had truly been fixed. A few more days of driving from Palmwag as our base and I would be confident of its reliability.

That evening in the bar Clarissa told Jurgen where we had been and of the rhino spoor in that far-off valley. "Ask him if they've seen any there recently", I said as I pointed out to Jurgen on my map where we had been. Jurgen looked quizzically at the track I had marked on the map before replying.

Clarissa listened and then told me what I wanted to know. Yes, there were occasional rhino sightings in that area, and a little further along in a secluded valley there was a good fountain where lots of game could be seen.

The next few days we travelled every track within reach of Palmwag and my map started to sprout a network of pencilled-in routes. My confidence in the engine was mostly restored and after fully servicing the vehicle, I declared that, to the best of my knowledge, it was fit for the next stage of our travels. The idea was to camp out, gradually getting further and further into the wilds of the Kaokoveld. We filled all our jerry cans and water containers, packed enough food for a week and, the following morning, set off early down a track that was now becoming very familiar.

The gully that had caused us such consternation on that first day was traversed with the practised ease of an old hand and by midday we were past our furthest known point. Here I experienced again that momentary feeling of

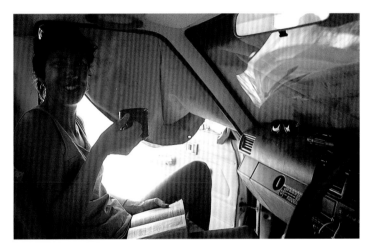

panic that I had occasionally felt during the past few days. The spectre of a breakdown in these conditions always hovered in the back of my mind. There was always that thought, "What if the engine dies again? What if I can't fix it?"

The further we went, the more barren the terrain became. Igloo-shaped and light green, the ubiquitous *Euphorbia damarana* bushes were scattered on the open plains, while other hardy plants bunched together in the sandy rivercourses. Here mopane scrub and tamarisk bushes clustered so densely that when we walked along one of these riverbeds we had the illusion of being in a forest. Away from these ribbons of vegetation, it was all rock and sand. Mountains reared on all sides from the flat valley floors and distance became hard to judge. As we progressed further away from Palmwag, the track grew rougher. On

Our vehicle and tent perched atop a tiny plateau in a remote Damaraland valley. The view from our 'veranda' could not have been bettered for, as we breakfasted, we could see in the distance small herds of Hartmann's mountain zebra and gemsbok, and a giraffe. The perfect camp at dawn, however, was not so perfect an hour later when the sun had risen and began to blaze mercilessly down from above.

The hours between 11 a.m. and 3 p.m. were the toughest of the day. Every animal would vanish from sight and the heat become unbearable, and so this was time to stop and rest until the cool of the late afternoon. In other parts of Africa we would have been able to find a suitably shady tree, but here it was different. A tarpaulin would be dragged over the vehicle to provide some meagre shade. Then, with the canvas carefully tucked down so that no piece of the dazzling sky could be seen, we fitfully read books, nibbled biscuits and dozed in the oven-like confines of the vehicle.

A midday stop in the wilderness of Damaraland. Red-coloured boulders and pebbles are one of the striking characteristics of this part of the world, and the redness seems to be accentuated by the lush green of the common *Euphorbia damarana* bushes.

two occasions, washaways in the steeper sections had to be filled in with boulders before we could continue on our way, and beyond these the track showed not a single sign of recent use. At last, we were well and truly on our own.

By the end of the day we were, by my calculations at least, close to the fountain that Jurgen had mentioned. The mountains and hills around us seemed to correspond to where I thought we were on the map. Moreover, in front of us was the long, steep-sided valley where the fountain was supposed to be located. Our destination was close enough now for us to stop and make camp.

Our first night out under the Kaokoveld stars was one to savour, for this, at last, was the real thing. Not since the 1970s in the Ngwezumba Valley in northern Botswana had I felt so alone in a wilderness inhabited by big game. This was indeed a place with a similar atmosphere, but here there was also the delightful pleasure of camping where one pleased. Just off the track, in the bed of a wide dry watercourse, there was a beautiful sandbank, and it was here that we stopped.

As the sun set behind one of the western ranges, Clarissa put up the tent while I checked the vehicle for signs of trouble. Rosemary, always one to explore the surroundings first, went off in search of some wood for a fire. Far up on the slopes of the valley wall a herd of gemsbok cantered noisily along a path on their way to drink. Their destination, the fountain, was a kilometre away: through the binoculars, a splash of green on the ochre terrain could just be seen. In among the green patch

there was a glint of water but, alas, no rhinos. The dry riverbed in which we were camped, however, bore many signs that elephant and rhino had used it recently as a thoroughfare.

That night, as I was preparing to go to bed, a slight sense of unease momentarily disturbed my contentment. Outside, it was so quiet that it hurt the ears. You could hear your heart thumping loudly. We were surrounded by a silence that had not often been disturbed in thousands of years. Now and then a Hottentot or Bushman party would have hunted the valley. Countless thousands of rhino had trod this way to drink at the fountain. The track had probably been blazed when this was part of Etosha, and later used by poachers when it was not. Now, a vehicle passed very occasionally with modern-day visitors intent on seeing or conserving. But for all of that, the silence and remoteness of this far-flung place remained complete.

In the early hours of the morning Clarissa shook me awake. A second shake and she had my full attention. Outside, we could hear a scraping of sand and a sharp snap as a branch broke. Quickly now, I zipped down the door of our tent and shone the torch into the darkness. A few yards away the looming grey mass of an elephant materialized from the gloom. It had its trunk up, scenting the air as it slowly but deliberately moved towards our encampment. Hastily, we scrambled out of the tent and towards the safety of the car. The light of the torch, our whistling and then our shouts did nothing to stop its approach.

"I wonder why it's so curious?" marvelled Clarissa as it still came on. "We have to do something – this isn't the place to have an incident!"

This was easier said than done, as it knew of our presence and was indeed very curious. In Botswana I would have tried rushing at it, shouting at the same time, and been fairly confident that it would have turned tail and run. But here, our remoteness and the uncertainty of the reaction I might get dictated caution. Instead, I tried a trick that seems invariably to deter elephants: I bowled a large stone along the ground aimed at its feet. To elephants, who rely on their hearing more than their sight, the impression is that they are being attacked by something that quite literally runs beneath their legs. Confused by this aggressive tactic, they invariably turn and run. True to form, this determined elephant turned and ran from its imaginary attacker. As the behemoth departed in undignified haste, I turned to Clarissa and bowed theatrically.

"Encore! Encore!" she declared, laughing at my antics. "I always knew I was in good hands!"

The next morning, we rose and breakfasted before sun-up. Closer examination of the elephant tracks revealed that the curious animal had closely approached our camp twice from different directions before we finally awoke. Once, it had even been to within a trunk's length of the vehicle. At this revelation, Rosemary was incredulous and not a little irritated that she had yet again slept through another exciting episode.

"I'm missing all of the interesting things that happen at night," she mused, referring to the soundproofing effect of the vehicle's canopy. "The next time, please wake me up also."

As we pulled away from our idyllic camping place, I made a mental note that, if I could help it, there would be no next time. The unpredictability of elephants and the loneliness of our location were not a good combination. In future, we would camp far away from even the vaguest hint of a game trail.

Always the desire was to be off before the sun rose from behind the horizon, for this was the magical time of the day. The air was fresh and jerseys were a necessity. The scenery was at its most benign and, best of all, we felt energetic. We knew that two hours later it would be a different story.

One curious aspect of the scenery had us all confused at one time or another: this was our inability to judge distances in a terrain where there was often a complete lack of familiar objects to use as a benchmark for scale. Quite often I found myself looking at the opposite wall of a steep valley, and because of the clarity of the air, would be convinced that it was only a few hundred yards away. Suddenly, an animal would bolt from a hidden gully, and there then followed a giddy instant in which the mind grasped the true scale of the scene.

We saw no signs of anything out of the ordinary that morning, although the scenery and the wildness of the surroundings would have normally satisfied me. I was, however, determined to see a rhino and this desire was beginning to spoil my ability to appreciate anything else.

By late morning, after a fruitless search of a rather

barren river valley, the heat from the sun's rays turned our thoughts to shady places. Amazingly, almost as if on cue, we found a single tree at the head of the valley. Although completely incongruous in the boulder-strewn landscape of that desert valley, its deep shade offered an ideal stopping place – ideal except for the fact that an elephant had already beaten us to it. When it heard the noise of our motor, however, it conveniently made way for us, departing with amazing speed over the tumbled boulders and sharp outcrops of the valley floor. Twenty minutes later, after an extraordinary climb along a steep mountain gully, it crested the ridge. For a moment it halted there with its trunk raised, a pinprick on the distant mountain skyline, and then it was gone, lost in the endless ramparts and valleys that lay beyond.

Several hours later, once the sun's strength had waned sufficiently, we set forth from the cool shade of the lone tree to search for game – but it was to be a disappointing afternoon. The valleys seemed strangely empty of wildlife and the track we were following was truly atrocious. There were some glimpses of distant giraffe and gemsbok, but nothing else.

By late afternoon, we found ourselves in the middle of an extensive and uneven gravel plain that was bounded on one side by towering, jagged mountains. As it crossed this plain the track became very indistinct, the two ruts only just discernible among the loose pebbles, and there was always the feeling that it was about to peter out completely in the rocky wasteland around us. In the midst of the plain, however, there was a tiny plateau. This overlooked a wide, forested riverbed which bisected the plain's vast expanse – a perfect camping place. Leaving the track and bumping slowly over the loose rocks, we were soon on the little

Chance encounters with elephants in spectacular locations are something to be expected when camping out in the Kaokoveld. On this occasion, a dawn walk to a ravine only a few metres from our camping spot revealed a herd of elephant quietly feeding in the giant tamarisk bushes below.

plateau and unloading the vehicle for the night.

When the sun goes down in the western reaches of the Kaokoveld, the daytime heat is replaced very quickly by a chill wind that blows from the coast. Jerseys and jeans are quickly donned and it becomes hard to imagine that, only four hours earlier, the sweat had been flowing freely from every pore. On the bare rock the tent pegs could find no purchase and so the guys were tied to convenient boulders. This was no place to sit out under the stars and so, after a supper in the cab, Clarissa and I retired to the tent. Exposed as we were on our little plateau, our tent flapped incessantly all night in a rising gale. As the blackness of

the night set in, the sense of the place's utter loneliness was heightened by the moan of the wind over the rocky wastes. We were indeed far from home and our little encampment was but a speck in the vastness of the Kaokoveld wilderness.

By dawn the next morning the wind had dropped and, as we roused ourselves from beneath piles of sleeping bags and blankets, a rosy glow over the western mountains heralded the beginning of a new day. From our elevated position there was a splendid view of the surrounding plains. Our 'veranda' vista was more spectacular than any luxury lodge could have provided and, as we breakfasted in the pre-dawn light, the plains around us stirred with life.

In the distance a lone giraffe made its way towards the mountains. Closer, and suspicious of the movement coming from our little hill, was a group of ostrich. Beyond them, a herd of gemsbok cantered off, leaving a plume of dust hanging in the still, morning air.

Rosemary, who had risen earlier than we, had walked the two hundred metres to where the edge of our plateau afforded a good view of the rivercourse. A few minutes later there was a muted shout and she beckoned to us. Clarissa rushed off and I followed a few seconds later with my cameras and sketchbook. As I approached the lip, the rocks clinking loudly beneath my feet, Rosemary turned and put her finger to her lips. Creeping closer, the riverbed came into view, and directly below us a group of elephants could be seen browsing on the stubby bushes inhabiting the sandy bed. In the tamarisk forest beyond, there were more elephants, all of them unaware of our presence thirty metres above them. Then, as the sun crested the mountains and the scene below us was flooded with a wash of yellow light, they began to move along the bed of the river. One by one, they gradually filed past our hidden vantage-point and gathered at a small pool a little further on. Finally, with only the faintest of scuffling noises, they disappeared from view around the nearest bend in the river.

Back at the tent, and encouraged by the amount of game that was about, I carefully scanned the surroundings with binoculars for the telltale silhouette that I longed to see. Surrounded as I was by such natural splendour, I should not have felt disappointed, but I was when the search proved fruitless. There was a further disappointment in store.

"I think you had better come and have a look at this", declared Clarissa, beckoning me over to where I had placed our water-containers on the ground the previous evening. Around the one that should have been completely full, there was a wide ring of damp sand. It was empty! A sharp stone had pierced the plastic and our reserve water-container had leaked its precious cargo into the desert earth. With only one full container of water left, there were no other options open to us – we would have to start back on the long two-day slog to Palmwag immediately.

The less said about that return journey the better.

Suffice it to say that by the time Palmwag hove into sight, I think we were all entertaining serious thoughts of Swakopmund. If you have ever seen a cat that has been spun until dizzy and then set down on its feet, you have a good idea of our state as we disembarked and moved towards the main building. With tortured visions of that first plunge in the pool, we were in a hurry to book in and get over to the campsite, but a diversion awaited us.

Just as we arrived, Jurgen was sitting down to lunch in the dining-room with some other members of the staff whom we had not met in the previous weeks. One of these, a delightful, bustling woman, had just come in from the kitchen with a huge tray of delicious food. I think she they must have noticed our hungry glances, for in no time at all we were seated at a table and wolfing down what I later found out to be a German dish called 'Kartoffelpuffer', made with potatoes, hot and dripping with fat. Seeing us take to the food so, we were soon asked what it was that we had been eating in the desert. From past experience we knew that this was a difficult question. A dilemma presented itself – should we tell them the truth?

Clarissa was always being asked this question, especially by women, and the kind lady who had plied us with the 'Kartoffelpuffer' was now waiting to hear what she had to say. The truth of the matter was that we were never hungry while in the bush; rather, it was the monotony of our bush fare that caused us to have such gluttonous tendencies when any delicious food was put before us. Moreover, the reactions of the enquirer to our way of doing things had long since caused us to fib for the sake of peace. When told

that we never cooked or heated anything – that we never in fact used plates at all – the concerned listener would decline to believe us. They were universally horrified when they heard that we would each open a tin, one of meat and the other of vegetables, eat half and then swop. This we jokingly called our 'balanced diet'. That would be dinner. For breakfast we each had a plate of cereal, and for lunch there would be biscuits with sardines or cheese. Tea was the only thing that we heated up. At this stage the listener would often become defensive, for somehow they always took it as a slur on the way that 'they' did things when camping. And a look in their vehicle would tell you why. There would be gas bottles, braai grates, fridges and freezers, boxes of spices, and huge amounts of fancy food and fresh vegetables – sometimes even the kitchen sink! They indeed ate well, spending most of their time in the bush preparing and cleaning up after meals under adverse conditions, and were exhausted afterwards. For us, it was a maximum of two minutes to prepare, two minutes to eat, and there was nothing left to clean. The listener would then depart, secretly convinced that we were, at the very least, eccentric.

As far as Rosemary was concerned, it was a similar story of strange eating habits, only in her case it was the amazingly small amount of food that she ate – enough to satisfy a sparrow – which caused universal disbelief. She cooked for herself and often an entire month's supply would fit into a small tin trunk!

So, back to our dilemma – should we tell them all this, and be regarded as mad? We declined to disillusion them and lied instead, saying, "Oh! we ran out of fresh veggies yesterday."

Later on that evening we were back in the bar and Mr Gruttemeyer asked the inevitable question.

"Any rhinos?"

"Not one."

"Too bad", he said. "Our clients have just come back from a safari and they saw two."

Outside, the sun was setting behind the palms of the oasis and his clients were all relaxing and talking of their adventures in the desert. In the vastness of the Kaokoveld there was only a small number of rhinos. The odds on finding one seemed to be getting longer.

That evening, one of the employees we had been introduced to at our lunch-time feast was behind the bar

The rare desert rhino – P.A.

and when ordering our drinks, I bought him one as well. A retiring person, he had parked his caravan well away from the camp under a solitary palm tree. He was very interested to hear that I was an artist and told me that he, too, was an artist, that he carved wood and had done so for a living. This was a conversational road that I had been down many times before, but as the drinks flowed and the evening progressed, I could see from the way he spoke that he must be a bona fide artist. Indeed, he was enjoying the chance of talking about himself and I came to realize that he was good at what he did: his confident 'art-speak' revealed a person comfortable with his talents. It was obvious, however, that a deep-seated grievance hovered just below the surface and his face darkened as he spoke of some incident in the past, when his work had allegedly been marketed and sold under another's name. Not knowing quite what to say in the ensuing silence, we both contemplated the moonlit Kaokoveld scene through the window of the bar. He visibly cheered up. "Oh well, I'll get back into it again some time." Then he went on to tell me of a stump of wood that he had behind his caravan and that it was just right for the carving of a kudu's head.

The next day we relaxed by the pool, enjoying the splendid luxury of splashing about in cool water under a hot desert sky. Then, as the other guests retired to their comfortable bungalows, we, the campers in steerage, returned to the campsite to swelter under tarpaulins or follow the small patches of shade around our mopane tree.

Clarissa and I made gallant attempts at working. It was an enormous effort for Clarissa to get out her reference material and retire under some bush to work, but she did so with a stoic determination that I found rather challenging. Then I had no excuse but to retire to the hothouse of the lean-to and continue on whatever painting was in progress. In all the time we had been at Palmwag, even when we had gone out on drives, I had been diligent in my artistic endeavours. The lightweight field-easel and my artistic materials were always to hand and all the midday hours were spent completing many small oil and pencil sketches. These were invaluable to me, for they would form the core of the material that I would use at a later date to create the larger, finished studio paintings. And so it went as we swatted flies, retrieved windblown sheets of paper, and, in my case, endured the stares of an enraptured Damara staff while I painted.

above – An attractive boardwalk over one of the Uniab's smaller channels. Took one to the bar at Palmwag lodge – a place where many tales & stories of desert game could be heard.

One of these Damara workers noticed some rocks that I had placed on the edge of our lean-to's table. These had been idly collected on one of our desert journeys; I had recognized them from my time as a geologist in the Karoo. He spoke to Clarissa in Afrikaans and she translated for me. He wanted to know what they were.

"Aragonite crystals, but they are not good specimens."

After listening to Clarissa he looked again at the rocks and then walked off.

Later on that afternoon the same man was back. He presented me with a small bag of what turned out to be beautiful examples of Aragonite crystals. Obviously, he had spent the afternoon scouring the hills in search of them. Equally obviously, the expectation was that I would buy his offerings. Looking at the man in front of me, I saw someone dressed in patched clothes, marginalized by his race and lack of education. To make matters worse, the poverty of his appearance contrasted sharply with the background of my shiny new vehicle. Bargaining with him (through Clarissa) did not take long and soon he had departed, with a jaunty step and 25 Rands for a bag of crystals that I did not want. The next morning another of the Damara staff expectantly arrived in our campsite with a huge bag of the same stuff which I had no qualms about refusing to buy.

The vast canyon between the rich and the poor was

The Aub River, one of the smaller tributaries of the Uniab, is a few hours' drive from Palmwag. At one location on the Aub the dry watercourse tumbles haphazardly through a small gorge and here several substantial potholes have formed. Set deep in the gorge, the potholes – and the glittering water within them – are tantalizingly inaccessible to the wildlife of the area.

Opposite
The clarity of the desert air, and the lack of familiar objects such as trees sometimes make it difficult to appreciate the grandeur of the Kaokoveld landscape: everything seems to be closer than it really is. Only when a large animal, such as an elephant, is seen wending its way along a distant game path does the true scale of the surroundings become apparent.

request was far beyond my capabilities. Their sewing machine had been broken for a while and it seemed that his wife was having to do all their sewing and patching by hand. He told us that their clothes were now starting to look very worn and tatty. To be poor like this is hard indeed. To be poor and then not be able to keep one's dignity intact, must be unbearable. The irony of it all is that the places in the world where nature is intact are also those where the inhabitants are poor. Surrounded by the priceless treasures of wilderness and wildlife, they are poverty-stricken, while it is in the cities and industrial parks that the wealth flourishes. This is how we humans value nature.

Determined to go out again, I pored over my map, unable to decide whether we should return to the area we had been in before the leaky water-container had forced us to return, or try another place altogether. I decided to question Gruttemeyer once again, but found he was away in Swakopmund for the day. Instead, in the office was a pilot whom I had not met before. Ever-persistent in tapping all possible sources of information, I went through my routine and then produced my map. This time I was amply rewarded for my persistence, for the pilot knew a lot about the whole area and did much to revive my flagging hopes. It seemed that we had been on the right track and that one of the valleys we had reached on our last trip was indeed a good place to see rhino. We had simply not gone far enough up it. When the track ran out, he suggested that we drive in the riverbed till we could go no further. Then and only then were our chances of seeing rhino considered to be good.

A few days later and at the end of a hellish two-day journey, we found ourselves halfway along the valley in question. Here we camped for the night and relaxed around the much-needed warmth of a camp fire. The journey had been a blur of heat-filled days, as we rattled and bounced over tracks that seemed to go on for ever.

At one point the track negotiated the steep side of a very deep valley. The rains of the previous season had eroded this precarious route and we were forced to build up the side of the road in order to pass. Lugging heavy, red-hot boulders in the midday heat had frayed the tempers, but this was soon forgotten as we then negotiated the shored-up section. With Clarissa driving and me walking in front to check that the rocks were holding, there was a

brought home to me by another episode in the lives of these Damaras. Next to where they lived, they carefully tended a small vegetable garden for their own use. On the night before we had returned from our last desert sojourn, this garden had been raided by elephant. We heard about this indirectly from a group of tourists in the bar who seemed to think that it was a huge joke, and they laughed heartily as they told us the story.

Indeed, another incident touched my heart as well. One day one of the Damara staff came across to the campsite and asked if I could help him. With Clarissa translating for me, the man brought forth a small metal part from their sewing machine. Examining it, I could see that it had worn down and snapped. "Can you fix this for them?" Sadly, this

bad moment when one of the boulders shifted. The vehicle leaned outward at an alarming angle and the front inside wheel lifted off the ground before righting itself. Shaken in more ways than one, nobody said anything as we moved on.

As we sat by the flickering flames of the fire, the effects of eight hours of travel slowly drained away. Rosemary was cooking her meal in the back of the vehicle. Clarissa and I shared our own supper, one of our notorious 'balanced diets'. Around us was the epic grandeur of a truly wild landscape. The riverbed was quite wide at the place we had decided to camp and densely populated by a kind of stunted mopane scrub. Around us, on the riverbank, were huge ancient *Welwitschia* plants. Beyond were the red boulders and shingle plains of the Kaokoveld.

The next morning we were off again, early as usual, and found that we had camped quite close to a spring of water (or fountain as they are called hereabouts). This was to be the best of many fountains that we would encounter in our travels in the Kaokoveld. Its spring water filled some small pools, and there was even a tiny rivulet that flowed for a few yards in the desert sand and supported a patch of coarse green grass and reeds. That there was plenty of wildlife was evidenced by the major game trails which could be seen snaking down the hillsides towards it. More exciting, among the numerous elephant droppings there was also fresh rhino spoor.

We kept to the vicinity of this fountain for the next few days and it was here that we saw our one and only Kaokoveld lion. Surprised while resting up during the heat of the day, the splendid, black-maned male bolted off through the *Euphorbia damarana* plants almost before we had realized what it was. There was just one good glimpse of it, as it turned and studied us for a few seconds from a nearby rise, then it darted behind some rocks and was gone. Shy by day, lions were, however, very vocal on all of the nights we spent in this fantastic place.

A disturbingly odd occurrence that we experienced here was also associated with the night. It happened when we had retired to bed in the tent. As I was drifting off to sleep, I clearly heard the very distant sound of a vehicle. When I drew Clarissa's attention to it, she declared that she could even make out the pauses when the gears were shifted. Listening hard to a sound that was only just at the level of being audible, I, too, found that I could make out the distinctive change in note of the motor when the gears were shifted. There was only one conclusion to be drawn from this – that, unbelievably, a vehicle would soon be approaching. Unzipping the tent, we tumbled out, expecting to see its lights as it slowly wended its way along the same track we had used to access this part of the valley. But we saw nothing at all. Standing on some rocks nearby, I was surprised to find the valley empty, and listening hard, found that the engine noise had, in the meantime, vanished as well. Frozen and tired, we listened for a while and then, still puzzled, returned to the tent. In my mind I was worried about the suspicious nature of this strange event; we did not want someone, possibly an armed poacher, to come stumbling unexpectedly into camp. The moment I zipped the tent closed, however, the sound of the vehicle returned. This time I put only my head outside the tent. With some experimentation we discovered that we could hear the ghostly vehicle only while we were inside the tent and only if the front flap was zipped. This had the effect of making the whole tent as taut as a drum. Presumably the shape of the tent and its tautness had somehow amplified the sound of that distant engine as it carried through the silence of the night. The next day I examined my map and found that the only road which could possibly have any traffic on it was eighty kilometres away and beyond several ranges of hills. The acoustic qualities of the desert had fooled us yet again.

One by one the days passed. We had seen many elephant, giraffe, gemsbok, and mountain zebra, but the desert rhinos continued to elude us. I began to feel that, actually, there were no rhinos at all in the Kaokoveld and, even if there were, there was a conspiracy to stop me

seeing them. Our supplies of water began to get a little low and I was sorely tempted to replenish our supply from the nearby fountain: this would save us a very long and uncomfortable drive to Palmwag. The bits of elephant dung floating on the surface of most of these pools did not deter me in the least. Indeed, I had boiled and used water far more polluted than that in the Ngwezumba area of Botswana and never suffered from any ill effects. It would have been easy to filter the water through towels and then boil it over an open fire. There were many persistent rumours, however, that some of the fountains had become infected with anthrax. Indeed, a rhino had already succumbed to the disease, and it was assumed that it had been infected by one of the tainted fountains. I felt it was simply not worth the risk.

On the last day before we would have to return to Palmwag for water, we set forth yet again in search of the, by now, almost mythical beasts. That evening we returned to our comfortable little campsite on the riverbank, disappointed and weary of the endless boulder-covered wastes. Irritatingly, the spoor and dung heaps of the rhinos were common in the vicinity of where we were camped. To me, their very profusion was a mocking reminder of my inability to find these elusive animals.

That evening I walked up onto the hillside above our camping place, following, where convenient, the curious game paths that led to the nearby fountain. Something about the paths had been bothering me and I then realized what it was: these game paths had the same function as those I had known in the sandveld of Botswana's Ngamiland. There, however, the game path was a seasonal thing. During the rains all the wildlife disperses away from the dry-season pans and rivers. As the year progresses, the smaller pans dry up. Then, in the dry season, the wildlife again starts to congregate around the perennial water supply. Increasingly, large numbers of animals use the most logical and easiest routes to and from their nightly feeding grounds. A game path subsequently develops and, at the height of the season, some of these paths become highways worn down by the daily passage of thousands of animals. When the rains fall again the animals disperse quickly and, after a month or so, the path has vanished totally under the growth of the new season.

The game path that I had been following along the contour of the hill had exactly the same function as a game

below – Many times, in order to continue onwards, we had to negotiate a careful path over rocks & boulders to reach the relative smoothness of a stream bed!

trail in Ngamiland, yet it differed in one important aspect. This was no seasonal path: the countless animals that had passed this way had created a permanent feature, a relic of the ages, and as old as Africa itself. These smooth pathways were not formed by the passage of huge herds, but rather by the daily movements of small numbers of animals over thousands of years. Up to a metre wide in places, they are completely free of stones. Step off the path and you immediately stumble over a terrain of shiny pebbles and boulders, where you have to walk very carefully to avoid a sprained ankle. Walk on the path and you can safely saunter along at a brisk speed, half-asleep if so desired. When all the Kaokoveld's elephants, rhino and giraffe have disappeared, their paths will remain behind as curious geological features. A thousand years from now they will still be there, ancient monuments to be marvelled at by some future generation of archaeologists.

Using one of these convenient ribbons of smoothness, it was an easy walk to the top of the hill where I sat down and began to scan the surrounding countryside with binoculars. As I panned slowly over the still scene before me, my attention was caught by something anomalous. About two kilometres away a small white speck on a plateau in the valley floor started to move slowly down the slope towards the fountain. Peering hard through the binoculars, and struggling to keep them steady on the distant object, I hardly dared to believe my eyes. There was no mistaking it: I was looking at a desert rhino!

Later on that evening, when I was contentedly sitting at the fire contemplating the 'victory', Clarissa told me that when I had come running into the camp, panting and babbling incoherently about rhinos "somewhere over there", she had thought that I meant there was one near the camp. She and Rosemary had then been surprised when I rushed off, camera in hand, and kept on going over the boulder plain until I had disappeared from sight over a ridge a kilometre away. Every moment counted as the light was fading and so, jogging along game paths and convenient streambeds, the half an hour that it took me to reach the little plateau seemed an eternity. As I drew closer to where I knew the rhino must be, I became very aware of the noise I was making – stones rattling, rocks clinking, and my heart thumping madly with excitement. At last, there it was, moving slowly down the steep face of the small plateau and only a hundred metres away. With

above – The Kaokoveld is criss-crossed by distinct game paths which are kept clear of pebbles & boulders by the passage of occasional big game

the first sight of the rhino and of its two curving horns, I was also, for the first time, very conscious of how open the country suddenly seemed to become – there are no trees to climb beyond the riverbeds of the Kaokoveld. The rhino progressed steadily down the slope towards me, browsing briefly from many of the small bushes along the path it was using. When it was thirty metres away from me, my courage failed. Nearby there was a convenient gully and, dodging into this, I ran, bent over, until my lungs felt like bursting.

After a short rest it took me forty-five minutes to walk back, only to be met en route by the vehicle. The headlights were on for it was almost dark, and when it pulled up next to me, two pairs of concerned eyes glared out. Clarissa, relieved and angry at the same time, rightly tore a strip off me. "Are you all right? You are! Well, please don't ever do that again. Do you realize that you've been

A desert rhino slowly picks its way down the side of a small plateau situated in one of the thousands of valleys in Damaraland. After several weeks of hard searching, we were on the verge of giving up altogether, but this was the first of several we would be lucky enough to find.

Opposite
Our second rhino, glimpsed as it traversed a vast tableland on the far side of a large, shallow valley. Although at least two kilometres away, this rhino was very aware of our presence and, after staring hard in our direction for several minutes, turned and walked briskly off in the opposite direction.

gone for nearly an hour and a half and we were getting really worried?"

'When it rains, it pours', the saying goes, and so it was with our luck, for that night, the rhino, having been joined by another one, lingered in the riverbed below us, making noises like a steam engine. Much galloping and squealing followed, accompanied by the sound of clattering pebbles. Occasionally, there were deafening snorts and, in the pitch-black darkness of a moonless night, the power of the imagination was such that on several occasions I was convinced they were about to blunder into our little encampment. But, again, it was the extraordinary way that sound carried through the desert air that deceived us and the next morning the only fresh tracks to be found were two hundred metres away.

I was up with the dawn and scanning the countryside from the nearby rise, almost certain, after the din of the previous night, that the rhinos were still close by, but the valley was empty of life. Back at camp, I again examined our water supply. Realizing that we would need more if we were to stay on safely, I decided that the unexpected turn of events justified the risk of using the water from the nearby spring. Thus the rest of the day was spent filtering water through towels to remove the pieces of elephant dung and springbok droppings, then boiling it in a kettle over a mopane-wood fire. By evening, all of our water containers were full, although the liquid they contained was greenish in colour and had a sharp saline taste that did not agree with Rosemary's discerning palate. "Hm, only in tea, I think," she declared with a grimace after sampling the unappealing stuff. Indeed, if we left a glass of the coloured liquid still for a moment or two, a green sediment settled at the bottom.

The following day we set forth early, illogically certain that we would be lucky again. It was one of those days when everything seemed to point that way: we had heard lions calling nearby at dawn, and as we breakfasted, a huge elephant bull had wandered unconcernedly up the riverbed in front of us. On a distant ridge a large herd of mountain zebra had watched us for a while before galloping off. More importantly, the previous evening, there had been much noise from the vicinity of the fountain, which suggested that the rhinos had been active again. Amazingly, it turned out to be a fantastically lucky day for us all – for each one of us sighted a rhino.

First, Clarissa saw one browsing the edge of a distant wash and we followed it for an hour, finally getting to within twenty metres of it. When it finally noticed us there ensued a sudden charge, which Clarissa, at the wheel, handled very coolly indeed with a long burst from the horn. At this, the rhino wheeled and tore off through the rocks and bushes; ten minutes later it was still running flat out as it disappeared over a distant ridge.

Rosemary was next. From the back of the vehicle, she spotted a rhino later that morning. This one was too far off and in a deep valley, so we pressed on in search of other sightings, excited at the prospects. Nevertheless, by midday we were ready to stop for lunch.

As was normal at this time of the day, we would drive into the dense mopane scrub of the riverbed and park beneath the best bit of shade we could find. I would then stretch a canvas tarpaulin over the vehicle, and we would weather the midday heat in moderate comfort. This, as usual, was what we did that day, but, while unloading some chairs from the roof rack, a movement under a nearby bush caught my eye. There was a startling crack as a branch snapped, and at that moment our third rhino of the day stood up and snorted, only to lie down again in a different position. Strangely, it seemed oblivious of our presence, especially as we had made considerable noise in unpacking. So, with the chairs out, we sat drinking tea and munching biscuits, revelling in the uniqueness of the occasion – for where else in Africa could one do this? We were truly privileged indeed. As we sat there, with the rhino only thirty metres away, the tension of the previous weeks seemed to dissipate entirely.

"Well, then," sighed Clarissa, sensing the change in atmosphere, "at last we can now relax a little bit."

The remaining days we stayed in camp, content to let the game come to us rather than have the fillings in our teeth shaken loose on drives. It had become a holiday at last, and

Our best view of a desert rhino, a beautiful example of what has become, in the last few decades, one of the most endangered of the larger African mammals. Possibly fewer than 3000 remain on the continent, maybe a hundred of these in the Kaokoveld.

I completed some of the best oil sketches I was to do in the Kaokoveld. Finally, when the food had begun to run a little low and only one container of the green water remained, we returned to Palmwag in high spirits.

We were late it seemed, and our long absence had been noted by the staff at Palmwag, particularly the kind lady who had plied us with Kartoffelpuffer on our previous return.

"Ah, so the Augustinuses have returned", was her abrupt greeting when she saw us. "One more day, and I would have had the police out looking for you!"

It was true – we were long overdue, and the ramifications of this had briefly occurred to me in the last few days of our stay in that distant valley. I could see now that we had broken an unwritten rule: always let somebody know when you will return, and never stay out beyond that day.

"Last year we had some people break down out there", she said gesticulating out of the window at the distant mountains. "When they had been gone too long for my liking, I called in the police. It took them two days to find them. Another day and I'd have done the same thing again for you. Please, you must tell me when you go and when we should expect you back."

The 'wood carver' was behind the bar listening to this. "And if you'd come back yesterday you would have been here when the lions came through the lodge last night."

It seemed that these lions had caused a great commotion as it was almost unheard of in these parts that they should have been so bold. Clearly, from the conversation at the bar that evening, Palmwag was unused to such night visitors.

"They roared all night", he continued. "One big male was calling from beyond the palms over there, where I have my caravan. Hell, man, it was so close I thought it was going to get into the caravan with me."

That night we were in the bar and I had the satisfaction of telling Gruttemeyer of our successes. I actually think that he was quite pleased by our perseverance, if by nothing else.

"Now," he said encouragingly, producing the photograph albums again, "you must see some real desert elephants. Look at this." He opened one of them and pushed it over to me. The page displayed some photographs of a beautiful valley. Its floor was densely forested with stately acacia trees, between which meandered the many dry channels of a wide riverbed. In some of the photographs there were elephant herds. These were the true desert-dwelling elephants of the Kaokoveld, the ones that actually ventured onto the sand dunes of the Namib. They were also the elephants that visited the bizarre lake called Auses in the dune belt – a place I longed to see. When asked about the localities depicted in the photographs, Jurgen confirmed my suspicion that it was indeed the Hoanib and was effusive when describing its great beauty. This was a different Hoanib from the one I had imagined. To find out that there was more to this valley than Auses and the dune-traversing elephants of which I had heard so much, was a revelation.

Back at camp that night, I looked at my map of the area with rising interest and the glimmer of an idea was sown. I knew the Hoanib Valley to be the home of the true desert elephants – this was where Owen-Smith had been so concerned about me disturbing those elephants. But the photographs had shown me a more important aspect of the Hoanib even than the desert elephants. Scenically, it was obviously the most outstanding area of wilderness in Namibia, if not in southern Africa.

The next day I again confronted Gruttemeyer with my map. I think that he was starting to get used to me, for he even smiled when I unfolded it on the counter of his office. When I left a little later, my mind was made up – it would be the Hoanib next. Gruttemeyer had been helpful and described how I could reach the valley. I even had a small sketch map of what seemed to be the most difficult part of the route: the stretch between Sesfontein and Dubis.

The road to Sesfontein is a good one, slightly wider than one would think necessary until one remembers that Sesfontein used to be a large South African military post. It is still, however, a Namibian road and that means that you can expect the hardest corrugations in Africa. The enjoyment of the journey to Sesfontein was thus coloured by the effects of those accursed corrugations. We were further aggravated by the 'whoosh' of those white government vehicles when they overtook us at autobahn speeds. Inside these, and in airconditioned luxury, the occupants seemed oblivious to the pounding that their vehicles were absorbing. We were rather jealous of them!

A hundred kilometres passed and we arrived in the vast elongated valley that precedes the vale of Sesfontein. Here, trees began to dot the landscape and we saw cattle for the first time. Much has been written about Sesfontein and its environs, but the reality of the situation is that there are now too many people and livestock in the area. It has turned into a dustbowl, and consequently all the wildlife has long since vanished from the vicinity of the road. Soon we were entering the town itself. This may once have been an interesting place, but sadly, this is not now the case. The old fort is crumbling and the irrigated garden for which this place was noted, has had its spring of water diverted and put to other, more mundane uses. We continued on and, after passing an abandoned military base, were soon out on the other side.

Here, according to my sketch map, I was supposed to find a track leading to the left off the main road and through a Herero village. Before long, however, we were

halfway up the mountains behind Sesfontein. Something was wrong with my sketch map: we had missed our turning and were now on the track to Puros instead. Yet this mountain track was indeed a scenic one, and interesting as well, for alongside it ran a tiny, green-fringed furrow of sparkling water – truly an extraordinary sight in those barren parts. Small springs at various levels up the side of the mountain feed this furrow, adding to the tinkling stream as it descends towards Sesfontein.

Rather glad to have seen this unusual water feature, we returned down the hill and tried again to find our turn-off. For a while I roved around in the village, searching for anything resembling a track leading westward, in the meantime nearly making some Herero women dizzy. Finally, I decided to keep going west as best as I could, and by following some cattle paths we managed to clear the village and its curious inhabitants.

Miraculously, the confusing network of cattle paths seemed to coalesce into several tracks all leading in the same general direction. Thereafter, our new-found route traversed what could only be described as a con-servationist's worst nightmare. Everywhere cattle and goats were huddled in the meagre shade of mopane trees. These emaciated unfortunates were surrounded by their own handiwork – the dustbowl of the Okambondevlakte. And a dustbowl it truly is, for as we continued further westwards, our route passed through drifts of what appeared to be chalk dust. A huge, white, billowing cloud was raised by our passage and often when we slowed to detour around a fallen tree or a soft part of the road, this cloud would catch up with the vehicle, enveloping it as completely as any white-out in an Alaskan blizzard. Unexpectedly, our chosen track would gave way beneath the wheels as we hit deep patches of this dust. The effect was the same as driving full speed into a stream, except that I would simultaneously have to struggle with the steering, change gear, and try desperately to wind up the window. One such drift of this noxious substance was worse than the rest. As we hit it, the vehicle sagged as though we had fallen into a hole. The engine stalled and a wave of white powder avalanched through the windows. Every part of the cab was coated in a thick layer of the stuff. From the back, there was much slamming of windows to the accompaniment of Rosemary's shouts of protest. All this activity came too late, however, for the inside of the

The entrance to the Hoanib valley at Dubis.

A Tawny Eagle surveys its harsh domain: the arid bed of the Hoanib River.

back looked like the interior of a frosty fridge, while Rosemary's flailing profile was only just visible through the still swirling mists. At this sight, and unaware of what she looked like herself, there were peals of laughter from Clarissa. Coated from head to foot, Clarissa's eyes stared out at me from a face powdered and ready for a black and white minstrel show, while each hoot of laughter brought a fresh trickle of more white powder from her hair and shoulders. Ten minutes later, the same thing happened again. After the third time, it had ceased to be funny and I became concerned that I might be on the wrong road. None the less, half an hour later we were past this hideous part of the Kharokhaobvlakte, and in front of us lay the vast ramparts of a mountain range – exactly as indicated on Gruttemeyer's sketch map.

Some knowledge of the recent geological history of the Hoanib is necessary in order to understand why this accursed dust exists. In the not too distant geological past, probably less than a million years ago, the dune belt along the lower part of the Hoanib, near the mouth, migrated over its bed and dammed the river. As the centuries passed, the valley all the way up to and beyond Sesfontein was gradually filled with the fine silt, which would normally have been dumped into the sea. Eventually, two to three hundred metres of this fine silt was deposited. Then, in the very recent geological past, maybe less than one hundred thousand years ago, the winds shifted and slowly the dune belt retreated. Once again, the Hoanib started flowing into the sea. Each year the silty deposits were eroded by the annual floods, so that the relict silt flats of the floodplain above Auses, the Okambondevlakte, and the Sesfontein Valley are now all that remain. Evidence of the earlier period, when the river was blocked at the mouth and the silt deposits two hundred metres deep, can still, however, be found high up on the gorge walls. Here and there these lofty relics of that era cling precariously in protected pockets, the loose sandy deposits still showing the characteristic ripple patterns of estuarine sediments. When man and his domestic animals arrived on the scene, however, the delicate cover of vegetation was quickly removed from the Okambondevlakte and the Sesfontein Valley. Grass cover that had stabilized these areas for tens of thousands of years was quickly depleted, and it was then that the dust clouds started to blow.

Once clear of the worst of the silt, the road visibly turned in a westerly direction. Also, the terrain on either side of our tiny track began to correspond with the topographic map that I had of the region. By midday, I knew exactly where we were and was able to say to Clarissa, with absolute conviction, that we were approaching Dubis, the fountain at the entrance to the Hoanib Valley. First, however, we were confronted by a wall of mountains and, as we proceeded slowly towards it, I was quietly relieved to see the entrance to the valley suddenly appear, almost out of nowhere. Soon the Hoanib River and the green oasis of Dubis lay before us, and beyond, a splendid gorge zigzagged out of sight into the mists of the Kaokoveld.

Where the track entered the bed of the river there was a long and refreshing pool of water. Emerald-coloured vegetation hugged the riverbank here, in startling contrast to the looming, black rock walls of the Hoanib gorge that lay beyond them. Downstream of that first pool was the entrance to this gorge, with a series of other pools, each forced to the surface from beneath the sands by the rock reefs made of the same folded material as the mountains beyond. A kilometre downstream, the perennial waters of the Hoanib, having been briefly forced to the surface at Dubis, submerge yet again beneath the sands.

Here and there, half-starved cattle stood motionless under the tamarisk bushes lining the pools, and piles of dung lay scattered on the short, green grass fringing the water. This dung was a mixture of cattle and elephant droppings, and herein lay the thorn in the rose, for this isolated oasis is ultimately a place of conflict between man and wildlife. It is also one of the three major watering-points that the true desert elephants use on their wanderings in the Hoanib and Hoarusib. Places such as this are few and far between. Indeed, Auses, the nearest of the elephants' other watering-points, lies a hundred kilometres downstream. Meanwhile, at Dubis they must

share the water with cattle, donkeys and goats, and occasionally the herders themselves. Of course there are not only elephants here: the water attracts other denizens of the Kaokoveld as well – hyena, ostrich, baboons, gemsbok, and the occasional rhino.

Desert lions also use the oasis, for the Hoanib, like the other major rivers of the Kaokoveld, is a highway along which these nomadic beasts move from the interior to the coast and vice versa. For some years, a pair of these nomadic lions had roamed the coast between the mouths of the Uniab and Khumib rivers. The Bartletts, film-makers of National Geographic fame, had even managed to film them on several occasions. These lions then moved inland, eventually turning up at Dubis. The owner of the cattle that watered at Dubis encountered them there and shot them both. Ironically, the stockowner was also a part-time employee of a safari company that operated in the Skeleton Coast. Worse still, the lioness was found to be pregnant with cubs. Stories such as these must surely become more common in the future, for Dubis, although the key to the survival of the Hoanib's wildlife, is also a place which will increasingly be in conflict with man's interests.

It was now midday and scorchingly hot. Having driven much of the way from Sesfontein with the windows up because of the silt dust, we were all irritable, tired, covered from head to toe in dust, and gasping in the intense heat of the valley floor. At the sight of these lovely pools, there was no resisting the powerful urge to throw ourselves from the vehicle and splash about in the water. Nevertheless, after a scant few minutes, the burning rays of the noonday sun and the airless atmosphere on the floor of the valley forced us onwards in search of shade for a much-needed rest. For the next kilometre, the track followed the riverbed and was in the water most of the time. So, wary of soft spots, I walked in front, with Clarissa following in the vehicle. Rosemary trailed along at the rear, enjoying the novel sensation of wading through water in a desert.

Soon the track emerged again onto the dry bed of the widening Hoanib Valley and here I noticed a solitary tree clinging to the bank. Unbeknown to us, we would shortly return to this tree, but on we went and, while eagerly searching for a suitable place to stop, encountered a large herd of elephants around the next bend in the valley. Our first true desert-dwelling elephants!

This should have been an auspicious moment, but such was the oppressive heat in the vehicle that, instead, it was the opposite. I remember that no one uttered a word as we stared glumly through the windscreen, sweating profusely in the oven-like cab. Directly ahead, a dark mass of about thirty elephants stood semi-comatose – and they were in the shade of the first suitable tree we had seen so far. More irritatingly, it was impossible to pass them in that narrow defile. They shifted about restlessly, and one or two raised their trunks in our direction. I inched closer in a foolish attempt to get past, but then one of the larger cows trumpeted and charged – a bluff, no doubt, but we were not in the mood for games such as this. When the dust had cleared and the cow rejoined the herd, I waited five minutes and then tried again. This time the cow stopped, ears outstretched and only a few yards away. There followed a shrill trumpet, and for a long moment, two red, pig-like eyes glared down at us. Then, turning slowly, it made its way back to the herd again. With Garth Owen-Smith's words ringing in my ears, I knew that I should have to leave them in peace.

Defeated and bad-tempered, we returned reluctantly to the miserable excuse for a tree that we had seen earlier on and here, enveloped in a cloud of flies, we waited for the cool of the day. At four we tried again, not really daring to hope too much, and found that the elephants had vanished. At last we proceeded into the forested section of the Hoanib Valley, heading downstream into what is, without doubt, one of the most spectacularly beautiful pieces of wild Africa left on the continent.

The sun sets early in this valley because of the towering walls of the gorge, and it was time to find a camping place. I had been warned that it was prudent to camp out of the watercourse and on one of the high shelves adjacent to the rocky walls. One had only to look at the base of the huge acacias to see why. There, wrapped around every trunk, was the tangled detritus left behind in the aftermath of sudden flash-floods. Soon we were unloading our gear onto a pristine piece of sand which we had all agreed was safe from the possible walls of water that might sweep unexpectedly past in the night.

Precautions such as these are not merely token exercises. Far from it, for in Namibia there are many horror stories of vehicles being swept away and lives endangered by flash-floods. These rare occurrences are the only time that the river actually carries any water and the suddenness of the event is also the tool that shapes the valley floor – for the flash-flood carves a new route for itself each time. Eventually the riverbed is criss-crossed with a braided pattern of many different channels – hence the name 'braided channel'. All of the riverbeds of the Kaokoveld are shaped in the same way and they are all braided streambeds. Curiously, this type of river is not confined to the arid parts of the world. It also occurs in high latitudes, downstream of glaciers – albeit with a daily cycle rather than a seasonal one. At night the streams stop flowing, but during the day meltwater from the glacier rushes down the riverbed and the characteristic 'braiding' occurs.

Before long, a crackling fire of driftwood was casting a rosy glow on the huge overhang of rock we had chosen to be our home for the night. Later, as we ate our supper, we found ourselves conversing in whispers, for the towering walls of the valley were like a giant Roman amphitheatre, where every slight noise made was magnified unbearably. Just opening our trunk of food seemed to unleash a cacophony of cymbals and drums. In that dark valley even normal conversation seemed abnormally loud, a slammed door, grotesquely disturbing. Beyond the fading glow of the fire's embers the valley's brooding silence was occasionally broken by the call of some distant night bird. Once, far downstream, there was the evocative and timeless sound of an elephant trumpeting. Then, timed to perfection, as if to remind us of reality, a donkey somewhere upstream at Dubis started to bray interminably.

The next day we moved further down the Hoanib, marvelling at the scenery and putting as many kilometres between us and Dubis as possible. The scenery of this valley is beyond the power of mere words to describe. The geology is ruggedly beautiful, the walls of the valley so precipitously steep. Indeed, there is a grandeur in all the elements that go to make up the uniqueness of this valley. Foremost of these 'elements' are the huge acacias that populate the braided bed of the valley almost all the way to the dune belt. Almost exotic in their lushness, their presence transforms what is in reality a harsh desert environment into a cool and eminently restful place. Yet, as dense as this cool forest seems when one is in the riverbed, in reality it is but a tiny thread of life.

That morning, leaving the vehicle in the riverbed, and with Rosemary wandering about somewhere nearby,

above – The tangled driftwood at the base of most Hoanib acacia trees is an indication of the strength of the rare flash-floods which sweep this valley.   P.A.

Clarissa and I had set out to climb the valley side. Once out of the riverbed there is an abrupt return to the desert. Sand and rock prevail and the further away one gets from the green ribbon, the more frail it seems. Small relict patches of Namib dune sand cling to the higher reaches of the valley side, and in the wide curves of the folded strata, black and purple rocks mingle with greenish shale and fractured quartzites. All the rocks of this valley have been folded in several different geological epochs and it is these folds that have given the valley its characteristic shapes – the Gothic curves of the mountains and the jagged, looping outcrops. Panting from the exertion of scrabbling up steep gullies filled with warm sand, we reached the top after a forty-five minute climb. Far below us, the Hoanib seemed small and insignificant surrounded as it was by the imposing black rock mountains that marched towards every horizon. Even the acacia forest, so apparently dense

from within, looked sparse, almost bedraggled, from our lofty lookout. Yet, sparse or not, this forest is a haven for wildlife.

Later on that morning, having returned to the vehicle and moved on down the valley, we began to encounter that wildlife in ever-increasing numbers. Gemsbok would gallop unexpectedly from the tamarisk groves, disturbed by our slow passage along the rocky bed. High up on the rocky slopes we saw giraffe picking their way along narrow paths like mountain goats. Steenbok peered from beneath tumbled bushes on the islands between the dry braided streambeds of the Hoanib's erratic course. Groups of ostrich were everywhere, as were springbok. Walking along the bushy riverbanks we were startled repeatedly as francolin flushed, at the last second as it were, from beneath our feet. Of course, lions were on our mind whenever that happened.

The Hoanib riverbed after a flash-flood. The force and suddenness of these floods are what shapes its course, and the result, over thousands of years, is the characteristic 'braiding' of the streambed.

This was indeed an artist's paradise, and in this valley I completed many small oil sketches of wildlife and landscapes. The main problem for me was simply that at every bend there was a painting begging to be completed. This was no unpleasant thing, for the shade beneath the huge acacias was dense and cool – there was no ordeal involved – but painting in the field is difficult at the best of times. There is the easel to be unpacked and assembled. Oil paints, thinners, paint mediums and brushes have first to be arranged conveniently and only then is the painting commenced. Speed is the final ingredient that is needed, for in a couple of hours the lighting of the scene will have changed dramatically. Wind is the artist's enemy at such times and in the Hoanib this ingredient is in plentiful supply.

"I wish I had a video camera", declared Clarissa on one windy occasion, hugely entertained by the fandango I was performing with my easel and canvas. When each gust had faded away and all the dust been picked painstakingly from the surface of the wet canvas, painting started again in earnest until the next gust came whirling down the valley floor.

On some of the longer stops, Clarissa worked on her thesis, and when the mischievous gusts of wind plucked at her table, it was my turn to be entertained as she tore hither and thither retrieving errant sheets of paper. Whenever it was time to move on, Rosemary was always the last to return, having wandered off on long walks. There would be much shouting and calling from Clarissa and myself before she would appear, far away down the valley, slowly making her way back to the vehicle.

And so it was some days before we approached the lower parts of the valley where the towering walls began to diminish in their splendour. Here the climate started to turn distinctly cool as we neared the icy influence of the Atlantic Ocean. One morning we awoke very late to find ourselves enveloped in the dank silence of a dense fog. Water ran in rivulets from the tent when we threw back the outside door, and as we spoke, clouds of condensation billowed forth. After we had made our breakfast and were bent over the tent, shaking it free of water, I noticed Clarissa straighten up very deliberately, all the while staring into the riverbed. Then, as I opened my mouth to ask what was up, the vast bulk of a magnificently tusked elephant loomed out of the mist only a few metres away.

Afterwards, when we had calmed down, we both agreed that the sudden encounter had literally transfixed us, the elephant included. What we could not agree on was the length of time that followed before any of us moved. It seemed like an eternity to me. Clarissa was adamant that many seconds had passed. In reality the pandemonium probably took place instantaneously. The elephant swung out its ears and trumpeted shrilly. The effect of this from so close and in the silence of the fog was almost paralysing. I say almost, because we proceeded to leap, as one, for the safety of the vehicle as the elephant lunged forward, passed us and disappeared into the fog. The next few seconds were truly frightening for all around us and invisible, more elephants made their presence known as they panicked. Trumpeting wildly, they crashed off through the groves of tamarisk and it was a few minutes before the cloying silence of the fog had settled, yet again, over our campsite.

The elephants of the Hoanib are an enigma. Why do these animals live here in such a hostile environment, a region where there is less than one hundred and fifty millimetres of rain annually? It was once thought that these elephants used to migrate freely between Kaokoland and Etosha but that human interference had permanently forced them deep into the most arid parts of the desert. There are, however, vast, uninhabited tracts of land in the corridor between Sesfontein and Etosha, but none of this group of elephants has shown any inclination to migrate in that direction. Most of the evidence seems to indicate that these elephants are occupying the area out of choice – that they are adapted to the harsh climate. This adaptation was graphically illustrated during the severe drought that affected the area from 1977 to 1982. During this time, the other desert-dwelling animals that shared their habitat, including such hardy animals as springbok and gemsbok, were reduced to one-fifth of their former numbers. Yet throughout that drought not one elephant had died.

It seems that the elephants' habits had given them an advantage. They graze as well as browse and can feed off the high branches of trees. Also, they can dig for water in riverbeds and are capable of walking eighty kilometres in a day to reach a distant waterhole. It would seem impossible that such large animals as these could not fail to have an impact on the fragile ecology of the desert, but, amazingly, this is not so. It may even be that their presence is crucial to the survival of many other species. For example, when

the acacia pods travel through the digestive tracts of the elephant, the hard coat is rendered more absorbent to water. They thus have a higher chance (fifty-seven per cent as compared with twelve per cent) of germinating. Consequently, in the arid environment of the lower Hoanib this may be a crucial factor in the propagation of the Hoanib acacias – especially after the rare, seasonal flash-floods. It is also known that these elephants do not uproot trees as do the savanna elephants, and aerial photographs have shown that between 1963 and 1983, there was no reduction in the numbers of acacias in the Hoanib. Even away from the riverbeds, only one fifth of the plants are utilized: during the drought some *Welwitschia* plants were stripped of their leaves, yet none of these plants died.

On the sixth day, and far down the Hoanib Valley, the hidden fault in the engine, which had been dormant since our arrival at Walvis Bay, manifested itself again. A worse occasion for this to happen could not be imagined, for we were over a hundred and thirty kilometres from the nearest help, and had only four or five days of water remaining. It was my worst nightmare coming true! At first I had hoped, that after the usual tinkering, the glitch would disappear. But this time, it was not to be. Thankfully, when the engine began the telltale splutters which I knew to be a prelude to trouble, we were near one of the shady acacias,

Opposite
The Hoanib River Valley is much more impressive when one is in it and on the braided streambed. There, you seem to be surrounded by a dense and shady forest of acacia trees. The view from above is far more revealing, however, for it is only then that you realize how narrow the forested strip really is. Far below us, our vehicle seems an insignificant dot on nature's magnificent panorama.

Below
On some mornings the Atlantic fog-belt penetrates far inland along the many river valleys of the Skeleton Coast. When this happens, dawn is a damp affair, a cloak of silence settles over everything and the Hoanib Valley becomes a brooding and mysterious place where elephants pad about like giant, grey ghosts. In these conditions, to walk too far from camp when heeding the call of nature is to risk getting hopelessly lost.

above – The Hoanib
river valley is not the
place to suffer from the
curse of an unreliable
engine.   P. A.

lights – we would need all our battery power for the following day. So we sat next to a flickering fire while I racked my brain as to exactly what it was that I was going to do the following day.

Lonely at the best of times, the Hoanib was now at its loneliest. The dark mountains surrounding us were ominous in their silence, and the sensation of being so far from anywhere was almost overwhelming. It was also a night of disturbed sleep for I tossed and turned, my slumbers tormented by the dream that always afflicts me in times of stress, that is, the cold nightmare of being unprepared for a vital exam and ultimately failing the test.

The next day I decided it must be the carburettor that was causing the problem, and that the only way to find out if this was true was to dismantle it completely into all its separate components. I would then wash everything in petrol.

My artist's table was taken out and the tools laid on it like an operating theatre. Soon the carburettor was lying on it in a hundred parts and each was dutifully cleaned in the noxious liquid. The hidden channels in some of the parts had to have petrol blown through them, and by the time that distasteful job was complete, I had accidentally sucked up mouthfuls of the stuff. Then came the task of reassembly . . .

At that moment, exactly when we were at our most vulnerable stage, a distant sound caught our attention. It was but a faint whisper that we heard – intermittently, like a sail flapping in the wind. Rosemary poked her head out of the back and pointed upstream at a tall column of whirling dust. "Look," she cried. "A dust-devil." Moreover, it was approaching fast! There then followed one of those frantic scenes which could have come directly from a Chaplin comedy. We rushed hither and thither in desperate haste, shouting instructions, slamming the bonnet shut, and closing the doors and windows. Then, with only a few seconds left, a tarpaulin was thrown over the table and Clarissa and I hung on for dear life as the whirlwind hit us with a vengeance. The vehicle rocked as the sandblast struck, and for a moment the table and its precious cargo was lifted bodily in the air, with Clarissa and I attached to the corners. I had a brief nightmarish vision of us searching for carburettor parts in the sand dunes for the next week, but then the vortex was gone. The incident over, we proceeded hastily to finish the job at

and it was here that we coasted to a halt. Every bit of wiring was checked, the distributor examined and the fuses looked at. The carburettor jets were infuriatingly clean. My repair manual was no help either and, after unsuccessfully attempting to restart the engine, I began to feel the pressure of the situation weighing heavily on my shoulders.

"Have you tried everything?" inquired Clarissa, as she peered over my shoulders at the shiny new engine. "What about the petrol? Maybe it's dirty fuel?"

"I don't think so, but whatever it is, it's not the electric choke. That damned poor excuse for a mechanic is going to pay for this."

Even Rosemary, usually so confident that problems such as these could always be fixed by me, began to show signs of alarm after we had been under the tree for four hours.

"Don't worry", she consoled as she brought me yet another unsolicited mug of tea. "Everything will be fine, I just know it." I knew then that it was time to really start worrying. Unfortunately, the sun was low and my attempts to fix the car were over for the day – I would try again at first light.

That evening there was no conversation as we all busied ourselves with the chores of making camp and, later, a meagre supper. Adding to the general gloom that afflicted us was the depressing inconvenience of having no

68

hand. Sweaty, burping petrol and covered in oil, I finally completed the assembly as the sun dipped low in the sky. Then came the dreaded moment. Would it start? Clarissa and Rosemary feigned nonchalance as I climbed into the cab and turned the key in the ignition. A cliff-hanger to the end, the engine roared into life only after the third attempt.

Our last night in the Hoanib was a cold and anxious one, and a fire was made, more as a diversion than for anything else. This was a suitable farewell to the valley, for the wind howling in the higher gullies was a sound that added greatly to the lonely atmosphere. And for us the last few days had been lonely ones indeed. From the moment that the engine had died, the true wildness of the place had been forcibly brought home to us. Yet even this was something to be savoured, for this was wilderness personified. The wind whipped around the fire and our eyes were slitted against the flying sand. As we sat there I noticed Clarissa glance up and stare intently into the inky blackness. She looked back at me, but to my raised eyebrows, I got only a shrug in reply.

The next morning as we cleaned up our campsite prior to departure, Rosemary gave a cry and beckoned us over to where she was standing. There, in the hard sand at her feet, was the distinct spoor of at least four lions. On closer examination, it seemed that these were the tracks of a lioness and three half-grown cubs. The tracks followed one of the braided streams and, where they passed close to our camping site, they had come up the bank for a better, closer look. Then, curiosity satisfied, they had continued on their silent way.

It was a fitting end to a fantastic experience.

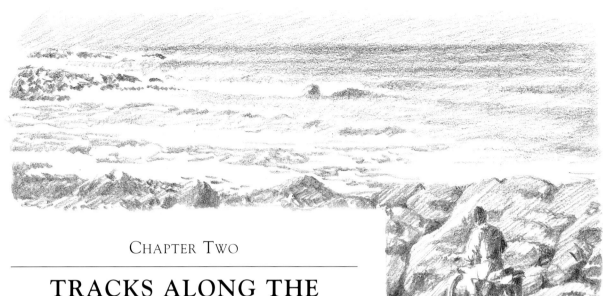

Rod Braby near the Uniab mouth

CHAPTER TWO

TRACKS ALONG THE SKELETON COAST

The wilderness experience of the Hoanib was the climax to our first taste of the Kaokoveld and our return to the comforts of the oasis at Palmwag proved to be an anticlimax. It was now time to think of other places to visit, for the dry season was well under way. In the remaining seven months before the advent of the rains, we had planned a month or two in Etosha before moving on to the Okavango. But I still had another old dream to fulfil before heading into the interior of the continent – to see elephants crossing the dunes at Auses. Yet another image had haunted me since our stay at Swakopmund. In a bookshop I had bought a calendar produced by a local conservation group and one of the images was unforgettable: that of a battle-scarred yet magnificently maned lion resting on a coastal dune. Behind him, waves broke along a dazzling Skeleton Coast beach.

These images had made a deep impression on me. It was not simply that I wished to see these things, but rather that I must and therefore would experience them for myself. Additionally, as a wildlife artist who has always tried to avoid the clichéd images of the genre, I felt that these bizarre subjects would make great paintings, having consistently stressed the overriding importance of true bona fides, if I were to paint these animals, then I must first have ventured in their paths.

When a pair of lions was resident at the mouth of the Uniab for several months, Rod Braby encountered the male on the beach while patrolling on a motorbike. The encounter was a surprise for both parties. In describing the incident, Rod told me that he had pointed the bike at the surging surf, only metres away, with the intention that if the startled lion charged, he could ride straight into the ocean. The lion, however, turned and bolted over the ridge that flanks the beach at the mouth. The next day Rod returned to the scene and followed the tracks, only to find that the lion had stopped on the ridge and watched his rapid departure from behind some rocks.

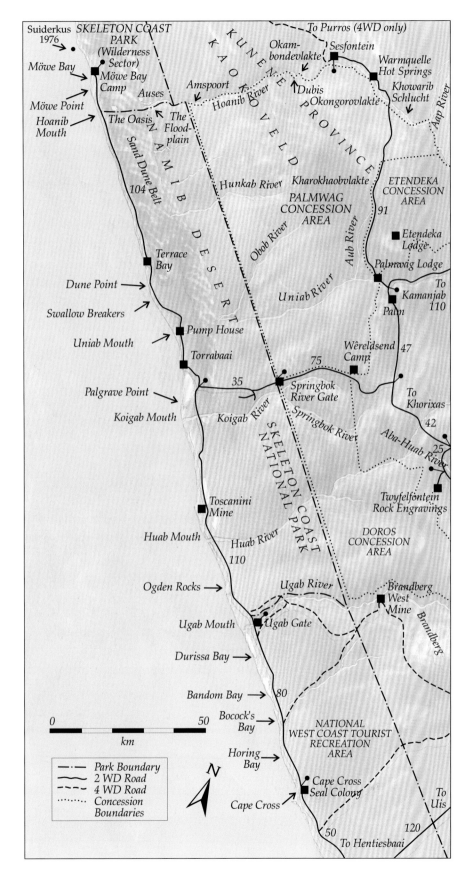

So we returned to Swakopmund, with the Skeleton Coast as our next goal. Of course, it is never a hardship returning to this delightful town. To the desert traveller, Swakopmund is the mirage that tantalizes with its visions of bitter winds howling outside cosy cake and coffee shops. As we were packing to leave, servicing the vehicle and doing all of the myriad things to be done before departing, Palmwag and its sweltering heat had seemed far away indeed from the salubrious climate of the coast. Yet two days later we found ourselves passing Uis and racing along the road towards the Atlantic Ocean.

That evening we were comfortably ensconced in two huts at the municipal camp. An icy wind was blowing, and the mist was settling in. Damaraland seemed a distant memory, but as we unpacked our trunks, the food and clothes within were still hot with residual heat from the Kaokoveld. Then, after wrapping up warmly, we were off to town, driving slowly through the gloom for a 'ritual' of tea and cake in one of the nearby hotels.

The following morning Clarissa and I sauntered down to the phone booth at the office. Unable to stand the tension of what she was about to attempt, I stayed outside as Clarissa dialled the number that Margie Jacobsohn had given her. The more I thought about it, the more I realized that we were really being rather cheeky. Here we were, telephoning complete strangers and hoping that somehow, when Clarissa had explained who we were, we would be welcomed with open arms. The more I thought about it, the more agitated I became. Through the glass of the telephone-booth door I could see Clarissa talking and taking notes at the same time. A few minutes later, she hung up and pushed the door open.

"Well, what happened?"

"Relax, we're in", and she broke out in a grin. "I don't know how I did that, but we've been invited up there to stay with them as their guests."

The phone had been answered by Sigi Braby. And we had been lucky in more ways than one, for she was due to leave for Möwe Bay that day – another few hours and we would have missed her. When Clarissa had explained who had given us her number, what we were doing in Namibia, and why we were phoning her in the first place, an invitation to visit them at Möwe Bay had followed. Sigi had warned her though that we would have to wait a few days as they were off on a patrol. So a date a week hence was agreed on, and she promised meanwhile to arrange the necessary permits that we would need to enter the Skeleton Coast Park as their guests. These we would pick up at the Ugab gate on our way.

I could hardly believe our luck. We were actually going to Möwe Bay and the possibility of getting to Auses was now very real. For the rest of that day I walked around on a cloud, my imagination running riot with all the possibilities that now presented themselves. Seeing my hopes soar, Clarissa gently cautioned me.

"Don't get your hopes up", she had said. "Remember, we've only been invited to stay with them at Möwe for a few days."

Of course this was true. The chances of my seeing a desert lion or elephant in the dunes of the Skeleton Coast were extremely slim, but, ever the optimist, I dreamed on.

In the meantime there were many things to be done. Food for a month was purchased, 'just in case'. All my oil sketches from the Kaokoveld were packed up and sent back to Durban, and the camping equipment cleaned. There was also the little matter of our vehicle, or rather, its infuriating, intermittent fault. It was under guarantee, so I contacted the local dealership and booked the car in on the clear understanding that they had to find the problem and fix it. On the arranged day I delivered it to their workshop and explained the problem to the mechanic.

"Don't worry, *meneer,* if there is a problem, we'll find it," I was told by a smiling man who was, at the same time, both noncommittal *and* reassuring. "Leave it to the experts", he continued, "After all, that's what we're here for." Somehow his reply left me feeling unconvinced and terribly helpless.

A week later, however, we were speeding along the coastal road northwards from Swakopmund. Again we passed the tiny settlements of Wlotzkasbaken and Hentiesbaai. The coastline hereabouts is but a vast flat plain that stretches inland all the way to the horizon. Here, unfortunately, there are no curvaceous dunes to add atmosphere to the scenery, which on its own is rather unexciting. Wlotzkasbaken and Hentiesbaai are equally unexciting. And empty for most of the year as well, for many of the houses are owned by inland residents and used only for holidays. Tacky would not be an unkind label for some of these buildings, but the mock gingerbread houses of board and corrugated iron do have about them a peculiar kind of Namibian ambience. Anything else would look silly here. Also, in a similar vein, but solely for the benefit of sport fishermen, campsites have been constructed along the coast almost to the mouth of the Ugab River. These concrete eyesores have been endowed with suitably uninspiring names and are identified by signposts such as 'Mile 26', 'Mile 30' and so on. This whole area of coastline is protected to some degree and goes by the incredibly dull title of 'National West Coast Recreation Area'. Actually a better title would have been 'National West Coast braai and off-road driving area'. This is because, to the passing traveller, the coast it protects seems to be one long braai park, where weekend warriors have defaced every hill in sight with their vehicle tracks – blemishes that will last for hundreds of years in the desert environment.

About halfway along the road to the Ugab River there is one place that is well worth visiting: the seal colony at Cape Cross. There is more to this locality than the seals. Its name betrays the fact that it is also a place of historic interest, and here, on this rocky headland, one gets a powerful feel for the earliest days of exploration of this dangerous coast.

When the Portuguese explorer, Diego Cão, landed here in 1443 and raised a small, stone monument on this windswept cape, it then represented the very limits of Portuguese exploration of the African coast. In reality, however, Cape Cross was but a stepping-stone in that process of exploration and rather unimportant in the years following, yet, by virtue of a carved stone monument, it is the only place along the coast where you are so obviously reminded of the exploits of those hardy seafarers. Here, in the protective lee of the rocky headland, it is easy to imagine a sailing ship anchored, and to visualize the first steps of Europeans on a land as remote to them as Mars would be to us today.

Diego Cão made two journeys down the coastline of West Africa for the King of Portugal. On his first, both of his ships carried a granite cross or *padrão*, which he had been instructed to erect on the distant shores of Africa. One of these was erected at the mouth of the Congo and the other at the furthermost point of that journey, Cabo de Lago, in present-day Angola. Eighteen months after his return to Portugal he set forth on the second of his expeditions and again the two ships under his command

A padrão. P.A.

carried two weighty granite crosses. The first of these was raised at Cabo Negro, on the southern coast of Angola. The second was placed at the headland we now know as Cape Cross. When Cão and his men departed this desolate place, the cross stood for hundreds of years before it was again seen by western eyes.

The image of the *padrão*'s lonely vigil is a powerful one. Countless storms had lashed its inscriptions, whole generations of Strandlopers must have noted its existence, and many a lion must have rested in its meagre shade with a kill from the nearby seal colony, before, some time in the latter half of the 1840s, that lonely vigil came to an end: Captain Messum, an entrepreneur searching for guano deposits, then rediscovered the cross, but sailed away leaving it unmolested. In 1879, Captain Warren of the English cruiser *Swallow* also came across the monument while searching for suitable anchorages and he, too, left it where it was.

Around this time also the Germans were consolidating their grip on the region and the gunboat *Wolf* was busy traversing the coast in pursuit of this mission and planting claims wherever possible. One of these was placed near the location of the cross, which was, again, left alone. However, the vigil of the *padrão* over the seals at Cape Cross was soon to be over. In 1893, when Captain Becker of the *Falke* was surveying the coast's most promising anchorages, he found the *padrão* and removed it. Eventually, it was taken back to Germany. Here it first was housed at the Naval Academy at Kiel, and later moved to the Institut für Meereskundee in Berlin where it suffered bomb damage in the Second World War. It now resides in Berlin at the Museum für Deutsche Geschichte. In 1895 the Germans erected their own replica of the original cross at the same location, but with the German eagle prominently engraved on it. This little piece of imperialistic sculpture still stands on the spot where once stood, one can only assume, its original namesake.

On this vast coastline of long, sandy and exposed beaches there are very few headlands and capes offering shelter for ships. The rarity of these protected anchorages is what attracted Diego Cão ashore in the first place. Indeed, between Swakopmund and the Kunene there are only two similarly rocky headlands. Others also seek the protection of these rocky refuges in the form of Cape Cross's other star attraction – the seals. Cape Cross hosts a gigantic colony of Cape fur seals and is the most northern place on the African continent where these seals rear cubs.

The most northern colony of all is further up the coast at Cape Frio, but for some reason the seals do not rear pups at this place.

The seals at Cape Cross have long been culled for their skins and for some body parts that are sold to the Far East for 'medicinal' purposes. Recently, this culling has been the subject of much controversy. The pros and cons have been hotly and emotionally debated in the newspapers. In the past as many as 3500 cubs and 1000 adults were culled annually at Cape Cross, but, despite this, the populations of seals seemed to be stable. In recent years, however, their numbers have fallen drastically along the whole coast. This decline has been blamed on many things, including a possible virus. The commercial fishermen operating along this coast favour continued culling, even though many thousands are shot illegally in the fishing grounds – and all of this despite the decline in seal numbers. The seals, they argue, are aggravating their low fish catches; understandably, fewer seals would mean more fish for them. The backdrop to this argument is, however, the unassailable fact that the fishing industry has already destroyed the offshore stocks largely through its greed. Thus, as the meagre stocks of fish diminished, the fishing industry came into direct competition with the seal population. As usual, when the vested interests of man are in conflict with those of nature, it is always nature that comes off second-best. The seals, despite massive die-offs along the coast, continue to be culled on a commercial basis.

The sun shone on the day of our passing visit. It was one of those beautiful days when the mist lifted, the wind dropped, and the long Atlantic swells were glassily smooth. The car park at Cape Cross is only a short walk from the low retaining wall that separates the seals from the visitors.

Two things become immediately apparent when you open your car door here. The first is the noise: a constant wailing roar, it rises above that of the thundering surf. The second is the smell, which is so pungent and repulsive that it has an almost physical solidity. Both are created by the colony. At first glance, the extent of the colony is not immediately obvious as the seals' shape, colour and smoothness resemble, and blend in with, the boulders on which they lie. Then, as you look harder, there comes the realization that the rocky headland is entirely covered in a

mass of blubber. Everywhere we looked there were seals and more seals. Thousands upon thousands of them lay packed on the headland. Best of all, in the blue surf beyond the rocks, the sea was alive with many thousands more. In the sky above this chaotic scene, flocks of seagulls wheeled and dived, each adding its own call to the general din.

The largest of these seals are the bulls, and these attain their maximum weight of 220 kilograms (500 lb) just before the rutting season, which can last up to eight weeks and during which they fast. The cows are much lighter and weigh in the region of 180 kilograms (300 lb). It was once thought that these seals eat their own weight daily in food, but it is now known that they eat only a maximum of four kilograms of fish, lobster and small crustaceans a day.

Obese and clumsy on land, these smelly creatures are not endearing to look at and at Cape Cross the visitor is able to see every revolting detail of their bodies as they crowd close to the low wall. Secretions dribble from eyes and mouths or cling to salt-encrusted whiskers, ghastly odours waft forth, and they scream incessantly at one another in vying for the best basking sites. In the water, however, they become a different animal. Offshore, thousands of them, and as graceful as ballerinas, surf and dance in the powerful waves that crash on the rocks of the Cape. This spectacle alone is reason enough to visit this place.

An hour after leaving Cape Cross we were at last approaching the entrance to the Skeleton Coast Park. The small office found here and indeed the gate itself have a homely, cluttered appearance, more akin to a tiny

Cape Cross and its seal colony should not to be missed on any visit to Namibia's Skeleton Coast. Here there is the opportunity to view seals in their tens of thousands, and watch as hundreds of them dance, as gracefully as ballerinas, in the crashing waves beyond the colony.

shipbuilder's yard than the main entrance to a National Park. And thankfully so, for when distant deskbound bureaucrats start to 'improve facilities', the results are usually clichéd edifices suggestive of great efficiency. No worry about that here, however, for this entrance has its own unique personality. Inside the office, our permits were awaiting us, and when the formalities were completed, we moved on across the Ugab River and into the park proper.

Unfortunately, despite the size and extent of this park, its boundaries make no ecological sense at all. Politics alone have created the shape that appears on modern maps, and it remains a thin strip of land along the coast which on its own cannot support any permanent numbers of desert elephants, lions and rhinos. These animals spend most of their time in the hinterland – the Kaokoveld, the very terrain that we had visited in the prior weeks. However, the lower reaches of the Hoarusib, Uniab and Hoanib rivers pass through the park and are essential to the survival of these animals. Thus they enter the park as visitors only, intent on the water to be found at Auses on the Hoanib, the gorge in the Hoarusib, and a very few other places on the coast where fresh water is to be found.

This national park has an interestingly convoluted history. In 1907 the German Colonial Administration created three game reserves, one of which was Etosha. The vast area encompassed by this reserve stretched from the environs of Etosha Pan to the coast, and from the Kunene River to the Hoarusib, amounting to some 93 000 square kilometres, and thus one of the largest game reserves ever to be proclaimed in Africa. This grandiose example of line drawing on maps did not, however, account for the fact that people lived in many of the areas covered by the so-called 'reserve'. The Kaokoland portion of this was later excised in 1947 and after that only a small portion of the Kaokoveld and the coast was protected within the reserve. That small portion was the strip of desert between the Hoarusib and the Hoanib rivers. In 1958 a commission found this strip of land to be insufficient to support the desert elephants and rhinos inhabiting the region, so the reserve was enlarged, in a southerly direction, to include vacant land (nearly 6500 square kilometres) lying between the Hoanib and the Ugab rivers. Not for long, however, as the Odendaal Report of 1963 entirely removed the whole of the Kaokoveld from the reserve. The portion to the north of the Hoanib was incorporated into Kaokoland,

while the portion to the south of the river was used in the creation of Damaraland – for the use of the erstwhile Riemvasmakers. All that remained after such radical surgery were two isolated reserves: Etosha and the Skeleton Coast, a strip of protected land 30 to 40 kilometres wide, running from the Ugab to the Kunene.

In 1963, however, the newly enlarged Kaokoland was earmarked for economic development by the South West African Administration. Slowly, the cogs of progress began to turn and an entity called the Sarusas Development Corporation came into being from the ashes of several previous ventures in the region. This Corporation owned the mineral rights to the region and it proposed to develop the area. Unfortunately for them, however, there were many changes taking place on the Namibian political scene. South Africa flexed its muscles, taking over many of the state departments of the Administration of South West Africa, including Sea Fisheries. Thus, when the Sarusas Development Corporation called for tenders to build a harbour on the coast as a logical part of their plans, the directors were soon summoned to Cape Town where they were abruptly told to drop their plans for a harbour. Ostensibly, the reason for this was that any new port on the coast would put pressure on the already established but ailing fishing ports of Walvis and Lüderitz. It must be remembered that the centre of the fishing industry was then Walvis Bay, which was officially if not geographically part of South Africa. As the new administrators of the Territory, the South African officials withdrew their support and the project was scrapped. Subsequently, the Corporation donated their buildings, vehicles and other equipment to the Department of Nature Conservation for the purpose of developing tourism in the area. This was successfully used as an incentive by the Director of this Department in tabling the legislation necessary to implement the recommendations of the Odendaal Report. The Skeleton Coast was declared a National Park in 1971 and its ecologically unsound boundaries remain in that state to this day.

With such a splendid and evocative name, the Skeleton Coast National Park evokes images of pristine beauty and of a region little disturbed by man because of its hostile environment. Nothing could be further from the truth! The coast is dotted with the detritus of many failed mining projects, none of which is old enough to be interesting on

Rosemary examines a rusty wreck on the Skeleton Coast. P.A.

its own. Also, virtually all the facilities within the park are for fishermen and most of the places that an independently minded traveller can visit unaccompanied are associated with man's influence on the coast – rusty wrecks and mining ventures. These are located along the main road en route to either the campsite at Torra Bay or the lodge at Terrace Bay – again, two destinations of interest only to fishermen. The really interesting places are kept out of bounds to visitors and all because the authorities worry, with some justification, about the potential damage that owners of four-wheel-drive vehicles will inflict on the sensitive environment. Instead, the authorities tell us, films, videos and books will be the way in which we can experience those forbidden areas. The northern and most interesting part of the Park is completely off-limits to visitors, except for the clients of a small, exclusive, tented camp situated near the Hoarusib. Thus, the independently minded traveller, not interested in a guided 'tour', can only look at the books and calendars and sigh with resignation. Aware of all this, and with the permits arranged for us by Sigi safely in hand, we drove northwards feeling very privileged indeed.

Forewarned of the dullness of the park's southern half meant that I had no real interest in the little lay-bys that we were soon passing. Here, when we deigned to stop, signs described points of interest – for example, a wreck or a fallen oil rig now host to a colony of birds. These and all of the other carefully signposted 'attractions' are manmade intrusions into the genuine but natural attractions of the Namib. Incidentally, the wrecks seen here are all too recent. My own experience is that visitors are disappointed by them for a very simple reason: the much-touted 'mystique' of the coast is unfairly suggestive of wooden, masted sailing ships, while the reality is of a coast as littered with recent rusty hulks as any other dangerous coastline in the world. Along the road between the Ugab River and Terrace Bay there is, however, one genuine and wholly natural wonder which is easily accessible to all: the mouth of the Uniab River.

The dry watercourse of this important river enters the park 30 kilometres inland and then soon afterwards is lost from sight as it goes underground beneath the dunebelt of the Namib Desert. It appears again on the other side of this formidable barrier with only a dozen or so kilometres left before it finally reaches the sea. Here there is a small but

ancient delta. In eons past each of the distributaries of this delta had its day of importance. Then, as those eons passed, geological movements, combined with the random fickleness of nature, conspired to change its course over time. It is in the main central channel where the waters of the Uniab, flowing beneath the sandy bed from as far away as Palmwag, rise up in several springs. The miracle of this place is that, in the midst of a sandy desert, a stream begins to flow towards the sea. I had been told of this place. I also knew that if I parked at the intersection of the road and the riverbed, I would then be able to walk the last few kilometres to the mouth.

When we arrived, it was mid-morning. The sun-drenched landscape appeared warm from our cosy cab, yet opening the door brought in reality with an icy swoosh. Hastily we donned jerseys, windcheaters and the like. Clarissa literally disappeared beneath layers of wool and Goretex. At this spot there is also a small pumphouse, a working relic from the days when the coast was not part of any national park. There was a diamond mining operation at Terrace Bay and the Uniab springs were its source of fresh water. Luckily, diamonds were never found in the same quantities that were being dredged from the ocean in the south around Lüderitz, so that the venture soon collapsed. When the park was established, the houses and buildings were converted into a fishing camp and the Uniab water is still used by the camp today.

The Uniab delta is an important place for wildlife, and surprising numbers of game come here to water. As we walked slowly in single file down the rocky bed, springbok watched us from far-off dunes. Cheetah are occasionally seen here, and in the distant past this was a very important place for that mysterious race of people called the

A. Skeleton coast wreck. P A

Gemsbok & Flamingos at the
Small freshwater lagoon to be
found at the mouth of the
Uniab River.   P.A.

At the mouth, the waves crashed on the gravel bar and it was here that we sat for a while revelling in a scene so different from anything one would expect from the game fields of Africa. We were buffeted by an icy wind, yet at our back there was a burning desert. At our feet a stream of fresh water mingled slowly with the salty ocean brine. Our nostrils were filled with the strong smell of the ocean and of rotting seaweed, yet above us on the ridge, just visible over the tops of some hardy coastal plants, we were conscious of a herd of gemsbok examining us intently.

Then the peaceful nature of the surroundings changed abruptly when Rosemary called us over to a mudbank where the stream entered the lagoon. Here she pointed out a distinctive set of spoor superimposed on the myriad tracks left behind by gemsbok and the like.

" That's a bit big for a brown hyena, isn't it?" she asked.

I looked down at the tracks suspiciously. "That's not hyena, that's lion."

Alert now, although none of us had the skill to tell with accuracy how fresh the tracks were, it was obvious that a lion had recently passed by this way. I looked over at the nearby reedbeds with renewed interest. The idyllic scene had taken on a strangely different, almost electric atmosphere. Almost as one we decided that it was time to start back to the car, which suddenly seemed to be very far away indeed. No one talked on that walk back and only when we had regained the reassuring solidity of the vehicle, did we mention the lion spoor again. Naturally, here we could afford to be brave about it, but it was uncanny that each of us had been convinced that we were being watched on that long two-kilometre hike back to the car. Of course, this was probably our imagination getting the better of us, but imagination is a powerful thing – so much so that, when we were halfway back, a gust of wind had fooled my brain into thinking that a lion was charging us from behind. So complete was the illusion that I was utterly convinced that I heard a low growl followed by a grunt. Then, in a flashback to Botswana ten years previously when I had nearly lost my life in an unexpected lion encounter, I leapt forward involuntarily. When I turned around, there was nothing to be seen but sea and sand!

Strandlopers (Khoikhoi who roamed the beaches of southern Africa in search of seafood). It has been said that this place might be the Olduvai Gorge of Namibia and some recent archaeological finds bear this out.

Soon we came to the springs. Here the crystal-clear water literally squirts up from the sandy bed in small jets. Then, gathering strength, it starts to flow as a small stream towards the sea. The muddy edges of this tinkling stream were imprinted with the spoor of game, both large and small. And yet when you raise your eyes from this cool scene, there is only the bare rock and sand of the raw desert. In the distance rise the scalloped ridges of the dune belt, dotted with small tufts of hardy bushes and shrubs. Presumably this was enough to support the amount of wildlife indicated by the mass of criss-crossing tracks. Further on this stream comes to a shelf where it cascades into a narrow red gorge before cutting a serpentine way through a series of ochre platforms. Here and there, rustling beds of *Phragmites* reeds startle the eye with splashes of bright green. Finally, having flowed along the edge of a low escarpment, this miraculous stream reaches the sea and there, at the beach, a lagoon forms. As we scrambled towards this idyllic finale, a group of gemsbok startled us all by spooking from a bend in the stream. They had been watering, oblivious of our approach. Beyond them, in the waters of the little lagoon, a flock of flamingo rose up and flew off in a blur of glorious pink.

Between 1894 and 1900 Dr Georg Hartmann, a geologist in the employ of the South West African Company, made a thorough exploration of the whole coastline north of

Cape Cross to the Kunene. The intention was to find suitable harbours and search for guano deposits. For this he gathered together a team of men to help him and one of these, a Captain L. von Estorff, was assigned the Uniab. Von Estorff did not find the Uniab delta to be an attractive place. Near the mouth of the Uniab he encountered a group of Bushmen, who soon afterwards decided to make an encampment close to his own. He noted that these Bushmen did not possess bows and arrows, rather they hunted game by trapping and snaring it. They did, however, own crude implements, some of which were made from elephant ivory, although whalebone implements were more common. These implements were used to peel the fruit of the narra plant, which was also an important source of food to them. Von Estorff recorded that, although there was abundant spoor, he saw little game for himself, but describes having seen some quagga. This can be explained by the fact that the game of this desert oasis was being regularly trapped for food by the Bushmen. He also found the water to be brackish. Somewhat naïvely, he asked his neighbours how it was that they could stand living in such an awful place. To this they retorted that, on the contrary, they thought the Uniab a beautiful place. And why not? In the vastness of the Namib coast, this was a paradise of fresh water and wildlife, the very necessities of survival.

Soon we were on the road again, passing first over the relict beds of the ancient Uniab and then a little later, past the campsite at Torra Bay. In Swakopmund I had heard a typically Namibian story about this place. Often empty for long periods, this campsite is sometimes opened only during the Christmas holidays. Then the entire farming community from the Kamanjab district adjacent to the Etosha Park migrates en masse to Torra Bay, where they set up a little tent city for the duration of the school holidays, with streets laid out between the various families' tents. So organized is this annual trek to the sea, that this tightly knit community deputizes their own police to patrol the streets. In this way and with typical pioneering thoroughness, order is kept intact during the revelries of the Christmas celebrations.

After a short while we were driving through the Terrace Bay camp – but more about this strange place later. Beyond, the neatly kept roads suddenly deteriorated for we were now entering the so-called wilderness part of the park closed to tourists.

An hour later we arrived at our destination – Möwe Bay. This place was named by Captain Hoffmann in 1884 while he was searching the coast north of Cape Cross for a suitable landfall. In the employ of the German Imperial authorities he was intent on doing all of the imperialistic things that nations do when confronted with vacant lands – they wished to plant the German Imperial claim and raise the flag. They were successful at Angra Fria, much further to the north. However, going south again, he was soon inspecting another landing place in a tiny rocky bay near the mouth of the Hoanib River. This he called Möwe Bay after his sloop the *Möwe* and it is now the location of the tiny outpost that administers the wilderness portion of the Skeleton Coast Park. It was here at Möwe Bay that the Sarusas Development Corporation wished to build their harbour, one capable of taking large ships. As mentioned previously, this project was scrapped, but as late as 1995 plans were put forward by the Ministry of Trade and Industry to resurrect the project, with the Government looking for money to do a feasibility study and more than 80 million dollars to build the harbour itself. So much, then, for the area's status as a National Park.

Lion tracks at the Uniab. P.A.

Near the mouth of the Uniab River. P.A.

It was nearly two o'clock when we coasted to a halt outside one of the three houses that made up the settlement of Möwe Bay. I did not know it then, but I was later to discover that Möwe Bay was the most desirable place that any Namibian could ever dream of visiting. The fishing was legendary, and there was the added attraction of the Hoanib and Hoarusib and their desert elephants. Of course, the fact that this place was off-limits to all but the chosen few was the final dab in the honey pot.

Möwe is an austere place – the buildings themselves have 'government accommodation' written all over them – but that is not to say that this place is lacking in atmosphere. It is definitely a working National Parks camp, but one that has a magnificently wild coastline at its door. This is reflected in the bric-à-brac lying about. Against the wall of the nearest building were bits and pieces of old boats intermingled with the skulls of desert game. I later found out that this was the office. Straddling it on either side, were three houses and some rondavels. There seemed to be no one about, but as we contemplated what to do next, a vehicle arrived and parked next to ours. From this there alighted the sun-darkened man whom we would come to know well in the next few days. This was the irrepressible Hannes. When we explained who we were, he brightened up considerably and then told us that the Brabys should have been back from patrol the day before, but that they were now expected later that afternoon. Meanwhile, he directed us to a third house beyond the office and told us to make ourselves at home. This, he informed us, was where the visitors stayed. As we were unpacking, we were immediately aware of the musty smell of the building allocated to us. It smelled strongly of damp and salt and was peculiarly evocative of the past – especially of school holidays.

Later on, when the vehicle had been unpacked and all of our equipment safely stored indoors, Hannes returned. He insisted that we accompany him on a short trip to a place nearby. "There is a little lake there. And high dunes as well." It was where all the visitors were taken, he assured us.

With commendable foresight, Clarissa and Rosemary piled in the front with Hannes. Foolishly, I chose the open back of the pick-up, electing to stand among loose wheels and fuel drums for the sake of a good view of the terrain we were about to traverse. This was a mistake, for the next

half an hour was just a blur of impressions seen through slitted, tear-streaked eyelids as I hung grimly onto the roll bar. This was my first experience of the speed at which these parks people travel in the desert. Back along the road and over the Hoanib we went, then turning inland to travel many kilometres across the gravel plain that lies between the beach and the main body of the dune belt. Here, the violent rattling that had accompanied our passage vanished and we swished smoothly over expanses of sand at a speed that gave me the feeling I was attached to a low-flying aircraft. Finally, as we crested the highest dunes Hannes slowed down, stopped and then leapt out of the vehicle with all the enthusiasm of someone who had never been there before. At this stage I had almost frozen solid in the frigid blast of the slipstream, my hands nearly iced in place on the handrail. Noticing my pinched features and wind-blown hair, Hannes just grinned. "A bit cold, was it?"

Mumbling something about being O.K., I had then tried to leap off the back as nonchalantly as I could – only to fall flat on my face in the sand. As the others dismounted and I dusted the sand off my clothes, I was suddenly transfixed by the sight of what lay spread out before us. Below us, nestling up against the high dunes, was a vast expanse of green reeds looking weirdly out of place in that desert scene. To crown it all, in the centre of this green mass, the blue waters of a small lake, known as the Oasis, glittered in the afternoon sun. Far away over the gravel plains behind it was the Atlantic Ocean.

Hardly had this epic scene sunk in when we were off again, as our guide threw himself down the steep slope. Slipping and sliding in the loose sand, we followed Hannes down to the reeds to commence a crazy search for a boat that he said was moored somewhere on the shore of the lake. What ensued was almost comical. We struggled through the reeds in the wake of the energetic Hannes and for half an hour floundered around like fish out of water, disorientated by the towering walls of vegetation. When we finally emerged, we were all cut and scratched by the razor-sharp edges of the reeds, and still had to run to keep up with our guide.

Luckily, there were opportunities to catch up with him and these came when he would stop suddenly in his headlong rush to point out the tracks and droppings of the various animals that frequented the area.

Hannes finally found the old lifeboat from the wreck of the Suiderkus. Soon we were scooting about on the shallow waters of the Oasis – the dunes of the Namib towering over us!

"Hmm, that could be lion!" Then he would be off, only to stop again a little further on. "Hmm, look at this. That might be brown hyena!" And so it went. Thankfully, in the end the boat was found and dragged to the water's edge and we were soon paddling around that bizarre desert lake in a vessel that had until recently been the lifeboat from a wreck on the Skeleton Coast. How relaxing it was. As Hannes and I paddled, cormorants rose noisily from the water to circle slowly over the dunes. Nearby, on the grassy edge of the lake, a lone springbok watched our progress warily. What a strange place the Namib is!

The sun was low in the sky as we set off for home. In the back I again hung on for dear life and contemplated our imminent introduction to our hosts. Eventually, we arrived back at Möwe Bay, unsteady, and in my case, frozen and not a little nervous of the coming minutes. As we pulled up in front of the office, the Brabys were sitting out on their veranda, enjoying the last rays of the evening sun.

My first impression of this couple was of a very handsome pair. Both of them were good-looking and tanned, with that healthy, outdoor look so envied by the city-bound. As we disembarked they came over to the truck, and what could have been an awkward moment somehow passed as we introduced ourselves. Rod was slightly offhand in the beginning, and I later found out that Sigi had had a hard time selling the visit to her husband. Before the night was over, however, we had all become friends – they would invite us back many times in the years to come – but at that first moment I felt really guilty that I had been unacceptably pushy.

Rod and Sigi were the perfect hosts. Later on that evening I spoke to Rod about Auses and desert elephant and he casually mentioned that in a few days' time he was going there for the day and we were welcome to come along.

Over the next few days we amused ourselves fishing and going on long walks up the beach as far as the wreck of the trawler Suiderkus. This hulk, lying rusting and broken on the boulder-strewn shore, was already nearly gone – reduced almost to nothing by the Atlantic waves since it came ashore in 1976. On the beach and in the rocky wasteland that lay inland jackals were common, one or two of them following us like stray dogs as we wandered about. Interestingly, the fresh spoor of brown hyena was everywhere, but when I mentioned this to Rod I was

surprised to hear that in all his years there he had seen them only once or twice. In the evenings we lolled about in their living-room and swopped stories. Once Rod brought out his collection of photographs and we were suitably impressed by the superb pictures he had taken of coastal lions sitting on the very beach we had walked on that morning. The pair of lions he had photographed had often visited Möwe Bay and, during the nights of those visits, would hang about in the vicinity of the houses. These were the same coastal lions that would appear in the Bartletts' film Survivors of the Skeleton Coast, and that would later be shot by a herdsman at the Dubis oasis in the Hoanib, not far from Sesfontein. The Bartletts, acclaimed film-makers for the National Geographic, were also based at Möwe Bay and their house was another, more isolated building about a kilometre away and closer to the sea.

The fishing along this portion of the coast was legendary and we all longed to try our luck for the tasty fish galjoen or black bream that abounded just beyond the breakers. On the first suitable day for fishing, Clarissa, however, toiled in the sun for far longer than either Rosemary or I and paid the price for her enthusiasm. The sun, shining down through the crystal-clear air of the desert, had silently wreaked its insidious damage on the only exposed part of her body – her face. That evening, she was in bed, writhing in agony from the worst case of sunburn that any of us had ever seen, nor ever wish to see again, for her face and lips had puffed up in the most alarming fashion. The next morning, the day that Rod had said he was going to Auses, she lay supine, saturated with

The last remnants of the Suiderkus

painkillers, her face swollen out of all recognition. Desperately disappointed, she decided that she could not bear the thought of bumping about in a vehicle for the entire day. Rather, she would remain behind as Rosemary and I went off to Auses with Rod.

In my mind I still clung to the hope that I would get to see a desert elephant walking on the dunes – after all, we were bound for the place where it would be possible for this to happen – but Rod warned me that in all his years at Möwe Bay, he had only once seen them crossing the dunes to Auses.

At breakneck speed we hurtled back along the track that Hannes had taken to the Oasis. Here, at the foot of the dunes, Rod lowered the pressure of his tyres and we were soon off and into the vast sand sea of the Namib wastes. Our route was only just recognizable as the course of the Hoanib River where it had carved a sinuous path through the undulating dunefields. Occasionally, a rock poked through the reddish sand or there was an isolated clump of bushes, but nowhere was it obvious that floodwater had once flowed through the bleak landscape. Indeed, in some years the sand dunes block the bed of this river and the floodwaters never make it to the sea. The rolling dunes then become a confusing maze of dead-ends and a trap for the

inexperienced traveller. These are the elements that conspire to make this a journey tackled only by those who know the way with complete certainty. For the next hour Rod confidently navigated a route through this apparently featureless desert, seemingly always knowing which way to go when confronted by a towering dune or a stretch of treacherous sand in his path.

Presently, some rocky hills came into sight, punctuated with patches of vegetation. Suddenly, we rounded an outcrop and entered a dense forest of tamarisk bushes, following a track that cleaved a winding path through this startling change of scenery. A herd of gemsbok, spooked by our presence, thundered off through the undergrowth and then we were out in the open again.

The scenery here was equally surprising, for now a vast green plain spread out in front of us. This, Rod informed us, was the 'Floodplain', formed by the lowest of the silt deposits laid down by the Hoanib River. There, however, all comparisons ended. Unlike the similar deposits that formed the Okambondevlakte and the vale of Sesfontein, further up the Hoanib, where cattle and goats have destroyed the stabilizing vegetation, the Floodplain is untouched by the ravages of man and his beasts. Here, only the wild animals of the Skeleton Coast are to be found, and the silt is held in the ancient grip of natural vegetation. There are no drifts of the dreaded chalk dust, and no 'white-outs' to be endured.

Off to our left we glimpsed a splash of colour and Rod drove towards this along a well-used track. Presently, a small camp came into full view. This idyllic spot proved to be one of the Bartletts' fly-camps. There was also a neatly laid-out airstrip on which were parked two fixed-wing microlight aircraft. Nearby, tucked in the bushes, was a small encampment. Rod did a quick spot-check of the camp and then went over to the two microlights where he made sure that the anchoring tethers were still secure. Satisfied, he returned to the vehicle. "Everything seems to be O.K. here. Let's go and have a look at Auses now."

I was surprised at how close this was to the Bartletts' camp – literally only a few minutes away. It lay, however, on the other side of a towering dune and the last part of the journey was up the side of a vast sand slope. It was late morning and the firm surface of the dune had become softened in the heat. Halfway up the slope the vehicle sank in a soft patch and stalled, so we got out and walked on foot

The route to Auses from Möwe Bay takes one through sand dunes for thirty kilometres. With no defined track and virtually no landmarks, this a journey where your vehicle sails across soft sand as a boat would on the sea.

with Rod to the crest. There, below us, as we panted from the exertion of the climb, was a spectacular dune-bound lake of crystal-clear water – the magical lake known as Auses.

The Oasis, the Floodplain and Auses are all terminal manifestations of the Hoanib River. Even though it is a kilometre away from the Hoanib's main channel, the lake at Auses is nevertheless derived from that river: it is filled by water from the seasonally inundated Floodplain seeping in under the intervening dunes. No planktonic material can exist in these sterile waters so the lake is perfectly clear, the yellow sandy bottom easily seen through its limpid waters.

As we stared admiringly down at the shimmering water, Rod pointed at a small antelope struggling its way up the nearby slipface. "Look at that – a springbok! I've never seen one do that here before." For the next few minutes the lone springbok toiled upward against a river of descending sand which its own efforts were making worse

by each step. Finally, it was level with us and after a brief glance in our direction it was off, bounding down the slope towards the Floodplain. Several waterfowl swam on the surface of the lake and these, too, had sighted us for they began to call agitatedly to one another. The clarity of the water was such that the nervous birds seemed to be floating on thin air, suspended far above their shadows, which bobbed about on the sandy floor of the lake. Then, as they made their take-off runs, the water became visible as their wakes painted the bottom with a sparkling display of interference patterns that were a delight to the eye. On the far side of the lake the slipface of a dune was scarred by the tracks of several large animals, and huge rivers of sand had cascaded down in their wake. "See those tracks over there?" declared Rod, pointing towards them. "Those were made by elephants sliding down the sand to the water. Looks like they've been here recently!"

Eventually, when we had absorbed as much of the place

There can be no more exotic location for a sparkling lake of clear water than among the towering sand dunes of an arid desert. Such is the spectacular location of Auses, the name given to the small lake that is formed where the floodplain of the Hoanib River penetrates the sand-dune belt of the Namib Desert.

83

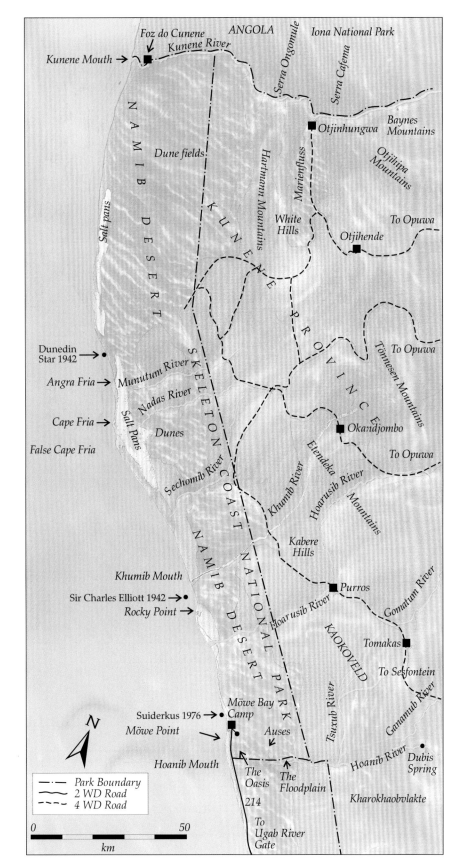

Map legend:
- ·─·─ Park Boundary
- ─── 2 WD Road
- ─ ─ ─ 4 WD Road

0 ——————— 50
km

N

Opposite
For the wildlife of the lower Hoanib Auses is of great importance – desert elephants, gemsbok, the rare desert lions, and springbok negotiate the steep dunes to get to and from the water's edge.

as was possible in the time available to Rod, we reluctantly returned to the vehicle and he reversed down the dune.

That evening, Clarissa was visibly over the worst of her sunburn and she needed much consoling when we recounted the experience of seeing Auses. She had missed what was likely to be our only opportunity to see something of Möwe Bay's fascinating environs. That night, however, Rod came in from the office after a long spell on the radio and said that he would have to make a quick trip northwards up the coast to Rocky Point. Again, we were welcome to come along for the ride. Clarissa was determined not to let another opportunity slip through her fingers, and decided that, no matter how she felt, she would accompany us. The next morning we all set off, on what Rod promised would be another long day.

This time our route was along the beach just above the waterline. This type of travel was a new experience for us and I marvelled at how coolly Rod dodged the incoming surges and yet managed to maintain speed through even the softest stretches of sand. Beach driving is not for the faint-hearted or the inexperienced: to prove it, the beaches of the Namibian coastline are liberally dotted with the rusting remains of vehicles whose owners had neither the experience nor the ability to use such treacherous highways – or were simply out of luck.

Near the mouth of the Hoarusib, we came off the beach and, gaining a faint track, crossed the riverbed. There was a surprise for me here. The ocean was almost in sight, but elephant droppings were scattered in abundance on the salty, and damp, bed of the river. Never in all my travels have I come across so unlikely a haunt of elephant, and yet they clearly frequent this barren place. We could not stop here for long, however, as Rod had arranged to meet someone at Rocky Point, so we continued past this fantastic place, but with the promise that, if there was time on the way home, he would take us up the Hoarusib itself. Hoping against hope, we were thrilled to find that this actually came to be because Rod's rendezvous at Rocky Point did not materialize. After a few hours of waiting in vain for the other party, we started on our return journey. When we reached the Hoarusib, I held my breath and said nothing, but, true to his promise, Rod swung the wheel and the Nissan accelerated up the winding valley along a faint and rutted track.

It is extraordinary what different characters all the

various rivers of the Skeleton Coast have. Since they are all constructed from the same materials and in the same environment, one would think that some uniformity of appearance would be logical. This is not so, and each is delightfully different from the other. The Hoarusib, particularly where it is close to the sea, is very picturesque and entirely different from either the Uniab or the Hoanib. Here it is broad and contains one or two small pools of fresh water. Red-coloured slipfaces of the dunebelt rise steeply from a bed which also boasts a green, grassy cover in many places. This grass and the water explain the abundant elephant droppings. But there is other game here as well, and, as we proceeded through this idyllic scene, gemsbok and ostrich cantered warily away and out of the valley, disappearing in clouds of dust up small craggy gullies.

A few kilometres further on the bed narrowed and high, black rock walls pressed in close to form a deep gorge. Here the green banks of reeds and grass appeared almost luxuriant in the midst of such stark scenery. Having flowed

silently beneath the sandy bed of the Hoarusib, water is forced up to the surface by rock reefs along the floor of this gorge, or the Hoarusib Poort as it is better known. Pools form and they are connected by little streams, some of which begin to run along the very ruts of the track. The final touch to this bizarre scene is the startling sandfalls that cascade from some portions of the gorge's southern walls. When the circumstances are right and the winds blow hard, small delicate rivers of sand trickle over the edge to fall through space as water would over a waterfall. The yellow cascades waft about in the gusts and dance from shelf to shelf as they follow the pull of gravity. At the bottom and on the green grass of the floor, they build huge cones of red sand over the course of the year – only to be conveniently removed when the Hoarusib comes down in spate and the whole process starts anew.

Here and there in that narrow gorge we came across more gemsbok and small herds of springbok. Everywhere we looked there were the silent calling cards of the desert elephant – and in amazing amounts considering the small numbers of these animals that regularly frequent this place. It was hard to believe that all the dung had been created by the very desert elephants we had seen in the upper Hoanib earlier that month, but Rod assured us that this was indeed the case.

Further up the Hoarusib, beyond the Poort, Rod stopped the vehicle and pointed towards a gap in the rocky sides of the valley. Here the all-powerful dunes had poured over the lip of the valley and Rod drew our attention to several long, sliding furrows marring the face of the slope.

"See those?" Rod said. "This is where the elephants strike the Hoarusib after walking across the desert from the Hoanib Valley."

After sliding down the slope like kids in a playground, the elephants would then head eastward along the riverbed towards the water and grass to be found there. After that, they would retrace their steps back to Dubis via Auses and the Hoanib. And so the cycle would continue, week in, week out, year after year.

In the past the elephants of the desert fringes were also able to water at another fountain on this river. This place, lying far up the Hoarusib at Purros, is the locality for a settlement of semi-nomadic Herero and Himba pastoralists. When the region was excised from Etosha, however, massive uncontrolled hunting took place and the last elephant resident in the vicinity of Purros was shot as late as 1981. Since then, the successful anti-poaching campaigns of the early 1980s seemed to have brought the situation under control and, in 1986, elephants returned to the Purros area. Naturally, the conservationists were delighted, but the Hereros and Himbas were not so happy. Competing with an elephant for water from the spring, or having precious vegetable gardens raided at night seemed to be all that they could look forward to. However, Garth Owen-Smith and Margaret Jacobsohn are doing some fantastic work. They have been the catalysts in a project involving the Himbas and Hereros with regard to the fate of the wildlife of the Hoarusib Valley outside the Skeleton Coast Park. The broad plan is that tourism, fuelled by the return of game to the area, will develop in such a way that the people of the area will reap the benefits for themselves. This is hardly a new concept, but it is hoped they will have as much success here at Purros as with the rhino populations of the adjacent areas. Apart from the prospect

of bettering their poverty-stricken lives with some revenue from tourism, Owen-Smith and Jacobsohn also found hopeful signs that the Himbas and Hereros at Purros might regard the return of the game as symbolic of better times they had enjoyed in the past. One eighty-year-old woman they interviewed told them that they now had few cattle and there were no elephants and they were poverty-stricken. Yet in the good old days they had been rich with many herds of cattle and that these had peacefully shared the water with elephants.

The famed 'sand castles' of the Hoarusib are another of the strange sights to be seen in this valley and these lie a few kilometres upstream of the Poort. They provide a graphic example of the ancient silts that were once laid down in this river valley in the same way as the similar deposits found in the Hoanib. These 'castles' are the eroded relics from the eons following the time when the river was cut off from the sea by dune migration. What remains is, in some places, strikingly similar to the architecture of medieval castles, and with a little

The Hoanib Valley is one of the favoured haunts of the true desert-dwelling elephants. Numbering seventy or more individuals, most of these elephants have been identified and documented by Sigi and Rod Braby during their years in the Skeleton Coast Park.

imagination it is not hard to see the shapes of towers and crenellated battlements. Close examination, however, reveals the true nature of their origin – the ripple marks and flow patterns of sediments laid down in estuarine conditions.

Beyond the castles, the bed of the Hoarusib becomes more arid and more typical of a desert valley, yet it has no acacias like the Hoanib. There is not a hint to be seen that further downstream and closer to the ocean, there is grass and water in abundance. Logically, it should be the other way around, and this assumption must have been uppermost in the minds of the first white men to have travelled that way.

These consisted of a group of men from the Thirstland Trekker colony at Etosha Pan and are part of a larger story which will be dealt with in detail in the next chapter. With their leader, a man called Gert Alberts, they had been sent westwards in 1879 from Etosha in search of a more suitable site for a settlement. Etosha's environs and the fickle nature of the springs along its shoreline had proved to be far from ideal. So the scouts set off and, after leaving the plains of Etosha, headed into the mountainous region of the Kaokoveld. Some weeks later they reached the springs at Otjitunda and Kaoko Otavi in the hilly region to the west of Etosha Pan. They found the country surrounding these perennial waters to be ideal – it was virtually uninhabited and teeming with game. Instead of returning immediately to Etosha with the good news, however, they pressed on westwards into the very heart of the desert. Amazingly, they crossed that vast expanse of rock and sand and reached the coast, a distance of 150 kilometres.

If you have ever crossed the dunebelt in a vehicle, you will quickly realize what an extraordinary feat that was. Much of the final part of the journey is over the dunes, a landscape as featureless as the surface of the ocean. Today, the journey over that dunebelt can take upwards of an hour in a vehicle and, with the inestimable advantage of knowing its extent, it is a simple affair. These hardy individuals, however, rode it on horseback, with no knowledge of the extent of the hostile country they were traversing. For all they knew, it might have been ten kilometres – or a thousand!

One afternoon, they crested the top of a large white dune and heard a strange rumbling in the distance. None could agree on the source of this ominous noise. An earthuake, distant thunder and galloping herds of game were all mooted as the cause, but one of the group who had lived at Port Natal suddenly realized what the noise must be: the sea. Remounting, they continued westwards for a few kilometres and after crossing a dune, were confronted by the blue expanse of the Atlantic Ocean. This was the first time that many of them had ever seen the sea. After this they turned southwards and travelled down the coast to the mouth of the Hoarusib, where they moved inland again. Following the course of the Hoarusib up through the Poort, past the sand castles and the fountain at Purros, they avoided the difficulties of the sand desert and eventually crossed over to the Hoanib Valley to reach Sesfontein. Thereafter, they were soon across the mountain ranges of the escarpment and home to Etosha. What a fantastic journey! And yet, little has changed in the Hoarusib since then. As we stood there under the sand castles, I could easily imagine a group of weary men cantering past, stopping to look up at the strange formations before

The Kaokoveld is a barren place of rocks and pebbles with no grass, yet even in this hostile environment there was a surprising amount of birdlife. Often, when walking across what seemed a lifeless terrain, Burchell's Sandgrouse would flush from beneath your feet with a startling flurry of wings.

continuing on into the dusty wilds of the Kaokoveld.

Only as the sun started to dip low in the sky did we have thoughts of home. We retraced our route down the Hoarusib and as we came to the coast, the sun sank below the foggy horizon. Although the rest of that long journey home was in the dark, Rod was unperturbed by this and navigated as surely as he had by the light of day. We bumped and scraped along under a starlit nightscape for what seemed like hours and then, just as I was beginning to question the reliability of this apparent confidence, the cheerful lights of Möwe Bay winked into view.

I think that the Brabys must have enjoyed our avid appreciation of their domain. I say this because, on the evening before our departure to Swakopmund, Rod proposed that we return at a later date. He was planning to go on a patrol into the hinterland to locate some rhinos. "Come back in a couple of weeks and you can join us", he had said with a grin, knowing full well that we would leap at the prospect. We would really see some wild country then, was his promise. So, with light hearts, we returned to Swakopmund, safe in the knowledge that we were not yet finished with the Skeleton Coast.

P. A.

The Braby house at Möwe

Back in Swakopmund, Clarissa and I and Rosemary made ourselves at home in the fishermen's huts for the third time that year. Although the massive swelling from sunburn had faded at Möwe Bay, Clarissa's face had since crusted over in the most appalling fashion, making her look as though she was suffering from some dread disease. Huge swaths of dried skin had stared to flake from her mottled face so she looked like the kind of nightmare monster one would encounter in a science fiction novel. However, Clarissa handled the situation with more aplomb than I would have had the same thing happened to me, and insisted on behaving as though there was nothing to see.

On the way back, we had stopped at Terrace Bay to buy some petrol, and Clarissa, in search of a pullover, had gone into the small tourist shop inside the main building. Her appearance provoked a dramatic reaction from the staff – the salesman literally backed away from the counter as she approached. Arriving at Swakopmund, I remembered the curious faces pressed to the windows of the Terrace Bay building as we had left, and insisted that she stay in the vehicle while I went into the office at the municipal camp. I was convinced that if anyone saw her, we would be

refused accommodation. As it turned out, it was two more weeks before the last of the after-effects had disappeared and she mostly stayed indoors until then.

The days at Swakopmund sped by, and soon we were loading up our vehicle with provisions and petrol for the days ahead with Rod and Sigi. The weather was gloomy as we departed and when the sun did eventually come out, it was accompanied by a howling wind, the strength of which I have never experienced before or since. The openness of the desert exposed the vehicle to the full force of the gusts which were so strong that on two occasions it was necessary to pull over and wait for the worst to pass. Even while stationary, the whole vehicle shook like a leaf and one of the rubber mud-flaps was twisted by the wind in such a way that it was torn from the bodywork. Later on that day the gale subsided and we were able to resume our journey, albeit at a slower pace, for another manifestation of the storm's ferocity had become apparent. With the sun in front of us it became impossible to see through the windscreen for it flared and sparkled like frosted glass. It had been perfectly sandblasted by Mother Nature, as had the bull bars at the front of the vehicle. The forward-facing

Skulls and bits of old wood
lay outside the museum, some
of which was from the wrecks
of old ships. P. A.

parts of this now shone brightly as bare metal, the black paintwork having been stripped off by the onslaught of flying quartz grains.

At Möwe, we settled in to the visitors' house as though we had always owned the place. That evening we were introduced to Rod and Sigi's three daughters, Chantal, Justine and Nicole, who were home from school on holiday. One could not hope to come across three more delightful children. Apart from being the best-behaved children I have ever met, they were totally self-assured in their wilderness home and capable of amusing themselves for hours on end. Wandering off on long jaunts on their own, they would pick plants and examine insects. They introduced us to another, albeit temporary, member of their household: Suri, the suricate. In later years, Suri would become famous worldwide after featuring prominently in the Bartletts' National Geographic film of the region.

Suri belonged to the Bartletts and they had taken Suri everywhere with them while they were filming. As they maintained a small base camp at Möwe Bay, they would often leave Suri with the Brabys when they had to go to Windhoek on business. It may be that we are burdening this species with our own anthropomorphic sentimentalism, but there is no denying that they are just irresistible. In the coming days when we were on safari with the Brabys, Suri was the clown that kept us all amused.

Of course, it must be expected that a home like the Brabys would be a menagerie as well. Constantly, there were surprises! On the afternoon of our return we were having tea with Sigi, when Nicole rushed in and plonked a little 'statue' down on the windowsill next to me. "This is Chomp", she informed me. Under her other arm, Suri struggled to escape. Next to my arm the 'statue', a shapeless object of dun colour, began to move very slowly and I realized that it was some kind of weird reptile with which I was completely unfamiliar. Sigi laughed and told us that Chomp was a grossly deformed chameleon that the kids had found and were now looking after. These little girls did not have dolls' tea parties: instead they went out and hunted in the desert for insects to feed Chomp! I was not surprised to find that neither Chomp nor Suri would be staying behind the following morning when the patrol was due to depart.

Late that afternoon I wandered next door to the office where Rod was working. On the walls were maps and photostatted memos. Files of paper and the other paraphernalia of a working office lay scattered on the desk and a radio crackled in the background. Listening to the cryptic conversations that issued from this, I was treated to several cameos from distant places. Tantalizing snatches of conversation were audible to my unpractised ear, only just discernible through a babble of interference: ". . . the capture vehicle isn't serviceable but . . .". There was more crackling, then: ". . . I'm bringing Johan in as his malaria . . .", or ". . . be at the airfield when . . .". And so it went as I listened in to the little dramas being enacted all over Namibia at that moment.

When he had finished his office chores for the day, Rod took me over to a nearby hut where they maintained a fascinating museum. Leaning against the outside walls of this museum were many wooden artefacts. "Those are from very old sailing ships", he confided, picking up a weatherworn length of turned wood from a pile of similar objects. Inside, there were shelves of interesting objects that had all been picked up along the Skeleton Coast. The most intriguing of all was the desert-blasted remnant of an ancient sailing ship's figurehead. Only the head had been found, but the carved features of the face were still quite visible. Here, indeed, were the remains of wrecks more in keeping with the mystique of the Skeleton Coast.

"Where did this come from?" I asked as he showed me the head.

"Somewhere in the north", he replied with a smile, replacing the head in its container. And that was all he would say on the matter. A couple of years later and on another stay with Rod and Sigi, I accompanied him on a drive along the beach far to the north of Möwe Bay. In the middle of nowhere Rod had stopped the vehicle and got out. "I want to show you something", he said as we walked inland over a shelf of sand that was only just above the high-water mark. This dry shelf extended many kilometres inland before encountering the rocky foothills of the hinterland. A couple of hundred yards inland Rod started to cast around in dry jetsam covering the entire shelf and stretching as far north and south as I could see along the coast. In a few minutes he had found a wooden artefact from an ancient ship. It seemed that the shape of the beach was such, that under very high spring tides, flotsam was carried inland for considerable distances and beyond the capability of the ocean to reclaim it – hence the

Paul Augustinus

collection of artefacts from the past. Here at last was a place that lived up to the Skeleton Coast's reputation for danger and mystery.

The museum was also packed with a variety of natural history exhibits. There were aerial photographs and shelves of skulls and bones from various desert game. Especially interesting was a human skull that had been unearthed at the mouth of the Uniab – a relic of a people long since disappeared from that coastal paradise.

The next day we packed and prepared for the journey ahead. Our vehicle was positively austere in comparison with the load that Rod was jamming onto the back of his Nissan 4x4. As Justine and Nicole ran hither and thither in their pursuit of Suri, Rod and his staff proceeded to load several sturdy tarpaulins, mist-nets, trunks of food, extra petrol, radio, tools, and dozens of other bulky items. All of these were carefully wedged around the significant bulk of a scrambler that Rod intended to use in an area inaccessible to the vehicle. When all the equipment was lashed down to his satisfaction, he fitted two sturdy planks to the railings at the back and informed me that they were the most important pieces of equipment of all. In the coming days I would see several demonstrations of their usefulness when we were stuck fast in heavy sand. Finally, the water tanks were filled and the preparations were complete. Then Rod, Sigi, Chantal, Nicole, Justine, Suri and Chomp levered themselves into the cab and we were finally ready to go. Rod leaned out of his window as I pulled alongside.

"When we get on the dunes keep your speed up and your revs on the red line. If it's soft and you slow down, then you'll get stuck."

With this piece of advice ringing in my ears, we moved off like a wagon train of yore, bound for adventure in the hinterland.

Once past the Oasis we climbed up into the dunes and, after lowering the pressure of our tyres, zoomed off over the sand bound for Auses and the Floodplain. This was my introduction – a baptism of fire – to the delights and hazards of driving on dunes. We sped over the desert, trying hard to keep up with Rod. After a while, I began to enjoy the freedom of racing across the windswept sand, but then we came to the difficult parts which began in a deep valley between some dunes. Beyond, there was the prospect of a long dune face to be climbed. Halfway up, I

could feel our vehicle sag and slow in the loose sand. I changed down, keeping the revs above the danger mark, and yet still we slowed! The top of the slope seemed very far off. Finally, in first gear, with my foot to the floor and the engine seconds away from stalling, we crested the rise, only to see an even steeper slope ahead. Of the following few kilometres the only recollections I have are of a screaming engine, panicky gear-changes, and a steering-wheel that seemed to have a mind of its own. But somehow we made it and, on the other side of the dunebelt and beyond Auses, finally caught up with Rod. He was busy pumping up his tyres again and so we did likewise.

An hour later we came to a crude signpost set on the boundary of the park and, without stopping, continued up the Hoanib. As we proceeded eastward the low rocky hills began to crowd closer to the river. Before long, these were towering over the Hoanib and occasional acacias were to be seen – we were now in familiar territory. Our route along the spectacular bed of the Hoanib was, however, to be a shortlived diversion, for in front of us, Rod's vehicle negotiated a steep bank and disappeared up a gully. We followed, and there materialized before us a gap in the valley sides; a small riverbed entered the valley at this point. Of course, when we left the grand scenery of the Hoanib, we also left behind the acacias and their soothing shade and regained more typically arid scenery. As we passed between some low hills, the desolation of the scene became complete and the track fainter – even the hardy *Euphorbia damarana* became scarce. However, it was soon to become even more arid and, once we had cleared the rocky scenery adjacent to the Hoanib, an undulating plain of pebbles and boulders totally devoid of any vegetation lay before us – a veritable moonscape. Our track was barely visible and had it not been for the sight of Rod's distant vehicle speeding along it towards some far-off hills, I might have thought that we had missed some turning.

"Well! They're not hanging around for us, are they?" observed Clarissa as we quickly set off after them.

"You're right, they're not and I think somehow they are testing us. You know, the macho thing."

Accelerating, and ignoring the violent rattles and bangs from the chassis, I raced after the Brabys' disappearing vehicle. In a short while all we could see of them was their fading dust cloud and by the time we approached the low range of hills, even this had disappeared from view. At the

Kaokoveld Scene   P.A

same time, however, the track became more distinct, started to follow a small riverbed, and was soon enclosed on all sides as the stream carved its way through a range of beautifully folded hills. Here, tamarisk bushes flourished and the telltale signs of elephants were everywhere.

It was getting late and, in front of us, the lonely track wound among boulders and bushes bathed in the light of a setting sun. We had fallen far behind, and for a while I began to entertain certain unspoken doubts that we might have lost them. However, as the sun dipped out of sight, and we rounded the next bend in the valley, there was a distant glimpse of the other vehicle.

We were indeed late – so much so that when we at last pulled up at the camping spot that Rod had selected, a fire was blazing merrily and a hive of camp-making activity taking place. Children were rushing back and forth, tarpaulins dragged around and boxes of food unpacked. The scrambler was already unloaded and parked nearby.

"We were beginning to think that you had got lost somehow", declared Sigi with a smile as I parked next to their Nissan.

It was three very weary travellers that fell from our vehicle that evening but, infuriatingly, Sigi and Rod seemed to have boundless energy, looking for firewood, preparing the evening meal. Suri, unleashed from the confines of their cab, scampered about investigating every hole in the ground while the children wandered off in search of insects to feed Chomp. As usual, Rosemary made herself comfortable in the back of the Toyota, and soon there was the merry sound of her gas stove being fired up for her first tea of the day. Meanwhile, Clarissa and I, envious of her already organized bedroom, did our best to assist Rod and Sigi in setting up camp.

A big tarpaulin was secured to their vehicle and stretched in such a way so as to form both a windbreak and a groundsheet. Their mattress was thrown down in the sheltered lee of this and their trunks of food and other equipment followed suit, serving double duty as weights to keep the tarpaulin in place. This, they declared, was their home while on patrol: they always slept under the stars of an open sky. This may sound terribly romantic, but when bedtime comes and an icy wind is blowing, romantic it is not. When we had been told of these hardy camping habits, Clarissa and I had privately discussed whether it would be polite to retire to the comforts of our tent, which

we had yet to set up. We thought not. Moreover, Sigi had pointedly noted that there was plenty of room on the tarpaulin for us. We decided that when in Rome, it would be better to camp as the Romans did, and as Sigi had even brought a mattress for us, it seemed that our minds had been made up for us.

Night fell and it was bitterly cold. Sigi had set up some chairs around the roaring fire and here we huddled for the rest of the evening, cooking, adding wood to the fire, and drinking an inordinate amount of Old Brown sherry. The colder it got, the more the sherry flowed. As is the case in such situations, our conversation grew louder and more fanciful by the hour. What more pleasant things are there in life than this? We had a roaring fire, food cooking, plenty to drink, and all around us was the untamed Kaokoveld. How much better can it get when friends who love Africa gather around a fire in the wilderness?

When it came time to go to bed, none of us was really capable of feeling the cold. Rosemary now returned to the cosy confines of the vehicle where she would sleep sealed away from the icy winds. Such luxury was not for Clarissa and I, however, and we joined Rod and Sigi on the tarpaulin. The children were already bedded down in the open back of the Nissan. Indeed, they had retired to bed

The day dawns at Dubis on the last day of our Kaokoveld journey with the Brabys. Sleeping and camping rough is the way things are done in this part of the world. Even if the night had been freezing cold, it was the irrepressible Sigi who was always up first.

Lunch break in the shade of the vehicle in the treeless wastes of the Kaokoveld. P.A.

much earlier and gone to sleep after much giggling and laughter. We tucked ourselves in, zipping up our sleeping bags as high as they would go. Somehow I had the feeling it was going to be a long night. Earlier on that evening when we had been marvelling with them at the way they camped, Sigi had explained to Clarissa that this was the way everybody in Nature Conservation camped in the Kaokoveld. It seemed that there were reputations at stake regarding these matters!

"What about hyenas?" I had asked Rod, with spotted hyenas in mind, remembering several occasions when I had attempted to sleep out in Botswana. Every time I had ended up sleeping in the cab after having woken to the sight of a spotted hyena looming over my bed.

" Don't worry", he had replied with a laugh. "I've never seen or heard them this close to the coast."

For a while we lay shivering in our sleeping bags, our hair tousled by the icy wind. The fire died down and soon only the glowing embers remained. Somehow, we eventually dropped off to sleep

At midnight we were all rudely roused from our slumbers by the whooping calls of hyenas. For a moment I decided that I must be dreaming, but then the hyenas repeated their performance and their lunatic calls echoed once again from the surrounding hills. Next to me, Clarissa sat bolt upright, while on the other side of the tarpaulin, and from beneath a mountainous pile of bedding, Rod's arm snaked out to shine a torch into the inky blackness. There, at the edge of the encampment, were the glowing eyes of several spotted hyenas which then proceeded to circle the camp. They were very curious and pressed ever closer until Rod had had enough. Leaping from his sleeping bag, he chased them off with a few stones. The hyenas soon lost interest and departed, moving down the valley towards the far-off Hoanib. I must confess, however, that Clarissa and I slept very badly for the rest of the night. I have an aversion, shared by Clarissa, to lying out in the open, unconscious and fully visible – and vulnerable – to large predators such as hyena and lion. Nevertheless, when I next looked out from my sleeping bag, dawn was breaking and we were all soaked from the morning dew.

Having extricated ourselves from our 'bed', stiff-legged and with aches and pains everywhere, Clarissa and I decided this kind of camping was not for us. Correspondingly, our awe of the Brabys grew greater by

the minute at the thought that they had been doing it like this for years! But the fire was already roaring, and Rod was up and making tea.

At the fire, Suri was luxuriating in its warm glow and chirruping away happily. Sitting there on its haunches in the way that suricates do, Suri constantly surveyed the goings on of the camp in an amazingly human-like way. First he would toast his stomach, then turn to do his back. And when I sat down next to the fire, Suri came over and nuzzled into the trouser leg of my jeans while I munched away at some of the leftovers in the pot and chatted to Rod about the rhinos he was hoping to find that day. It was here that the scrambler would come into its own.

The midday sun was burning brightly into our valley when we heard the distant sounds of his return and a little later he drew up in a cloud of dust next to the vehicle. A curt shake of the head was his reply to the inevitable question. However, we broke camp quickly and drove for a few hours along riverbeds and across open gravel plains to a tiny fountain – the very occasional watering-point of more rhinos that he wished to check up on. Desolate would be a kind description of this fountain's surroundings, the rolling rocky plains adjacent to the coastal dune belt. So barren were they that even the hardy *Euphorbia damarana* bushes were completely absent, and only a smattering of sparse shrubs hung on in the shallow streambeds. Yet here, Rod informed us, in this arid moonscape, there were a few rhinos. We made camp some distance away from the fountain and then walked over to have a look at it. Between the rocks, a few litres of brackish water lay in a bowl-sized depression, so insignificant that I could have walked over it without ever knowing. Yet this pitifully small pool of life-giving water was the very centre of the known universe for the wildlife that used it.

As night set in, we were all soon gathered around the fire. We had brought the wood with us and for a good reason: there was not a twig to be found within thirty kilometres, and, unlike the previous night where we had been sheltered from the wind by valley walls, we were now out on the plains – a fire was essential if we were to keep warm. The wind blew strongly and the tarpaulins flapped incessantly. The stronger gusts buffeted the vehicles, and sparks flew from the burning wood. Rosemary retired early, unwilling to brave the freezing conditions for long, and of course she had somewhere cosy to go. We of the 'sleeping-out' school stayed close to the fire and that evening our supply of Old Brown sherry was further diminished.

"You lot made some extraordinary noises last night," declared Rosemary the next morning as we gathered around the fire for breakfast. "Especially those huge snorts – what on earth were you doing?"

None of us remembered having made any animal noises and so this little mystery was soon forgotten – but not for long.

Later that morning, after having returned from another patrol on the scrambler, Rod walked over to the fountain to set up the mist-nets for a bird-ringing exercise. Here he discovered fresh rhino tracks which he was surprised to find led right back to our encampment. The fresh imprints of two rhinos halted but a metre away from where Rosemary had been sleeping – but on the opposite side of the vehicle from where we had been gathered around the fire. With notebook in hand, Rod measured the spoor and retraced the events of the night. It seemed that the two black rhino, one of which was a calf, after watering at the fountain, had then almost blundered into our encampment, halting only metres away from where we were sitting. Huddled as we were around the fire, buffeted by the wind and talking loudly – we hadn't heard their snorts of alarm, the noises which had so disturbed Rosemary!

The day passed slowly while Rod and Sigi methodically ringed the birds they caught in the mist-net. This was monotonous, uninspiring country and beyond the fountain there was nowhere to walk. Shallow undulating hills stretched off in all directions without variety, harsh and seemingly lifeless, yet a surprising number of small birds were caught by the meagre pool.

The next day we were on the move again, this time towards a mountainous region that lay just beyond the horizon. At first, much of the journey was along the ubiquitous riverbeds and over the trackless boulder-strewn foothills that are so characteristic of the Kaokoveld. For a while we bumped, shuddered and scraped our way over a flat region of dolerite boulders the size of grapefruits, which gave our suspension a thorough testing. So much so that it became a joke to try and talk as we jolted along. It was here that I decided, finally, that the mechanic in Walvis had been true to his word and solved the problem that had

plagued us in the past. The engine behaved perfectly and I could only assume that the episode of unreliability was finally over.

In this inhospitable terrain there was a surprising amount of wildlife. On the distant ridges, mountain zebra could be seen picking their way along precipitous paths. We also saw stately herds of giraffe slowly making their way through a shimmer of distant mirages. Then we entered the mountains proper and were free of the monotonous foothills and plains. The faint track that we followed in this treeless scenery took us along lofty ridges and, at the highest point, crossed a mountain range via an alarming pass. Here we had to negotiate a twisting, narrow gorge filled with large boulders and treacherous pits. In front of me, Rod's laden vehicle lurched dramatically at one of the trickier spots. It started sliding back, but then bounced forward as he scrabbled his way up the side of a tiny ravine. Having seen what he had done, I had to grit my teeth and force myself to complete the same, to me, almost suicidal manoeuvre.

Later, however, Sigi deflated my ego and told me that the pass was not considered to be one of the more difficult ones. It seemed that 'Divorce Pass' in the Doros region was the true test. The track which negotiated this long and terrifying pass hugged a steep valley wall and had a precipitous drop on one side. The story goes that the wife sitting next to the ranger proposing to use this route, after taking one look at the visually death-defying track, declared, "If we go up there, I'll divorce you!" Hence the name.

After the mountains had been crested, it was an easy downhill journey into the broad valleys that feed into the Okambondevlakte, and by evening we were approaching the Hoanib from the Sesfontein side along the dreaded chalk-powdered roads of the Okambondevlakte. On a sandy bank downstream from Dubis and not far from the forlorn tree we had used for shade a few weeks before while waiting for the elephants to move on, we made our last camp in the Kaokoveld. The next day we sped down the Hoanib and by late evening were parked in front of the houses at Möwe Bay.

Our Skeleton Coast adventures were not yet over, however. While we stayed on at Möwe as guests of Rod and Sigi for a few more days, one morning Rod came in from the office and asked me if I wanted to go to the

A view of our second camp on the patrol with Rod. It was here, during the night, that a pair of black rhinos wandered to within a few metres of our vehicles PA

Kunene River mouth on the Angolan border. What a question! It seemed that he was needed to accompany a survey team up the coast, their mission being to erect two temporary radio-beacon towers, one of which would be at the mouth of the Kunene. While they were engaged in this, he intended to ring birds. "Come along", he invited. "The Kunene is the wildest place in Namibia, and I know you would love it."

It would, however, mean driving over a couple of hundred kilometres on the beach, often through shallow seawater, and my precious vehicle was worth too much to me to risk ruining it for a few days on the Kunene. To this, Rod had shrugged. "Shouldn't be a problem. There will be five vehicles in the convoy – you'll fit in somewhere!"

The trip was a week hence and so it came to be that we stayed on at Möwe Bay until then. In the meantime we were running short of food, so Clarissa, Rosemary and Sigi went shopping at Terrace Bay. On their return Clarissa told me that there had been a wild party at Terrace Bay the night before and that the many of the fishermen staying there were all suffering from the after-effects. This in itself was not really significant, but it was one of the after-effects which caught my attention: badly bruised posteriors! On enquiring further Clarissa, had discovered that this was as a result of a traditional and unique 'game' played on some occasions at Terrace Bay. This game involved beating one another with a shambok. One by one the participants in this painfully macho game would drop out and finally the man with the greatest capacity to bear the pain would be left. Presumably this man, having suffered the most, would be the 'winner'! Clarissa could hardly believe the extraordinary story she had heard. To this day we do not know whether this was a practical joke, or yet another example of the roughness that many people do not realize lies just below the surface of much of Namibian society.

When they returned and I heard the story, I was reminded of my early days as a geologist and working with an exploration team in the Karoo. One of the field assistants was from Namibia and he was constantly telling me stories about his much-loved homeland and of his farm in the south of that country. One of these stories concerned his neighbours, three brothers who lived a bachelor existence of great boredom far from what they regarded as the bright lights of Keetmanshoop (the largest town of their district). He and they were often drunk at the weekend and fights would break out – not fist fights but gunfights in which they would pursue one another around their rambling farmhouse, shooting at random with their pistols. The same story was told to me repeatedly, and every time he would break down into uncontrolled mirth, the tears rolling down his cheeks. "It was great", he would say with a hint of nostalgia, for that was his kind of fun.

At the end of the week the survey team and their assistants arrived at Möwe Bay in a procession of vehicles. The team, a small group of Europeans and an American, set up home in the smaller of the two guest cottages. That night we met the people involved and a quick count confirmed that there would be room for only two passengers and that one of those would probably have to ride in the open back of one of the pick-ups. When told of the numbers, Rosemary realized that she was the one who would be staying behind at Möwe, and the following morning when we were all preparing to go, she was quite disconsolate as she waved us on our way.

Our departure from Möwe was a protracted affair with several false starts. This was another reminder of my days as a geologist, for the group was made up of the same kind of individualists that would be found in a geological exploration camp. The problem with individualists is that they are always difficult to organize, but a kind of pecking order gradually evolves and somehow things finally get done. The survey team appeared to be led by a capable, bustling German. Strangely, he became suspicious of Clarissa and me the moment he discovered that I was a wildlife artist and that Clarissa was an anthropologist. There was an English surveyor, and a Dane employed as a driver. The latter was in fact an ex-rally driver who had been hitching across Europe and got the job from his last lift. A second Englishman was their expert at erecting the towers. This was to be his last job before going home to England to open his own gym. Finally, there were a young French student and an enigmatic American who mostly kept to himself. Many of them had travelled extensively and worked in oil exploration in every corner of the globe. Because of this, most of them were very blasé. Nothing impressed them, and they were interested in neither wilderness nor wildlife. Rather, nature was merely something that stood in the way of the work of man. Had they encountered a desert elephant they would not have given it a second glance – to them, this was just a job.

One of the vehicles they had hired was a huge four-wheel-drive lorry to transport the bulky components of the towers and much of the electronic equipment. The driver of this behemoth was a cheerful Damara, who had never seen a perennial river in his life – the Kunene was to be his first experience of so miraculous a thing! The manager of the company that owned the truck, was also there in his personal vehicle. Ostensibly, his presence was needed to supervise the Damara driver of the lorry, but in reality he was taking advantage of a golden opportunity to go to the Kunene mouth – a forbidden area for most Namibians. He in turn had a friend along as well, a recently retired soldier from the South African army. It was indeed quite a motley caravan that set off to the Kunene that morning.

Beyond the Hoarusib the procession of vehicles took to the beach, which would be our road for the next two days. The manager accompanying the large truck had kindly allowed us to squeeze into the rear seat of his double cab. This was his pride and joy, and it was equipped with a powerful sound system which he played non-stop. Rod Stewart tapes were his favourite, and we must have heard one of these at least a hundred times before we reached the Kunene two days later. However, being a Namibian, he was well versed in the art of driving on the beach. Like Rod he knew exactly what to do and just how far it was possible to push the odds, and as we proceeded I decided that I had made the best decision of my life to leave our vehicle behind. It was a constant see-saw race against the incoming and outgoing surges of foam in an attempt to stay on the hardest sand, which lay right next to the water. Occasionally, there were unavoidable encounters with inrushing waves and the vehicle would splash through these, salty spray flying in all directions.

On one occasion, the convoy was making its way along the foot of steep sandy cliffs with the incoming tide surging between the wheels. Exhausted seals lay beached in the tiny space between the cliffs and the water and these flopped out of the way as we whined past in low gear. There was no doubt about it, this was alarming stuff, but for the drivers only. To be a passenger, as we were, was to be able to enjoy every minute of it. We were just along for the roller-coaster ride and it was all great entertainment.

The heavy transport truck stuck solidly many times that day. On each occasion there was much digging and giving of orders before we were on our way again, yet the manager

and the Damara driver seemed unperturbed when this happened, even when, once, the incoming sea was lapping close around the wheels of the bogged-down vehicle.

Late in the afternoon, and just when the tide was almost too high for the convoy to continue, the day's mad, headlong rush over the wet sand of the beach came to an end. North of Rocky Point, the lead vehicle of the convoy slowed down, pulled off the beach, and drew up on the shelf adjacent to the surging waves. This, it seemed, was to be the site of the first tower. The other vehicles followed, and were soon arranged in a small, protective laager against the wind. This was necessary, for a more exposed spot would be hard to imagine. We were poised between two great oceans, one of seawater and one of sand and rock. The beach, our highway for the past few hours, was arrow-straight at this point, and to the north and south disappeared from sight over equally ruler-edged horizons. A few metres away, crashing rollers sent surges of white-water up the slope of the beach to lick at the jetsam of the high-tide mark. Soon, a salty spray, brought ashore by a gusting onshore wind, began to settle on everything.

One of the towers was unloaded from the truck, but then, from one of the nearby Hiluxes, I heard muttered protests when Rod and Sigi began to unload their equipment from the Nissan.

"Bloody hell! We're not camping *here*, are we?"

By evening, the camp had been made, and many multi-

The only way to approach the mouth of the Kunene River is along the beach, but it can be a treacherous route even for those accustomed to this mode of travel. Bogged down in the softer sand near the high-tide line, the surveyors' truck is threatened by an incoming tide.

coloured tents stood in the shelter of the vehicles. The crew milled around trying to sort out the inevitable first-day confusions. Taking pity on them, Sigi cooked their meal for them while I watched from the corner of my eye and observed that cliques had begun to form among their ranks. Afterwards, when order had been restored and the various chores done, liquor was fetched from various vehicles and a huge fire made. This soon died down and one of the English crew members sauntered over to a piece of sandblasted wood nearby and began to drag it back to the camp. Seeing this, Rod leapt up from the remains of the fire and insisted he return the nondescript bit of wood to where he had found it. It was ancient wood cast up on the shelf, who knows when in the past, and was not to be touched for that reason. At this explanation, and muttering to himself, the sceptical crew member reluctantly returned it and wandered down to the beach to find wood there.

The next day the camp was a hive of activity while the tower was erected and the electronic equipment tested. Rod stayed to keep an eye on them, while Clarissa and I roamed around in an attempt to make something of the day. As the sun rose higher, however, we soon retreated to the shade of the tent and the vehicles.

This is a forbidding place indeed and it is easy to see why it can be a danger to a castaway, for there is no shade, no water, and not even a bush to shelter behind when the wind blows. The lack of this latter item was also to cause us some discomfort, as responding to the calls of nature required a kilometre hike in any direction just to get out of sight of the camp. A kilometre inland the first rocky outcrops of the desert proper were to be found. A walk to these silent sentinels, and into the rocky gullies beyond, was to experience fully the frightening nature of total solitude. There was the timeless feeling of an undisturbed wilderness and it was enveloped with an intimidating silence. A short while among those eerie rocks, with the occasional gust whispering in the crags, was enough to send one scampering back to the flats and the welcome sight of the distant encampment.

The next day we were on the move again. At Cape Frio we halted for a look at the seal colony and a little further on, at Angra Fria, we took a break for lunch. Here, just above the beach, is a roughly constructed wooden tower on the top of which perches a small covered platform with a view of the sea. When the Sarusas Development Corporation were looking for suitable harbour sites along the coast, they had not only looked at Möwe. They sent an employee, Ernst Karlowa, to build a small research station at Angra Fria. His mission was to determine whether the rocky headlands there might provide a suitable site for a harbour. This he proceeded to do, and the small platform we were lunching under was built so that he could sit and count the waves as they rolled into the bay – presumably to get some quantitative value as to the suitability of the site. What a mind-numbing job that must have been: all day long, day after day, counting the waves as they crashed on the shore.

In the afternoon we passed another interesting locality, that of the wreck of the *Dunedin Star* whose story is an extraordinary series of mishaps and disasters. In November 1942, the *Dunedin Star*, a British cargo ship with some passengers on board struck a reef a hundred kilometres south of the Kunene and foundered. The next day the ship's master, Captain Lee, ordered the stricken vessel to be abandoned, but after three trips of his only motorboat it broke down leaving 43 still aboard. Luckily, there were ships in the vicinity and these took the remaining crew on board.

On the beach, meanwhile, things were not going so well and the survivors had little shelter and no supplies. A search for water in the nearby desert had only revealed twelve skeletons in some half-buried shelters – an ominous discovery indeed! Moreover, a rough sea was preventing the ships offshore from floating in supplies, and radio messages were sent to Cape Town for these to be dropped from the air. One of the ships, the tug *Sir Charles Elliott*, became low on fuel and was forced to sail for Walvis Bay. Soon after that, the last ship departed, unable to help in the stormy conditions, but the same day a Lockheed Ventura bomber had landed near the castaways with supplies, only to become hopelessly bogged down in the sand. The luckless pilot had other news to report, for en route he had been surprised to discover the *Sir Charles Elliott* stranded on a shallow reef where she had been blown by a storm the previous night. Most of the crew made it to the shore and were eventually airlifted out of the area from Rocky Point.

While all this had been going on, a rescue convoy was making its way overland. This had been despatched from Windhoek three days after the *Dunedin Star* had gone aground, but beyond Kamanjab the convoy had been plagued by breakdowns, punctures and soft sand. Indeed, this had been a poorly prepared rescue attempt for they had set out with no radio and only one air pump – a hand one at that – which had to service every tyre. The leader of this convoy, a Captain Smith, earned the nickname 'Pump' Smith on this journey for obvious reasons.

For days they toiled on towards the coast and nothing was heard of them. Because of this and when news of the beaching of the *Sir Charles Elliott* and the mishap with the Ventura bomber reached Windhoek, a second overland convoy hurried forth, presumably to rescue the survivors from the *Dunedin Star*, the *Sir Charles Elliott*, and 'Pump' Smith's convoy. Actually, his convoy had struggled to within a few kilometres of the wreck site, but there they bogged down in a salt-pan and so he and two others set off on foot to reach the castaways.

The whole exercise was starting to look like a slapstick comedy, for the coast was littered with the hulks of sinking ships, planes up to their propellers in sand drifts, and trucks slowly slipping below the surface of salt-pans! Nonetheless, somehow the survivors were all gathered at Rocky Point a few days later and most were flown out from there. They had been nearly three weeks on the beach. The remainder, meanwhile, bravely returned to Windhoek with the convoys. Later on the grounded Ventura was reached by yet a third convoy and extricated from the sand. It took off, successfully, but forty-five minutes into the flight, an

The wave counting hut at Angra Fria

engine seized and the aircraft plunged into the ocean. The three crew managed to drag themselves ashore and proceeded to walk to Sarusas spring, fifty kilometres away over the dunes, and rendezvous with their convoy there. The remains of the bomber were later washed up on the beach and one of the engines can still be seen there today, a rusted relic of just one of the many stories to be told of the Skeleton Coast. The debris left behind by the castaways of the *Dunedin Star* is also still there, some fifty years later, and this was pointed out to us as we sped past the site of the wreck.

We were nearing the Kunene and the convoy seemed to gather speed with the end of the journey at hand. At this stage, too, we passed a school of porpoises heading in the same direction. There were hundreds of them racing through the rolling waves, seemingly intent on some unknown destination for they were travelling fast. So fast, in fact, that it was many minutes before we had overtaken the leaders as we raced along the beach on a parallel course. We sped on past that spectacular gathering to the deafening accompaniment of Rod Stewart, literally flying over bumps and splashing through the surges of the incoming tide in such a hurry that I dared not ask to stop for a better look.

Our arrival at the Kunene should have been a memorable occasion, but, sad to say, it was not! As we crossed the last reed-covered banks and the blue-green waters of the Kunene River came into view, Clarissa and I were still subjected to the thumping beat of a Rod Stewart ballad. Inexplicably, the volume was turned up even louder as we approached that last rise, and our host jived in his seat to the beat as we followed Rod's vehicle down the riverbank to find a suitable camp site. How tragic! We had arrived in Namibia's most remote and unspoilt paradise, and yet when the vehicle halted, we leapt from it, hands covering our ears, in what must have been unseemly haste. Around us the rest of the convoy arrived and soon the site was a milling mass of people.

We and the Brabys removed ourselves from this mêlée and made our camp a few metres away from the others. Only then were Clarissa and I in a position to appreciate where we really were. Slowly, we regained our sanity, soothed by the nearby waters of the Kunene as they swished past. Later, when we had pitched our tent, there was more time to absorb our surroundings. A few metres

away, fringed by reeds and dotted with sandbanks, an azure-tinted river flowed sedately towards the ocean – an attractive sight under any circumstances, but here, in this setting, it was spectacular, for we were surrounded by the sand and rock of a sweltering desert. Behind our encampment, scalloped dunes marched all the way to the horizon, and all about, there were picturesque outcrops of polished blue-grey rock. On the opposite side of the river, beyond the sandbanks and reedbeds, the stark boulder plains of Angola stretched northwards to disappear into the coastal mists of the Mossamedes Desert. We had indeed 'arrived' at a special place.

The following morning the 'crew' departed to do what they must and, in the ensuing quiet, we were able to have a breakfast that was more in keeping with this peaceful place. It was in fact Sunday, the sun was shining and there was no wind. There was a palpable feeling of tranquillity after the hectic rush of the previous days. Near us as we breakfasted was the Kunene, its slick surface hiding the strength of the river's flow. There was much evidence of

Opposite
Even though it is more than fifty years since the Ventura bomber crashed in the ocean after the *Dunedin Star* débâcle, one of its engines is still on the beach and looks remarkably intact, considering its exposed position.

The view from a range of hills north-east of Rocky Point and forty kilometres inland from the coast. Because of the crystal-clear air, vast panoramas such as this are the norm in the Skeleton Coast.

elephants in the spoor and droppings that covered the nearby mudbanks. Fresh lion tracks ran by the river's edge, neatly superimposed on the spoor of some gemsbok. The lion's pug-marks then entered the water and disappeared. Presumably, the lion had swum to the other side of the river, unafraid of the numerous crocodile. The presence of these signs of wildlife added greatly to the stirring scenery and charged the barrenness of our surroundings with a feeling that the place was vibrant and alive.

The headwaters of the Kunene River lie in the far-off plateau of central Angola. For half its length it flows southward before swinging sharply towards the ocean, and then cutting its way through several major transverse mountain ranges. Finally, after crossing the coastal plain, it reaches the ocean. The river received its name from the Hereros as they migrated into the Kaokoveld from central Africa. As they penetrated this harsh land, the river was on their right-hand flank and so it was named the *okunene*. This meant 'to the right', the 'large' or 'right' arm. Symbolically, to the Herero, the right arm of the body is the larger of the two. The land on their left flank they called *okaoko*.

Naturally, when the Herero people arrived here wildlife abounded. As was the case on every river in Africa until recently, huge numbers of elephant, rhino and plains game were found along its banks. Now, the last rhinos have long since gone, as have most of the other animals. Yet some wildlife does persist. The last fifty kilometres of the river's course are through the high desert of the Namib, totally inhospitable to man, and therefore, like the Hoanib and Hoarusib, the last refuges for these relict herds. A few elephant survive in this hostile environment, living off the

102

Later on I went with Rod to an isolated dune in the nearby desert. Here, under a bush, protected by a tarpaulin, there was hidden an outboard motor and the deflated bulk of a rubber dinghy. After much huffing and puffing, we managed to get the surprisingly heavy dinghy into the vehicle. Back at camp this was unloaded onto the sand near the water's edge and all of us took it in turns to operate the pump. An hour later the inflated dingy was bobbing at its mooring. Rod started the motor and, after one of his daughters had leapt in the back, declared that there was room for Clarissa and me as well. "Right, hop in and let's go and see what's about."

And so off we set up the river, weaving a path through the shallow sandbanks and keeping an eye open for the ubiquitous crocodiles. In the clear, shallow water of this final stretch of the river, we were forced several times to get out and push, bream darting between our legs as we struggled with the leaden weight of the dinghy. However, once across to the deeper channel and the high reedbanks of the Angolan side, we began to make more progress. Here, because of the familiar smells associated with verdant mudbanks, the rustling of the green fronds, and the constant calls of nesting birds, we might have been on any river in equatorial Africa – except that the dunes in the distance reminded us of our true location.

Soon, when we had rounded a bend in the river, we were passing the white buildings of the old abandoned settlement of Foz do Cunene. In Portuguese colonial times this was the station where fresh water was sucked up and pumped far up the coast to the town of Mossamedes (now known as Namibe). The inaccessibility of this place was such that it also became their 'Robben Island'. Here were incarcerated the politically unacceptable individuals of the Portuguese regime. Now, drifts of sand lie up against the sides of and between the derelict buildings. Passing close to this forlorn remnant of a not so distant era, we could clearly see, through the gaping windows and doors, the detritus of a vandalized past. The pumps were gone from the pumphouse and twisted machinery rusted where it lay. Unfortunately, the peace that presently reigns at this remote place is only thanks to the internal chaos that reigns in Angola. Some day, in a future, peaceful, Angola, people will return to reclaim the waters of the Kunene for man's use. Perhaps also when that time comes, the wildlife will flourish again along the upper reaches of this river,

The recent presence of a coastal desert lion was revealed to us by telltale pug marks in the mudflats next to the mouth of the Kunene. Intermingled with its spoor were those of a gemsbok and both sets of spoor entered the river at the same spot, leaving the end of the story to the imagination.

reedbanks that fringe the entire extent of the river's course. There are also gemsbok, springbok, ostrich and leopards, and at the mouth there is a lagoon where flamingos gather in large flocks and terrapins can be seen as well. The river and delta still hold large numbers of crocodile – indeed as we were sitting breakfasting on that first morning, one of these slowly pulled itself out of the water and onto a nearby sandbank to sun itself. The crocodiles are in fact the most visible of the Kunene wildlife and when the sun shines, large numbers of them haul themselves out onto the many sandbanks that dot the river adjacent to the lagoon at the mouth. Unfortunately, their presence also denied us the luxury of swimming or bathing; indeed Rod advised extreme care when we went to collect water. "There are some huge crocs here", he warned me, having seen me go down to the water's edge to shave and wash.

It was a strange sensation to travel up a flowing river of fresh water and yet be surrounded by the towering dunes of the Namib Desert. Rod Braby and his daughter in the rubber duck are just five kilometres from the Atlantic coastline.

because on the map at least, this is all part of a vast reserve – the Parque Nacional do Iona.

Beyond the Foz do Cunene we rounded another large bend in the river, to see the towering dunes of the Namib rising directly from the river's flowing water – but only on the southern side. On the northern side there stretched a desert of polished boulders, entirely devoid of one grain of sand. This is the 'sand shadow' phenomenon. The results of this phenomenon are strikingly obvious from the air or from aerial photographs and are seen to their greatest effect in the Kuiseb Valley, where the river is the exact boundary between the massive dunes that stop on its southern bank and the rocky plains that extend northwards from the opposite bank. This effect can also be seen in the Hoarusib and other rivers that cross the Namib on their journey to the sea. The effect is not mere coincidence. The prevailing winds of the desert tend to

move sand in a slow march northwards. When a major obstacle such as a river is encountered, sand accumulates slowly in the valley, but not for long as most of these rivers come down in flash-floods annually. These floods transport the accumulated sand to the sea and so the cycle starts again. The result is that any sand on the northern banks migrates northwards and is never replenished. All that remains is a rocky, windswept desert.

As we passed out of sight of the Foz do Cunene, Rod pointed to a patch of dense reedbanks. Here, he told us, on a previous trip with some high-ranking officials, he had come upon a herd of elephant feeding in among the reeds. Indeed, all along our route, the reedbeds were visibly battered from the attentions of these hardy elephant. As we proceeded further, these abundant reedbanks began to thin out, the banks becoming more rocky and the dunes higher. Then, many kilometres from the mouth, we passed an island of rock in the centre of the river. This was being used by cormorants as a nesting site safe from the predations of jackals. This rock reeked of the characteristic 'anchovy' smell of a seabird colony, and their droppings had painted their roosting place in a startling blaze of white. There was a noisy protest as we motored by and then they rose in a cloud to circle about in the updraughts above the river. It was then that Rod drew our attention to something high up on a dune behind the circling birds. "Look, baboons – up there on the crest."

Far above, a troop of dark-coloured baboons moved single file in a slow procession that took them out of sight and into the sea of sand, their barks of alarm barely audible above the noise of the motor. This must be the most unlikely place that I have ever heard their calls, so evocative of the more typical game fields of Africa, so out of place in a land of sand and seabirds. Even as we were looking at them, a disturbance on the Angolan bank behind us drew our attention. Between the tumbled boulders and out of a small bay, several gemsbok clattered away over the rocks to stand and watch us suspiciously from a distant rise.

Presently, the course of the river became more rocky and confined and soon rapids formed a barrier so we could go no further. Gunning the motor against the turbulence, Rod nosed the dinghy into a tiny bay and we alighted to walk about for a bit. Rod pulled the dinghy onto the sand and we scrambled up the rocky bank. "Hannes once saw a leopard hereabouts," he informed us, as he cast around for any telltale spoor. "And don't go too close to the water." This latter warning was an indirect reference to the several huge crocodiles which were regularly seen on that stretch of the river. Apparently, these wily crocodiles are very fond of baboons and, to confirm this, Rod pointed out baboon spoor leading down to the water's edge. There in the sand was written the story of a sudden scuffle. Needless to say, no tracks led away from the water.

We arrived back at camp at the same time as the survey crew, who were already opening their cans of beer. Rod was keen to be away from all the noise and chatter and he had therefore decided that his Sunday afternoon would be spent fishing at the mouth with his family, and Clarissa joined them. I, however, had different ideas. After pocketing a water flask, I set off to walk inland along the dunes above the river and an hour later I was struggling

through the sand to a position opposite the Foz do Cunene.

High up on the dune ridges overlooking the river and Angola, the view was magnificent. Everything seemed so clean and untouched, and the wind-blown sand was unblemished save for the spoor of the occasional baboon and springbok. The impression of cleanliness and freshness was almost physical and the silence so complete that each footfall had a deafening clarity. By the end of the second hour the effort of sliding down steep slipfaces and then scrambling up the slopes of the following dunes had begun to take its toll. Finally, I could go no further, and at the crest of the next dune fell exhausted and panting on the loose sand. Below me, beyond the Kunene, whose waters from this height were a deep blue colour, were the rocky wastes of the Angolan Namib – the Mossamedes Desert. All that lay before me, and far beyond the horizon, was the Parque Nacional do Iona, a triangle of proclaimed land that stretched two hundred kilometres up the coast to Tombua and a similar distance up the Kunene. How sad it is that this spectacular place is now the haunt of poachers and has been denuded of virtually every elephant and all of its rhinos. But from the heights overlooking that troubled land, none of this is obvious. Instead, there is

Although the sun blazed down on the bizarre scenery that we were travelling through, a bitter wind constantly blew off the grey Atlantic Ocean. Because of that wind, Clarissa, like the rest of us, was suitably wrapped up against the cold in a fashion that would not have seemed out of place on a ski-slope!

Two desert elephants near the mouth of the Kunene River.

P. A

only a sweeping view of breathtaking scenery. The sand-shadow effect was also plainly visible. On my side of the river, mountainous sand dunes marched directly to the water's edge. On the Angolan side, there was simply a desolate, rocky plain decorated by the patterns imposed on it by exposed geological features – the folded strata and eroded fracture lines.

As I sat regaining my breath, a movement far out on the Angolan moonscape caught my eye. Two objects were slowly making their way across the plain and my binoculars confirmed what I instantly knew they must be: elephants! All my tiredness vanished and I felt a rising excitement as I watched them turn gradually and come closer to the river. Slowly, they picked their way through the jumble of rocks and were only a hundred metres away from the water when their path changed again to take them eastward towards the coast. In twenty minutes, they had disappeared in the heat shimmer, striding ever faster towards the distant Atlantic and the reedbeds on the islands at the mouth.

On the long journey back to the camp I rushed along, delighted at what I had seen. Finally, when I reached the camp it was late in the afternoon and Rod and company were back from their fishing excursion. I could hardly contain myself as I related what I had seen and nearly missed Rod shaking his head at my undeserved luck. He had spent many months camped at this place before he had seen his first Kunene elephants. When I was describing to Rod what I had seen, we were seated around the warm glow of the communal fire. So, too, were some of the survey crew, but they were totally uninterested in, even bemused by, my excitement. Later on, one of them asked me why I had been so excited to see some elephants.

"What's the big deal?" he demanded to know. "If you've seen one elephant, you've seen them all!"

That night the 'crew' got quite drunk and, becoming bored with their eurocentric arrogance, Clarissa and I went off early to bed.

The next morning they were uncommonly quiet as they breakfasted. They ate in silence and then went off to work. When they had gone, a grinning Sigi told us that, apparently, at midnight, insults had been traded among themselves, authority challenged, and there had been a brawl. Then, their leader, incensed, had fired most of the surprised crew members on the spot. That morning they all went down to the tower they were building and radio messages had flashed back and forth to their HQ. The upshot was that they were all re-hired there in the desert, but under stricter conditions. One of these was that there was to be no alcohol.

If the crew were restless that night, none of them showed it, but around the fire there was little of the usual chatter. Bored and subdued, these press-ganged members of the Kunene temperance society attempted to amuse themselves by trying their hands at braaiing meat. A lot of this was turned to charcoal and boerewors to bootstrings before their patience snapped and, with nothing to do, they wandered off to bed in frustration.

The next day, Rod was up early and, with his mist-nets set up near a bank of reeds, was busy for the whole of that day as he and Sigi collared numerous birds. The following day we would be returning to Möwe, and it would be the end of the first phase of the year's journeying, so Clarissa and I walked to the point from which I had seen the elephants the previous day – it would be our last opportunity. There was nothing there, however, but the silence and the rocks of the timeless Namib.

A few days later we were in our usual huts at Swakopmund. Now, at last, our thoughts were turning to other places in Namibia – to Etosha. Yet, even as we pored over maps of the areas we would be soon visiting in the hinterland, I found myself looking again at my map of the Skeleton Coast. Peering closer at the point where the Kunene intersected with the ocean, I found it almost impossible to believe that I had actually been at that place only days before; it seemed more like a hundred years ago when I had looked down on those dusty elephants as they trekked towards the beach at the mouth of the Kunene, Namibia's Shangri-la.

The Sandcastles in the Hoarusib River
P.A.

CHAPTER THREE

THE ETOSHA EXPERIENCE

Because Etosha is a very organized place – too many people go there and there are too many rules and regulations for my liking – it had long been crossed off the list of places that I wished to experience. This was mainly due to a terrible snobbery I have regarding those areas in Africa where wilderness and wildlife are found together. In the past, this meant that I would never go anywhere that the dreaded bureaucrats had been successful. Rather, my haunts were in wild country where I could camp as I pleased, or at the very least, leave the confines of my vehicle to walk. In the Kaokoveld we had experienced wilderness in the true sense of the word, travelling to places where a breakdown would have meant trouble indeed. But travelling on our own, far away from the nearest help, had also brought us close to some of the rarest animals on the continent. The risks were taken and our journey became an adventure. Having had experiences such as these in the last few months, how was it then that I found myself speeding down a tar road towards that stronghold of bureaucratic might called Etosha? I asked myself that question many times while we crossed the last of the Namib's desert scenery.

As we climbed the hills leading into the heartland of Namibia, the bizarre mountain peak of Spitzkoppe receded into the distance behind us. After the rugged beauty of the

A cheetah pair looks out over the vastness of the Etosha Pan from a vantage-point on the sandy ridge above Okondeka.

109

coast and the desert, this heartland is decidedly mono-tonous. Between Karibib and Etosha the country seems to be made up of the same few scenic elements: low brown bushes, stunted brown trees and occasional brown hills separated by vast, flat, brown expanses. Wild Africa does not exist here either as the area has long since been divided into fenced farms and ranches. Thankfully, the road is tarred and so the journey from Swakopmund to Okaukuejo takes only half a day at the most. Even the towns that one passes through are dusty, uninteresting places, with none of Swakopmund's character. At the end of the journey lies Etosha, a land of uniforms, rulebooks and tour buses. So why were we going to this place? I had no answer to that question. For their part, Clarissa and Rosemary were interested in experiencing the full spectrum of Namibia's offerings. Not so narrow-minded as I, they had balked at the idea of bypassing such a famous place. Personally, I caressed my compromised principles with the thought that I would find abundant material for future paintings. Indeed, the purist in me had already decided that that was the only reason I was going there!

"I could never enjoy such a place," I said to Clarissa as we slowed down at the Andersson gate. " Look at the name of the gate! They can't even get their history right. He passed through the Namutoni end of Etosha, not here!"

Inside the office our bookings had to be produced and I was asked to read the declaration that all visitors were required to sign. My hackles rose as I scanned the list of rules and regulations. But I was committed – indeed I had paid in advance for a month – so I gritted my teeth and signed on the dotted line. On we went through the boom and proceeded along a tarred road that led some twenty kilometres to the camp at Okaukuejo.

Immediately, we encountered a herd of zebra standing in the shade of a roadside tree, a patch of which fell across the road and was occupied by a knot of zebras that refused to remember they were wild animals. Rooted to the shady patch, they stoically continued to chew the cud even as we squeezed past them! Gawking like tourists, we pressed on and were soon approaching the low buildings of the camp.

Once inside, it took only a glance at the surroundings for me to realize that we were in bureaucrat country par excellence. In contrast to the quiet countryside, it felt as though we had stumbled into a human ants' nest. Worker-bureaucrats clad in green and khaki walked purposefully hither and thither. Cars came and went from the car park in front of the office. There were signs, buildings, shops and restaurants everywhere. The splashes and screams of children from a large swimming-pool floated over a nearby fence, and all around us families and tourists walked and chattered. Disgusted, I had let Clarissa go into reception, leaving me to stew in the heat of the truck outside. My prejudice had softened slightly, however, when we located our bungalow. It looked decidedly comfortable and very inviting in the oppressive midday heat – and it was even airconditioned!

"Hmm", I had thought, "great for painting in!"

Little did I know then, that this was the thin, insidious end of the wedge.

The bungalow was one of several located right next to a waterhole. In fact, it had an unobstructed view of the pan itself and, even as we were moving our luggage inside, there was a sudden burst of activity among the animals drinking there. Springbok, kudu and gemsbok scattered, tearing off through the bushes, and I was startled to see a lioness sprinting after them. As the dust settled we saw the lioness come back and melt into the shade of a bush less than a hundred metres from our veranda. Later, when the vehicle had been completely unloaded, we lunched in

The waterhole at Okaukuejo is one that the patient visitor will find very rewarding. From the comfort of a bench on the grass-covered lawn, with cool-drink in hand, you can expect to witness all the drama of the wild: lions ambushing kudu, gemsbok and springbok are nowhere more easily or comfortably seen than here.

Opposite
A lioness is on the verge of pulling down a kudu close to the low wall between the camp and the waterhole.

Below
This low wall in front of the waterhole is all that stands between visitors and the elephants, rhinos and lions that come down to drink every day.

At the waterhole at
Okaukuejo spectacular
wildlife events are a
common occurrence P.A.

airconditioned luxury, gazing out through the windows at the little dramas constantly taking place at the waterhole. That evening we sat out on our veranda, relaxing with ice-cold beers from our fridge. As the sun set behind a group of elephant drinking quietly at the waterhole, I realized that, unbelievably, I was starting to enjoy myself.

The most distinctive feature of this National Park is the vast, salty Etosha Pan whose salt was transported in solution by the waters of a river that once flowed from the north. Almost certainly, the upper Kunene was the original source of this water when, in the distant geological past, it flowed into the Etosha depression. This is not to say that it issued directly into what we now know as the Etosha Pan. Possibly, it fed a vast inland swamp between the pan and the present-day course of the Kunene and the Etosha Pan was the terminal sump. This is analogous to the present-day Okavango, whose waters do not reach the sea: the salty deposits of the Okavango are 'flushed' out of the swamps into the Makgadikgadi pans. In the Kunene's case, the erosive powers of a smaller coastal river eventually overcame the transverse mountain ranges that flank that region. In so doing, it 'captured' the larger river and its perennial waters.

A similar case of classic river capture has also taken place in the past in the northern Kalahari. Here the Kwando, or Mashi as it is known in Angola, once fed its

perennial waters into the Mababe depression. Until very recently, this huge depression formed a swampy area only half the size of the Okavango, yet it was to be doomed when the Kwando was captured by the Zambezi. And so it is also with the Kunene. Today no perennial rivers empty into the Etosha basin, but there are two or three minor seasonal streams, the most important of which is the Ekuma, probably the original watercourse of the captured Kunene. Like the Makgadikgadi, Etosha can flood seasonally, although only to a depth of a few tens of centimetres. This water evaporates quickly as the season passes, and all that remains is the white briny plain that forms the characteristic backdrop to all memories of this place. The extensive salt-beds were not, however, precipitated from the waters of the Ekuma or the Omuramba Ovambo – they were laid down by the Kunene when it flowed into this region and not to the sea.

Long after Etosha 'lost' the Kunene and in very much more recent geological times, there were large fluctuations in the climate. At present all of Etosha's water comes from the Indian Ocean in the form of meagre rainfall during the rainy season. None of this rainfall is derived from the Atlantic, and the very size of the subcontinent means that the winds bringing moisture from the Indian Ocean are depleted long before they reach the western coast, but just enough moisture remains to support the semi-desert vegetation and the animals that live in the Etosha area. This was not always the case. Recent Shuttle photographs have revealed a corduroy pattern of fossilized dunefields in the bush to the east of the Etosha National Park. These are relics of episodes in the Pleistocene era (which began three and a half million years ago), when the annual rainfall declined below 150 millimetres. At that point the vegetation was destroyed, and wind became the dominant force in shaping the physical environment. This whole region became part of a 'Mega-Kalahari', whose fossil dune systems have been detected in beds of Kalahari sand as far north as the Shaba province of Zaïre, an area that now receives more than 2000 millimetres of rainfall a year. Interestingly, there were three distinct dune systems in this 'Mega-Kalahari', each of which is distinguished from the others by differently orientated dune systems, having been formed at slightly different times in the late Pleistocene when the subcontinent was dominated by different circulation systems. Etosha lies within the Northern Dune System of this Mega-Kalahari. Here the east–west dune alignment was formed in a different era from that of the north–south orientated dunes of the southern Kalahari System.

Archaeological studies conducted in these areas indicate that the interior of the subcontinent has been occupied since the earliest of Stone Age times. There are, however, prominent gaps in the records, which indicate that this occupation fluctuated according to the different climatic conditions. Understandably so, for during the dune-making period this area would have been as inhospitable as the dunes of the Namib. Middle and Late Stone age artefacts have been discovered in this Northern Dune System, and these indicate that people survived there in the times when the climate was at least similar to that of the present. Some say that the present-day San Bushmen are the descendants of those Stone Age hunter-gatherers, who were undoubtedly the first custodians of Etosha. Then in the 1700s other peoples began to migrate into the region, from the heartland of central Africa. Now known as the Ovambo nation, they settled on the wide fertile grasslands between the Kunene and the Okavango rivers. Etosha and its environs fell within their influence and they herded their cattle far to the south of the pan. They were thus the second custodians of Etosha and they grazed their cattle in harmony with the herds of game that abounded on the wide plains. Then, in the mid-nineteenth century, the white man arrived from Europe to hunt and trade, and for a while, from the late 1890s to 1989, its custodians were people who had come from a different continent. Now, of course, all Namibians have become the custodians of Etosha.

The explorers Andersson and Galton were the first white people to behold the salty wastes of the Etosha Pan. The story of their journey there is not only full of adventure and hardship, but one that gives perspective to Namibia's recent past; it is an interesting prelude to the events that took place at Etosha in later years. Their journey of discovery through the unexplored country north of Gross Barmen to Etosha provides a fascinating example of how, even in those days, bureaucrats and officialdom, in the form of local tribal chiefs, can conspire to restrict the movement of adventurers. As they say, "The more things change, the more they remain the same!"

On 3 August 1850 a small schooner, the *Foam*, dropped anchor in the desolate harbour of Walvis Bay. On board were Francis Galton and Charles Andersson. They came from very different backgrounds. Galton was a perfect example of the English gentleman explorer and was one of those fortunate individuals who went by the label of 'financially independent'. He had already made one small journey to the Sudan and his appetite had been whetted for greater things. Lake Ngami had just been discovered by Livingstone, and London was host to many sportsmen and travellers who had current information on South Africa. Galton decided, therefore, that he would explore the country to the north of the Cape Colony and try to reach Lake Ngami from the west coast of Africa, whereas Livingstone had approached it from the east. In London he met Charles John Andersson, a Swedish naturalist, and persuaded him to abandon a journey to the Arctic and instead accompany him to South Africa. They made their way to Cape Town and after a few weeks sailed northwards to Walvis Bay.

From their anchorage they had their first view of the desolate wastes through which they would soon be struggling, and in a few days, they had made contact with some missionaries and a cattle trader who lived nearby in the settlement of Scheppmansdorf (now known as Rooibank). This was situated on an island in the bed of the Kuiseb River, next to a small stream of fresh water. Here a missionary, Mr Bam, had a chapel and house. Stewardson, the cattle trader, lived in another house beyond the chapel. The latter had

Beyond the grasslands lie the white plain of Etosha Pan. P.A.

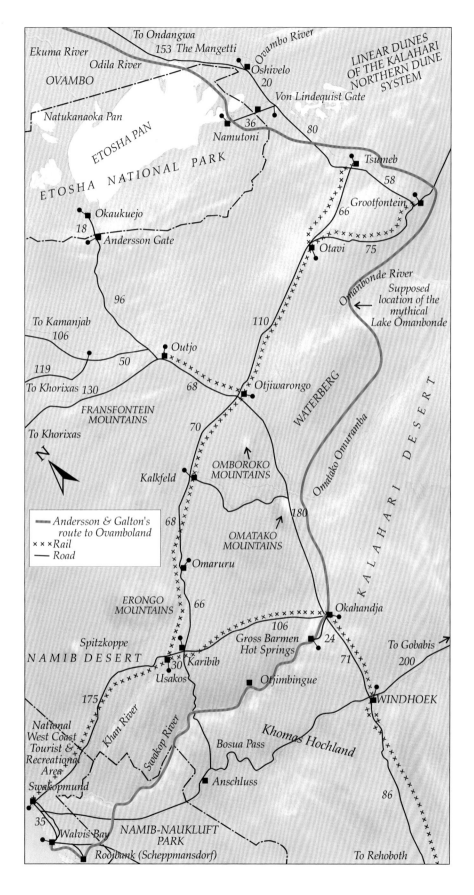

recently lost everything and so he, his wife and children could not afford to return to the Cape.

In a week or two Galton and Andersson had grown accustomed to the strangeness of the land and its people. This was especially so of their 'steeds', the ubiquitous ride-oxen. Also, during this period, all of their equipment was safely transported to Scheppmansdorf where they were given a small outhouse in which to stay and store their belongings. At night they were entertained by Mr Bam in his lodgings.

"The house", wrote Galton, "is a tolerably sized cottage . . . built of course by the Missionary himself, as well as he was able to build it; the workmanship was naturally very rough. . . . Chairs, a table, and a bureau were imported from Cape Town; the bed, bookshelves and so forth, made here. The wife does the whole house work, cleaning the rooms, managing the children, cooking the dinner, and, what I never liked, waiting at table. These ladies have the hardest and rudest of occupations, but, I must candidly say, they seem to like this life extremely, and I am sure that Missionaries must find great favour in the eyes of the fairer sex, judging from the charming partners that they have the good fortune to obtain."

A marauding lion was bothering the settlement, a coastal lion of the kind now only found north of the Uniab River. One morning Galton set forth with his gun, accompanied by Stewardson, for his first encounter with a lion. Looking sidelong at his companion, Galton mused that he would rather have had anyone else other than Stewardson, a failed tailor, minister and cattle dealer, for his guide, and also ". . . carried by any other kind of animal than my bucolic friend's" – Stewardson preferred his "trusty ox" to riding on horseback. They only glimpsed the lion, but on returning across the rocky plains, Galton noticed something that we in the present think is a modern affliction, caused by off-road weekend warriors. "As we rode back across the plain we saw vast numbers of old gemsbok tracks, although there are but few of these fine antelopes in the neighbourhood; but impressions made on this crisp gravelly soil take years to efface; they seem to be almost stereotyped; and a very few animals and wagons have produced an extraordinary number of spoors . . . the plain is covered with false wagon-roads in every direction. . . . Losing the way is the rule here, and not the exception; and a person who has crossed the plain without

doing so, rather plumes
himself on the feat."

By mid-September they were ready to
leave for the interior. They had purchased
and broken in the oxen and Stewardson had
consented to be their guide, at least as far as the
mission station at Barmen. The Naarip plain was
crossed and two days later they were entering the steep
valley of the Swakop River. To their delight, they found
green grass and a small stream of water. Numerous buffalo
skulls lay scattered about the place as well. Here Galton
started to notice a change in climate. His tent, so necessary
along the coast, was discarded and he began to sleep
outside by the fire.

On the 21st they moved on again along the Swakop's
winding bed. Poor Stewardson's reputation was sorely tried
soon after this when he let Galton's precious mules out to
graze in the riverbed. That night they were spooked by
lions and galloped off. On the following day the carcasses
of two half-eaten mules were found nearby. The presence
of the lions was again felt the next night when Galton was
recovering some of the meat from the dead mules from its
place of safety on a rocky ledge.

"I was busy tugging out the last shoulder of my trusty
steed, when the men called out, 'Good God, sir, the lion's
above you!' I did feel queer, but I did not drop the joint . . .
it was not till I came to where the men stood that I could
see the round head and pricked ears of my enemy, peering
over the ledge under which I had been at work."

Stewardson was by now as thoroughly alarmed by the
lions as those mules had been, for every night they came
and roared nearby. He was so afraid of them that, when, as

Ox wagons crossing the
flat desert plain between
Schappmansdorf and the
bed of the Swakop River.
P. A.

Galton
later realized,
they should have
been travelling at night, he
insisted that they should travel in the
heat of the day. Because of this, it was often late morning
before they were on their way.

One day, after one of these late starts, Galton heard a
faint call from behind. Turning, he saw Andersson lying in
the sparse shade of a tiny bush.

"I found him very ill, and with a racking headache,
under a tree to which he had staggered . . . and a very
lucky chance for him that he reached it."

Andersson had seen some interesting birds and gone
after them on foot. True to form, the naturalist had been
distracted and had fallen considerably behind. Then,
finding his companions gone, he had to rush after them to
catch up.

"I had only just caught sight of our party", wrote
Andersson, "when I was seized with sudden giddiness. . . .
Being fully aware of the danger, I collected all my energies,
and made the most strenuous efforts to overtake my friend.
But the stupor increased every moment, and my voice

115

Opposite
The sandy riverbeds that cut through the wastes of the Namib Desert formed convenient highways to the interior for the earliest hunters and traders who penetrated this region.

became so faint, that for a long time I was unable to make myself heard."

Luckily, Galton had heard him, and rode up. In a semi-conscious state, Andersson lay there for a while. By that evening he had recovered his strength, but was suffering from an intense headache which was to stay with him for the next few months.

On the 26th they were in the shadow of the Erongo Mountains and, after resting at a small spring called Tsobis, they set off for the mission station at Otjimbingwe.

Otjimbingwe was well situated for it had plentiful water and grazing. They found that the missionary there, Mr Rath, was busy building a sizeable house for himself on a nearby hill. Nevertheless, they were well received by him and his wife and Galton made his encampment nearby on 30 December. After this had been done, he went to spend the evening with Mr Rath and was very disturbed to hear news of the country ahead. Jonker Afrikaner, the leader of the Hottentot nation, had attacked the nearby mission station at Schmelen's Hope. Three days distant, this station was the last outpost and beyond lay the country that Galton had hoped to explore.

In the early 1700s the migration of pastoral people from central Africa via Botswana arrived in the area now known as the Kaokoveld. From here they spread south, seeking grazing lands for their herds, and eventually occupied all the land as far south as the Nossop and westwards to Gobabis. This came to be known as Damaraland and the people referred to themselves as Damaras (this 'Damaraland' must not be confused with the Damaraland of the present, which is a much smaller and artificial 'homeland' created in the late colonial era). At the southern extent of their influence they came into contact with the Khoikhoi (or Hottentots as the Dutch called them), who had already crossed the Orange River from the Cape some time after the 1750s.

Conflict was inevitable between the Damaras and the Hottentots and this finally occurred in the 1820s. There were disputes over grazing rights, and during a drought the Hottentots tried to push northwards into Damara territory. At the time of this trouble, to the south of Damaraland, yet another migration was taking place, that of the Oorlams, northwards into the land controlled by the Hottentots.

The Oorlams were of mixed Hottentot and Dutch blood. They spoke Dutch, wore western clothes and, moreover, they possessed horses and rifles. One of these Oorlams was emerging as a powerful force on the Orange River. This was Jonker Afrikaner. He had started to terrorize the communities on both banks, stealing cattle and dealing in arms and ammunition. This man was approached by the Hottentots to help them in repelling the Damaras. In return, he would be granted grazing and residence in the north. Being well armed, he defeated the Damaras in three battles, and, much to the irritation of the Damaras, then settled at a place within their traditional lands. It is thought that he named this place Winterhoek, later shortened to Klein Windhoek, after the mountains close to his original home in Tulbagh in the Cape.

For many years Jonker Afrikaner was the undisputed leader in Damaraland, and Windhoek became a centre for trade, with large cattle herds exported overland to the Cape. But Jonker then began to drink, and, as a consequence, fell into debt so that he had to return to his old habit of raiding cattle and terrorizing all the inhabitants of Damaraland. It was the Damaras who suffered most from this new turn of events, but occasionally he was tempted by the riches of the traders who were now starting to penetrate inland from Walvis Bay. In 1848 he even trekked down to Walvis Bay in search of loot because he had heard that a ship had been wrecked there. When he discovered, however, that the stricken ship could not be reached, he returned, frustrated and angry, massacring whole communities of Damaras along the way.

For Galton, news of the attack on the Damara settlements gathered around the mission station at Schmelen's Hope was a serious setback, for this was exactly the country he had intended to traverse in search of the unexplored terrain beyond. Even though Jonker had tolerated the presence of white people, he had never allowed any into the lands beyond Schmelen's Hope. Once, when the missionary Hahn was preparing to explore the interior, Jonker had sent a group of his followers to detain him until the dry, travelling season was over. Now, with the attack on Schmelen's Hope, the situation had worsened. To add to the complications, the indigenous Damaras also regarded the whites with some suspicion because Jonker had tolerated them: the white-skinned people were considered akin to the Hottentot, almost as spies for Jonker.

"At the Cape", wrote a frustrated Galton, "my plans had already been thwarted by the emigrant Boers, who chose to cut off all communication with the north by the one side of the Karrikarri [Kalahari] desert; and here were the Oerlams [sic], their offset as it were, trying to do the same on the other. The cases were as similar as could be; both parties were guided by British subjects, – both were effectually barring out civilization and commerce from Central Africa, and what I felt most peculiarly vexatious, both were barring out *me*."

Also living at Barmen was one Hans Larsen. This man, a Dane by birth, had originally been a sailor, but had left his ship at Walvis Bay and then worked for some traders living at Scheppmansdorf who had eventually bankrupted themselves. Larsen had received his last payment in cattle and he now lived as an independent man, travelling a bit, and doing odd jobs for the missionaries. He had also done a good deal of hunting and, after seven years in the Kuiseb, had virtually shot out all the game there. He was also dealing in oxen and it was to Larsen that they went for this latter item.

"I found him in the neatest of encampments, with an old sail stretched in a sailor-like way to keep the sun off, and in an enclosure of thick reeds, that were cut and hedged all round. The floor was covered with sheep-skin mats: shooting things, knick-knacks, and wooden vessels were hung on the forked branches of the sticks, that propped up the whole. A very intelligent English lad was acting as his 'help'. . . . Hans sat on an ottoman, looking like a Mogul."

Not only did Galton end up buying oxen from him, but he also hired him to take charge of the oxen during the forthcoming expedition.

Galton, leaving Andersson and Larsen to take care of breaking in the oxen and bringing up the rest of their equipment from Scheppmansdorf, now travelled backwards and forwards between Barmen and Otjimbingwe in an attempt to rectify the situation to his advantage. Over the next few weeks he wrote several letters to Jonker Afrikaner, threatening him with the wrath of the authorities in the Cape. Meanwhile, he waited, his patience wearing thin at the lack of progress. Little of consequence happened, however. Sometimes at night lions roared around their boma, and once there was a report that a Damara party had crept close to Otjimbingwe.

In an effort to amuse himself Galton went hunting in the vicinity of Otjimbingwe but to little purpose. Indeed, Hans Larsen had been active here as well, for the game was very skittish. Large herds of zebra would come down to the spring every afternoon, but he soon gave up trying to shoot them. In addition, "there were four or five hangers-on about the place with their guns, who would run down and have their shots; besides these, there were savages with their bows and arrows. Often, after an hour's hard and careful manoeuvring, the game was seen to be startled, and a ball from a zealous sportsman was whizzing at them from some ridiculous distance. The captain of the werft [settlement] made good and steady bags of game with his bow and arrows, getting a zebra about every other day. . . . The lions also killed several, and they supplied the natives pretty well. The Damaras were always on the look-out, and, guided by the vultures, appropriated in the morning whatever beasts the lions had left half eaten."

Every night he dined with Mr Hahn who told him much about the Damaras and the Hottentots. From the kraals nestled close to the mission he interviewed many men as to what lay beyond Schmelen's Hope. One of them mentioned a great lake called Omanbonde ten days away. It is possible that in London, Galton had been overly influenced by Livingstone's discovery of Lake Ngami. It was his greatest desire to discover something comparable and he leapt at this news.

"This was just what I wanted – a point to aim at, something to search for and explore. It seemed so very absurd to bring a quantity of men and oxen, and charge the scarcely penetrable hakis thorns which hemmed us in on

below – the ruins of the Rhenish mission station at Gross Barmen. The station was established by Carl Hugo Hahn in 1844. P.A

every side, without something definite to go after. The name was pretty."

So, at long last, after all their weeks of toil in the desert, Galton's expedition now had a goal, albeit one that was unimaginatively similar to one of Livingstone's successes.

Meanwhile, Jonker Afrikaner had sent an unsatisfactory reply and Galton retorted with a more threatening letter. Galton again waited for a reply, which came in the middle of December and in which Jonker invited him to visit his 'capital'. Galton eventually did exactly this, and arrived at Jonker's kraal in a suitably dramatic fashion – he charged in on his ride-oxen and halted with the horns of his 'steed' straddling the door of the chief's house.

In the coming months Galton had many meetings with Jonker and somehow organized that meetings also took place between the chiefs of the Damaras and the Hottentots. Both the Hottentots and the Damaras were of the same mind – that things had gone too far. No planting or sowing was going on. There was no law in the country. At these meetings even a few laws were drawn up. Subsequently, Galton received a friendly message from Kahikene, the Damara chief who ruled the land through which Galton wished to pass on his way to the mystical lake he had set his mind on finding, and "Matters now looked more sunshiny".

Early March found them on their way at last, and they set out, bound for the unexplored country north and west of Schmelen's Hope. By mid-March they had struggled through the impenetrable thorn bush of the area to meet with Kahikene, the chief who had been attacked by Jonker at Schmelen's Hope and his people widely scattered. Kahikene informed him that the next chief along Galton's proposed route, Omugunde, had already let it be known that he would not allow them to pass and that they would be attacked instead. When Galton's own Damara staff got to hear of this, they became quite panicstricken and refused to continue. Galton, Andersson and Larsen persevered, however, and, by taking a slightly different route, persuaded their men to continue. In the event, they also found out that Omugunde might be persuaded to let them pass and three Damaras who knew the area agreed to guide them to Omanbonde.

By mid-March the high cones of the Omatako Mountains were sighted on a distant horizon and here they saw their first large herds of game. By the end of that month they were looking up at the south-eastern side of the Omuvereoom Mountains, known today as the Waterberg plateau.

"Huge jagged rough stones, many as big as a small house, were piled up, and thrown about in all directions, with deep fissures between them. . . . There were some giraffe-spoors high on the hills. Giraffes are wonderful climbers. . . . From the hill we swept the country with our telescopes, and caught the glimmer of distant water between the trees: there was to be our next halt. . . . We 'marked' the vlei as well as we could, and took the wagon there, – three hours' travel before breakfast. . . . I had been hoping to see fewer thorn-trees, but here they were worse than ever. My oxen would not face them: . . . [they] plunged and tossed, and got their heads out of the yokes; and often the wagon-men could not get up to the fighting creatures on account of the thorns. . . . From eleven a.m., till night-fall, we were labouring through the thorns, that threatened soon to become impervious. Our clothes and hands were sadly torn. . . . Not a blade of grass was to be seen; and when we outspanned, a pitch dark night had set in; the oxen were roaming about, – we could hardly see them in the thick cover. When the morning broke, a few oxen remained, and the rest were gone. Away went half the men, without any breakfast, running a steady pace, for we feared the oxen might get back even to Kahikene's werft. They were overtaken beyond the vlei, as they were walking steadily back. In the meantime I had gone on to see how far we were from the stream. . . . To my delight, I found it close by, only an hour and a half off, full of running water, and like a trout-stream, with meadows of grass about it. It came out from a cliff of Omuvereoom."

On 30 March they were moving forward again. Following the foothills of the Waterberg, they proceeded northwards and found several deserted Damara villages. One morning they surprised a group of Bushmen as they foraged in a vlei for food. From two of these they obtained more information about Omanbonde. This, they said, was "as broad as the heavens". This was music to the ears of the two men, who could almost see the newspaper headlines in London, proclaiming their great 'discovery'!

"Well, Andersson, what should you suppose this lake's greatest length to be, eh? . . . Surely it cannot cover less than fifteen miles anyhow; and as for its breadth, it is no

A giraffe in the rocky country below the Omuvereoom mtns. known today as the Waterberg.

doubt, very considerable, for the Hottentots declare that if you look at a man from the opposite shore, he appears no bigger than a crow."

Soon after this they came to a village that had not been abandoned. After some parleying, they managed to convince one of the villagers to guide them to the lake. One day and they would be there, they were told by their willing guide. In anticipation, Andersson and Galton carefully examined their mackintosh punt (a fabric-covered canoe) to see if it was sound – for the next few weeks they intended to spend on the shores of the lake, in order to enjoy some fishing and shooting. The next day, 5 April, they toiled through a dense forest and that afternoon they emerged on the long, flat bed of what appeared to be a dry watercourse. Andersson was the first one out of the trees.

"There!" shouted one of their guides, "there is Omanbonde!"

"Omanbonde!" echoed Andersson, almost in despair, "but where, in the name of heaven, is the water?" Shattered, Andersson could do little but sit down and wait for Galton to arrive with the wagon. When the rest had arrived, he told Galton that the lake was in front of him.

"Nonsense!" he replied; "it is only the end or tail of it which you see there."

They struck off down the vlei and when they came to some reeds and their guides began to search for water, they realized the truth. They had been chasing a rainbow.

When they had recovered somewhat from their disappointment, and presumably packed away their punt, they began to consider their situation. They were now without a definite object. Should they return, with little to show for their troubles, or should they push boldly on? At this point Andersson wrote that Galton lost his enthusiasm for the task at hand, for to go forward meant committing themselves to months of travel in the drought season. The scarcity of water thus far had been bad and they could correctly assume that this would worsen as the season progressed.

As is the way of things, however, they found a reason to continue. Discussing their situation around the campfire, they remembered that over the last few months they had heard a great deal about the Ovambo nation far to the north of Damaraland. These were a people very different from the Damaras and Hottentots: they were an agricultural nation. Nangoro, the king of these people, ruled over a vast and powerful nation. After a short reconnoitre of the immediate country ahead, they decided that they would go to Ovamboland and meet this king. The guide they had recently hired told them that he would take them part of the way there. Thus, after a few days at Omanbonde they set forth again, battling their way through the thorns, ever in search of the next watering place for the cattle.

On 17 April they arrived at a spring called Okambuti. This, located near present-day Grootfontein, was, according to their guides, the northernmost extent of Damaraland. The chief, Chapupa, of the Damara village that they found at the spring flatly refused to give them the guide they needed for the last part of the journey into Ovamboland. Undeterred, Galton then proceeded to another, nearby, spring that was frequented by numerous elephants. The wagons were in a bad state of disrepair and many things needed fixing. They decided to wait there, do some hunting, and all the while look for someone prepared to guide them into Ovamboland.

On their way to the spring, however, they had had their first real setback when they broke the axletree of one of their wagons. Galton was furious with himself.

"I ought to have premised that the character of the country had entirely changed; instead of small bushes some magnificent timber trees began to appear . . . offering a very considerable impediment to wagon travelling . . . there was a stump in the way; it looked a rotten affair, such as we had constantly crushed over, but it really was a hard sound piece of wood. The off fore wheel of the large wagon came against it, and crash went the axletree . . ."

Andersson, surveying the damage, knew that the repairs would take several weeks and "as we had a journey of several months' duration before us, it was necessary to make the work as permanent as possible. . . . None of us had much experience in carpentry; but Hans was, by far, the most practical hand, and he boldly undertook the task."

Galton and Andersson now decided that they would continue on the ride-oxen and leave the work of making a new axletree to Hans. Moreover, these plans were furthered unexpectedly by the arrival of a man who offered to take them to Ovamboland. So on the 26th, Galton, Andersson and two of their servants set off. The guide soon deserted them, however, and they wandered around

Andersson was the first to arrive at the dry bed of the Omanbonde River. The vast lake that they had expected to find was nowhere to be seen. PA

the hilly country for some days, suffering considerably from thirst and not a little disgusted at their predicament. Just as they were considering retracing their steps to the wagons, they came across some Bushmen, one of whom they pressganged into service as a guide, and again they turned northward.

The next day, 30 April, they were overtaken by a group of men who looked very different from any that they had seen so far in their travels. They were in fact Ovambos, who had been aware of their presence for several days. Galton and Andersson were instructed to return to the wagons and wait for permission to proceed to Ovamboland. On 22 May this permission was received and they set forth yet again, leaving the wagons behind, with the Ovambos as their guides. Over the next few days they were surprised to find their caravan had swelled in size to over one hundred and seventy souls, many of them Damara women who were travelling to Ovamboland to barter goods there for beads, tobacco and corn. Leaving the hills of Damaraland behind them, they entered a vast flat country.

Five days after leaving the wagons they arrived at Omutjamatunda, the first of the Ovambo cattle posts. Here the surrounding country was swarming with cattle and

there appeared to be thousands of people. The Englishman and the Swede were the first white people that any of them had seen and so poor Galton and Andersson became objects of great curiosity. Meanwhile, the Ovambo guides were welcomed home in fine fashion. For two days their caravan was detained here, and Galton and Andersson amused themselves by shooting the wildfowl that abounded at the splendid spring nearby.

"It was a refreshing sight", wrote Andersson, "to stand on the borders of the fountain, which was luxuriously over-grown with towering reeds, and sweep with the eye the extensive plain encircling the base of the hill; frequented as it was, not only by vast herds of domesticated cattle, but with the lively springbok and troops of striped zebras."

The land he was surveying was what, sixty years hence, would become the Etosha Reserve. Thus it was that the first westerners saw this place. A short distance away from the spring was the vast salt-pan that gave its name to that future refuge. This they sighted on the first day's travel northward from the Omutjamatunda spring, and they wrote but a few lines of this event.

Andersson and Galton went on to meet the king of the Ovambos and, on 13 June, were ordered by the king to leave. The long road back to the coast lay before them and

Herds of zebra & domesticated cattle mix near Omutjamatunda

P.A.

Paul Augustinus

this journey would take them a further six months.

On 31 December Andersson waved farewell to Galton at Walvis Bay.

"Galton appeared delighted with the prospect of soon returning to civilized life. Though he had proved himself . . . it was evident that he had enough of it."

It had taken Galton and company twelve months and much hardship to travel from Walvis Bay to Etosha. In our Hilux we had done the same journey in less than eight hours – such are the realities of twentieth-century travel. Another reality is that Etosha National Park is now an island surrounded by the farms and beasts of man with a game fence enclosing the whole park. Its gene pool has therefore become isolated, always a dangerous situation. As previously mentioned, this park's predecessor was the larger game reserve proclaimed by the Germans in 1907. The subsequent whittling away of that vast entity by the German and South African regimes has left it with its present status – an island incapable of communicating with other islands, because the original movements of the herds of game have been severed.

The size of the park is often proudly touted in the brochures as being still among the largest in Africa. Unfortunately, this is misleading as the vast salt-pan of Etosha is useless to wildlife: it is more hostile than the driest parts of the Namib Desert. In fact, virtually all the wildlife is concentrated in the area south of the southern shoreline. Thus, not only is Etosha an island, it is a small island and, as such, it has to be managed by man like a farm. As in any farm, when the stock becomes too numerous for the pastures, the excess is removed either by slaughter or sale. Here elephants are culled according to the specifications of scientists who have determined exactly how many elephants the 'farm' can carry.

When the fence was erected in 1973, the wildebeest were the most affected: they were forever denied the use of their ancient routes. Also, road-building in the park created small gravel pits where anthrax thrived. Both zebra and wildebeest are particularly susceptible to anthrax and many died of the disease. In the early 80s, with carcasses lying everywhere, lions, which are not affected by anthrax, flourished. Moreover, pumped waterholes were established in many places and at each a lion pride developed, thereby increasing the stress on zebra and wildebeest as they now

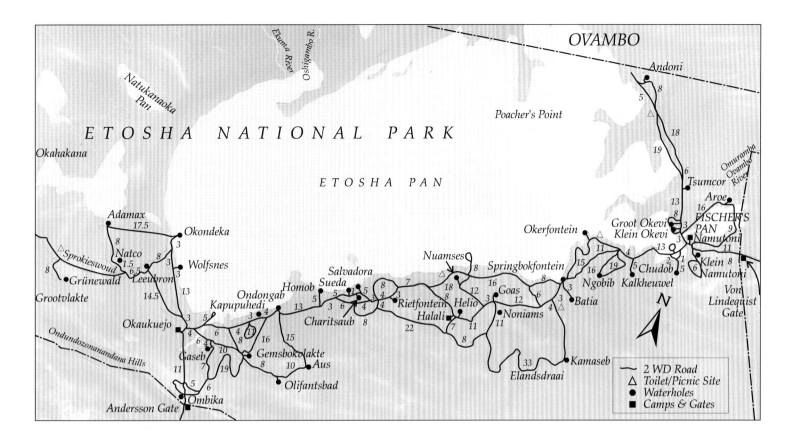

had to run the gauntlet of lions before drinking. It is thought that in this period cub mortality dropped off markedly, which led to the ratio of predator to prey becoming unnaturally high. The scientists discovered that lions were increasing and prey animal numbers dropping. They also noticed a dramatic decline in other predators. Cheetah declined from an estimated 1000 in 1923 to fifty in 1986, wild dogs from more than 2000 to less than twenty. Were the lions to blame, the scientists asked themselves? "Yes", was the conclusion and culling the lion was then considered as a possible remedy. This option was not in fact followed as the scientists and bureaucrats decided that it was a paradox to kill animals in areas set aside to preserve them; there would also be genetic loss; it is unaesthetic in protected areas, and so on.

In an article about the controversy it was stated: ". . . wilderness areas untouched by man, should be maintained in their natural state with management kept to a minimum." The inherent contradiction of this statement is laughable. How can it be managed if it is to remain a "wilderness area untouched by man"? This is of course a perfect example of the scientist's definition of "wilderness".

After putting up the fences, inadvertently causing an anthrax epidemic, drilling boreholes everywhere, and having totally disturbed the ecology of the area, they still consider it a wilderness! Worse, they blame the imbalances on the poor lions in their 'wilderness'. Give scientists the opportunity and they will dart, radio-collar and paint numbers on the flanks of everything in sight. And then they will proudly describe what they have done as "managing the wilderness". A serious reality check is needed here. Etosha is a farm, albeit a large one, with the scientists and the bureaucrats as the farmers. There is no wilderness here. And the lions? Researchers have even considered the possibility of putting them on the pill.

For all that, Etosha is without doubt a great place to observe animals in action doing things that it would be impossible to see elsewhere. In ten years of camping in some of Botswana's finest game country, I witnessed only nineteen lion chases, six of which ended successfully. In just one month at Okaukuejo we saw twenty-three chases and three kills, all within a hundred metres of our comfortable lodgings.

There is an element of the Roman *circus maximus* about

Opposite
Three Doublebanded Sandgrouse search for seeds in the scrub and sand of the Etosha bush. In the dim light of late evening, or the cool grey of early dawn, these birds would flock to waterholes, where, to the accompaniment of their characteristic warbling calls, they cascaded from the skies to the sound of thousands of whirring wings.

the waterhole at Okaukuejo. A small pumped pan is set twenty metres from the viewing area inside the camp. All that separates the guests from the wildlife is a low wall and some unobtrusive angled fencing. The wall would need but a small hop for the lions should they wish to enter the camp, which they do on occasion. The wall with its viewing area curves around one side of the pan and is flanked by a green lawn and some shade trees with benches scattered about. It is quite possible for the visitor to lie in the shade of one of these trees, book in one hand and iced drink in the other, looking up only when a lion makes a kill or a herd of elephants comes down to drink. The waterhole is also floodlit at night, and because of this facility many incredible things can be seen. Wildlife appears out of the night and vanishes again, seemingly oblivious to the watching crowd. Life and death dramas are played out as you sit comfortably a few metres away, a mug of coffee in hand. You can recline there, as arrogant as a Roman emperor, while the gladiators of the African bush battle for their lives around the edge of the pool. This is literally the case – as we were to find out on our first night.

The sun had set and the sandgrouse had come and gone from the water's edge. For an hour nothing moved in the pool of light cast by the floodlights. Rather enjoying our new-found decadence, we had eaten an elegant supper on our veranda. Nearby, the benches drawn up to the wall were slowly filling with spectators. Then, as we were clearing the plates, the crowd had suddenly fallen silent. A large animal walked out from the darkness on the opposite side of the pool. Raising her binoculars, Clarissa leaned forward for a better view. "My goodness," she hissed through the window to me, "that's a black rhino!" Dinner things forgotten, we rushed over to join the growing crowd at the wall.

The rhino was not alone: out of the dark came a half-grown calf. Several minutes went by while they stood there with their ears swivelling like radar antennas. Finally, after what seemed like an eternity, they moved down to the water to drink. Meanwhile, a ripple ran through the crowd as, from another direction, a third rhino made its entrance: a bull! Slightly bigger and more heavily built, it also sported a magnificent pair of horns. Puffing like steam engines and snorting explosively, the cow and the bull closed ranks and crossed horns. After a while, the half-grown calf nervously approached and joined in. Through the binoculars I could clearly see their pig-like eyes almost rolling with the excitement of the encounter. Then, from the dark, a rattling of stones heralded the arrival of a fourth rhino, a female with short stubby horns. Instantly the other rhinos swung round, strutting stiffly and snorting at the interloper. For a while the arena was occupied only by the motionless statues of four rhinos. Eventually, the latest arrival went down to drink. This done, it began to wander slowly about in the area between the pool and the wall. Suddenly, two Blacksmith Plovers fluttered up from the grass and let fly the shrillest whistling alarm call I have ever heard issue from a bird. The rhino froze and, mobbed by the plovers, proceeded to back slowly away. The plovers' indignant cries subsided and the rhino walked casually right up to the wall and began to browse from a bush only a metre away from our bench.

Rosemary, the closest to the rhino, turned around slowly and her raised eyebrows said it all. The crowd became quite excited then, and the former hush was broken by enthusiastic tourists as they pressed closer. As we sat there, the rhino browsed happily at the bush, giving us splendid views of its prehensile lips as they plucked delicately at the shrubbery, and an even more splendid view of the startling pink of its mouth, unconcerned by the chatter of the swelling crowd of tourists or their flashing

cameras. After a while, it moved further along the wall to other bushes while the crowd, now chattering loudly, followed it backwards and forwards for half an hour. Eventually, it disappeared into the darkness, and was later followed by the cow and the calf.

Soon the bull had the water's edge to itself, but not for long. As it turned and stared aggressively into the dark, more clattering of stones could be heard from the murk beyond. This time not rhinos but elephants emerged from the bushes. When they found the rhino in their path, all but one of them were careful to choose a wide detour. One, a young bull, did not and a confrontation took place. The elephant stepped forward, flapped its ears and flung out its trunk. Instantly, the rhino charged and the elephant retreated ignominiously, breaking wind as it went.

While all this gladiatorial activity had been taking place, a jackal had made its unseen entrance. It seemed to have appeared out of thin air. At an easy loping run it patrolled the water's edge, darting in and out of the elephants as they trumpeted in irritation. The rhino stood like a statue, head high and stiff-legged, until the jackal ran too close. Then there was an explosion of movement and the jackal accelerated away, yapping like a whipped dog. When this jackal approached the clump of grass where the plovers lay silently, it, too, was set on by the screaming birds. Ducking and cringing, it ran off.

After about an hour the elephants and rhino wandered away and the area round the pool fell silent. Slowly the spectators grew bored and by ten o'clock only a small hard-core group was left. When we finally went to bed that night I was convinced that we had arrived on a good day – that we had just been lucky. The following days, however, were to prove this assumption wrong and every night we would declare, "It can't get any better than this – can it?" Yet it did. The simple truth is that Okaukuejo is unique in Africa. There is no better place where it is possible to watch big game so close, from ground level, and in such decadent comfort than here in this camp. Moreover, it is the only place in Africa where black rhino can be observed so easily or so intimately.

If the nights were enlivened by the antics of rhino and elephant, then the days belonged to the lions. The lion chase we had seen on the first day did not prove to be unusual either. Every day a lioness would come down early to drink and then retreat to a bush at the edge of the pan.

There she would sink into the shadows and disappear from sight, her head pressed to the ground. As the sun rose higher in the sky and the heat of the day began to set in, springbok, gemsbok and kudu would begin to appear in the distance, slowly approaching the pan. They were nervous, but driven on by their rising thirst. Their long day was just beginning.

Our own working day had started as well. Clarissa occupied one side of the lounge, her thesis papers spread out on the coffee-table. I set up my 'studio' at the other side of the room and started to work on one of the three paintings that I would complete at Okaukuejo. Just a glance away through the window, however, was the pan and I was constantly monitoring the unfolding dramas taking place there. Slowly, the tension would build as the herds crowded closer and closer. Nevertheless, we would attempt to work, and Clarissa from her seat would ask me at regular intervals, "What's happening? How close are they?"

Sometimes it would take the more nervous creatures an hour to cover that last 50 metres to the final ring of bushes before the water's edge. Peering hard and long at every scrap of cover, the skittish animals would gather, poised, just beyond the last bushes between them and the water. Finally, a few brave individuals would file between the bushes, coiled like springs and ready to flee at the snap of a twig. Infected with the rising tension, Rosemary would burst into the bungalow. "What are you doing? The lions are about to make a kill!" Then we would drop everything and rush down to the wall.

Once the first few brave individuals had tiptoed nervously down to the water and started drinking, others quickly followed suit, many filing past the very bush where the lioness was secreted. The tension would now be at breaking point. The expectation that the lioness would burst forth was almost unbearable, and this could go on for half an hour or more. Finally, when the whole waterhole was a milling mass of watering animals, the climax would come. The lioness would rise, throw herself through the branches of the bush, and charge. Every animal at the water's edge would bolt, splashing and bouncing in all directions. The lioness would fixate on one individual, then sprint hard after her chosen prey. More often than not the attempt would end unsuccessfully, with the predator standing panting in the burning sun as the dust

settled before turning and walking wearily back to the cover of the same bush. Then the whole process would begin again. On one day this happened five times. In four weeks we saw over thirty chases and only three of these were successful.

The Blacksmith Plovers that had mobbed the rhino on our first night were also active in this way during the day. The following morning I had taken our binoculars and followed their movements in the grass a few feet from the water. There was always one plover sitting on a specific patch, and occasionally the other would come over to it and they would swop places. They were nesting! How wonderful it is that two tiny birds can nest so successfully within a metre of a major waterhole frequented daily by thousands of animals. They handled their task with amazing aplomb, calmly sitting on the nest as elephant walked by. If the elephant came to within half a metre of the nest, there would be but a brief flutter of the wings and a sharp call. Glancing down suspiciously, the elephant would always move off a short distance and the plover would settle back on the nest. Every approaching animal, whether rhino, jackal or kudu, was treated with impunity.

Blacksmith Plovers nesting at Okaukuejo within metres of the water's edge.

127

Opposite
The waterhole at Okondeka.
Here, at the contact spring that
issues forth from beneath the
calcrete, there is a constant
procession of wildebeest,
giraffe, gemsbok, and ostrich,
all of which are constantly on
the alert for the lions of the
resident pride. The seemingly
endless expanse of the Etosha
Pan provides a scenic backdrop
to the life and death dramas that
are played out daily.

One day the two plovers started chirping madly and fluttering about next to the pool. Calling plaintively, they darted back and forth. The reason soon became apparent when I brought my binoculars to bear on their antics: the chicks had hatched. Three tiny chicks were hesitantly tottering after them as they followed the calls of their parents. The parents led them to the very shoreline of the waterhole and it is here that they stayed over the coming days. Incredibly, they survived, dodging the feet of elephant and antelope alike. Sometimes a herd of springbok would rush down to the water, too fast for the parents to lead the chicks to the other side of the pan. The chicks would then be lost among the hundreds of hooves, only to appear again after the herd had departed, seemingly none the worse for wear. One by one, however, the chicks disappeared, perhaps victims of owls or snakes. I would wake up in the morning and, scanning the pan from my bed, would find one to be missing. A few days later the same would happen again. Sadly, by the time we were due to leave for Namutoni, all of the chicks had vanished!

Some days we went out for a drive, having become saturated with the events taking place at the waterhole. The country surrounding Okaukuejo is dominated by scrubby acacias and short, stunted mopane thickets. As you proceed northwards, however, the scenery becomes much more pleasing to the eye. The trees thin out and the plains begin. Also the white salt plain of the Etosha Pan comes into view and it soon becomes the dominant feature in an unbroken vista of yellow grass. There are waterholes here,

natural ones, which have served the needs of wildlife for thousands of years. At some places on the sharp distinct shoreline where the grassland meets the salt plain, there are calcrete outcroppings. Here a few springs occur whose water trickles forth onto the pan to form small pools. These springs are the gathering places of huge herds of wildebeest, zebra, ostrich and springbok. Smaller numbers of giraffe and elephant also use these waterholes, but more on this later. Beyond these gatherings of game lie the white expanses of the Etosha Pan. The views at these springs are unique, and although very similar scenery is to be found on the larger Makgadikgadi pans in the northern Kalahari, nowhere there has similar gatherings of wildlife.

Continuing northwards over the plains, you soon come to the shoreline of Etosha and here there is a spring called Okondeka. Dense acacia bushes have colonized the nearby sand ridge and these provide much-needed shade to a pride of lions which has made this place its home. These lions are very easily seen, and in the evening when they rouse themselves, they walk slowly down from the dunes to drink at the pools of the spring. Surrounding the water there is a startlingly green fringe of short, closely cropped grass. Beyond, on the white vastness of the pan, there are always numerous jackal and ostrich as well. Unfortunately, the only way to appreciate this place is from a car park set near the water. Here, along with other vehicles, you watch the scene through the windscreen like the patrons of a drive-in cinema. Irritatingly, some of those patrons kept their motors running for their airconditioning. Conversations would be clearly audible through the open windows of other cars and thus one became unwilling participants in a 'group' experience. Our neighbours, seeing the Durban number plates, would invariably lean out and yell across, "How's it, Durbs!" But sometimes we were lucky when we visited this place and there was no one else there. Only then was it possible mentally to block out the whitewashed pebbles of the car park from the mind and listen to the calls of the plains game as they came and went from this ancient place.

There are other waterholes near Okaukuejo and some of them are natural, but many are artificial monstrosities. My 'favourite' among the latter was a long concrete trough set on a bare calcrete plain. Nearby, a solar pumping station glinted in the sun. Here, zebras lined up like battery chickens to drink. We visited this trough only once in

A procession of cars & buses near Okondeka.   P.A.

Near the waterhole at
Okaukuejo camp. P.A.

ignorance of its pedigree, and, disgusted, we sped away, never to return. Nonetheless, this was our reality check, lest we forget that we were really guests on a farm.

One day at Okaukuejo was more special than the rest – so much so that, subsequently, we referred to it as 'The Day!' It had started much like any other day. Always early risers, Clarissa and I were often up and about before dawn.

Throwing back the sheet which I used to protect my studio area from dust, I was confronted by my wet canvas – a nearly finished painting of some elephants at the water-hole. My art materials were retrieved from a tin trunk and set on the table nearby, paint squeezed onto the palette, and clean brushes selected from the large jug near the sink. Clarissa likewise arranged her papers on the dining-table. In luxury lodgings such as ours, these chores were infinitely easier to do and, along with breakfast, they would be complete long before the sun rose. So, on 'The Day', we had been up a while and the eastern sky was brightening rapidly. Soon, the first glimmers of light were touching the tops of the trees. Usually, few animals ever came down at that time of day and little happened until an hour or so after dawn, so that the seats near the wall were empty.

There was a problem with the elephant's tusks in my painting and while contemplating this, I glanced idly out of the window at the pan. Much to my surprise and delight, a sinuous shape materialized from the bushes on the other side of the pan and slunk down to the water's edge – a leopard! So perfect was its camouflage that when it stopped moving, I lost sight of it among the rocks. Only when Clarissa had found our binoculars were we able to watch it as it drank. It stood up and stared intently into the bushes. Then, almost before we had a chance to appreciate what we had seen, it was gone.

Immediately on its departure, a lioness walked slowly out of the bushes on the opposite side of the pan. A low, mewing call carried softly across the water to our waiting ears and then, almost on cue, a pride of lions filed down to the water's edge. Their muzzles were bloodied and they all drank deeply. A few minutes later they were joined by a magnificently maned male, who waited until last to slake its thirst. The first of the sun's rays now touched the muddy fringes of the pan and in this glowing light, all but one of the lions walked slowly back into the bush, calling softly as they went.

The lioness that remained behind sat for a while in the weak sun before, disturbed by a shout from the camp, walking purposefully over to the usual bush. Slipping beneath it, it flattened its head to the ground and disappeared from sight. Clarissa and I returned to try and work and Rosemary, taking advantage of the cool of the morning, went off for a walk. Meanwhile, I puzzled over the shape of the tusks in my painting and then, in a flash of irritation, removed them completely from the canvas with turpentine and a rag.

For some time after this nothing happened. The morning advanced, and Clarissa and I worked away in our respective corners of the lounge. The cleaners came and went and the sun rose higher in the sky. Twice I repainted the tusks and twice more removed what I had done. It grew hot and the first kudu and springbok appeared among the distant bushes. Slowly, they meandered down the many paths leading to the pool and all the while Rosemary, who was keeping an eye on the proceedings, kept us informed with a running commentary from the veranda.

A group of female kudu approached and, without hesitation, walked right down to the edge of the water. At that point, having almost completed my third attempt at the tusks, the distraction was too much and, throwing down the palette and brushes, I followed Clarissa over to the wall. By now, the seats there had begun to fill up and some people were sunning themselves on the lawn behind. Suddenly, the lioness burst from beneath the bush and charged at the kudus, which scattered in all directions. One of them, hotly pursued by the lioness, galloped around the edge of the water and, passing close to where we sat, escaped. The lioness, visibly frustrated, walked back to the bush while we went back to the rondavel and tried to settle down to work. We had hardly finished 'settling', however, when a gemsbok blundered down to the water and drank, oblivious to the danger it was in. Rosemary rushed in and dragged us out again. A few scant minutes later the lioness repeated its act, but the gemsbok also escaped, and stood snorting explosively from a distance, while the lioness stoically returned to its bush. After the third chase, I packed away my art materials and covered my canvas. Clarissa, likewise, loaded all her papers into the tin trunk and admitted defeat for the time being. We were captive onlookers, dangling on a string that was being yanked too often by the lioness for us even to pretend that work was possible.

The little group of onlookers had now swelled to a fair-

sized audience and there was constant chattering along the full length of the wall. We were a very cosmopolitan crowd that day, with French, Italian and German being the main languages spoken. Most were tourists from Europe and many were very blasé about what they were seeing. It was almost as if they had expected nothing less. After one of the chases, the fourth that morning, they had burst into applause as the springbok escaped. The polite clapping lingered until the panting lioness had flopped down, exhausted, under its bush.

A sideshow then arrived in the form of a black rhino. This caused another ripple to go through the crowd, followed by an expectant hush. Fifty pairs of eyes swivelled from the lioness to the rhino and then back to the lioness. The rhino appeared suspicious and proceeded to investigate every bush thoroughly. Eventually, it came to the bush where the lioness was hidden. Instantly, there was

a deafening snort and the rhino charged. Leisurely springing out of the way, the lioness then strolled in a slow circle around the rhino to another bush where it settled down again. Again, the rhino followed and the process was repeated. Soon, however, the rhino tired of this game, watered and then went over to a nearby tree. Here, to the accompaniment of a wave of titters from the crowd, it proceeded to rub its bottom against the trunk. Then it abruptly lay down. The lioness meanwhile went back to its favourite place and disappeared yet again. For a while peace reigned, and the kudu and springbok pressed closer and closer.

By midday the heat was intense, and the water's edge was thronging with animals of all kinds. Only a few metres away the lioness lay quietly in wait as we all held our breaths expectantly. But still nothing happened, the minutes turned into an hour, and then one hour into two.

This lioness would not relinquish its kill in the face of a very inquisitive rhino.

131

In the midday heat of
Okaukuejo, a lioness misses
its prey in dramatic fashion.

Some elephants joined the throng by the waterside. On leaving, they passed the bush where the rhino lay. Either intimidated or offended, it scrambled to its feet and rushed at the bemused elephants. For a while, pandemonium reigned. There were snorts and trumpeting, with dust flying as startled springbok darted aside. Finally, the rhino and elephants disappeared into the bushes beyond, each going its own way. So, too, did the spectators and we also retreated to the cool comfort of our airconditioned lounge.

With feet up, we sipped at tall glasses of iced drinks, Clarissa muttering something about it being "hard work having fun here!" Indeed, it was turning out to be a long day for us, the weary spectators at Okaukuejo! However, we returned to our respective work places and I uncovered the canvas yet again. The problem with the tusks had me utterly confounded. No matter what I did, each attempt seemed to produce a result that was, somehow, wrong. Neither Clarissa nor Rosemary was willing to offer advice on this, as they had long since learnt that it was not worth the trouble to become involved in such decisions – especially when they turned out to be bad decisions. So I kept on trying, and as time went on the wet oil paint on the satisfactory parts of the painting next to the tusks began to become scuffed and marred with all the alterations. What had been such a promising painting was now turning into a disaster in its final stage.

Early on that afternoon the lioness made its move: almost before Rosemary had a chance to draw our attention to the drama about to unfold outside, it had sprinted out of the bush at a group of springbok which had waded into the pool to drink. Almost before I could blink an eyelid, it was all over, and the lioness was dragging a springbok back to the shade of a small bush. The chase was successful, but the exhausted lioness panted in the shade for twenty minutes before she started to tear at the carcass. The drama was not yet over, however, for she had only half-eaten the carcass when the rhino returned. With its ears rotating wildly, it advanced on the patch of shade where the lioness lay, but this time the lioness was in no mood for nonsense. With a low growl, the lioness rose slowly to its feet – and the rhino backed away to stand as still as a bronze statue at a respectful distance and watch. The lioness continued with its meal. After a while, I returned to the painting which by now was beginning to really irritate me. However, now that the

palpable tension that had hung over the pan all day was over, it seemed easier to concentrate, and with a glimmer of an idea brewing in my head, I picked up the palette and brushes to begin anew.

By four o'clock the shadows were starting to lengthen and the heat to fade. This is the best time of the day in the bush. The colours of the evening light have the power to transform the drabbest scene into a place of beauty. The long shadows add drama and, as the wind drops, the inhabitants of the bush prepare themselves for the long night of activity. Along the length of the wall people came and went after seeing the lion on the kill. New arrivals would rush down, asking the others already there, "Where's the lion? Did you see it make the kill? . . . Is that a black rhino?" and so on.

Inside the bungalow, I had finished at last and the wet, glistening painting was removed from the table where I worked and stood against the wall for a better view. Clarissa and Rosemary examined the finished results and there was a long silence before judgement was passed. Thankfully, they approved of the final result, and the painting was quickly banished to the vehicle where it would be able to dry and be out of my sight for a few days. At last the working day was over, progress had been made, and it was time for a sundowner.

As the sun dropped lower, the sandgrouse started to arrive in flocks, dropping down onto the shore in ever-increasing numbers, while the rhino still stood transfixed as the lioness finished off the springbok. Into this serene scene ran a large maned lion. There was no warning, just a bellowing grunt, as the huge male rushed at the lioness. The rhino backed off and a brief scuffle ensued between the lions. Then, out of the dust ran the male, the remains of the springbok in its mouth. Never has anything looked less regal than that huge lion lumbering off with its prize. One of the spectators rather more caught up in the proceedings than the rest, shouted, "Shame, shame" after the departing lion.

That evening, after the sun had set, the rhinos and elephants put on their usual show, and the lion pride that had watered that morning, returned to hover in the shadows just beyond the reach of the lights. In complete contrast to their daytime nonchalance, they were now skittish and nervous. They approached the pan from the side, close to the low retaining wall, and were on one

The end of a long day. P.A.

134

occasion only metres away from it. Here, in the stark light of the floodlights, they studied the closest spectators with steely eyes and uttered occasional snarls of anger. Two young immature lions, with scruffs for manes, became almost beside themselves with curiosity and lay facing the crowd, heads bobbing up and down as they peered intently at the onlookers.

Some of these, gaining strength from the numbers surrounding them, uttered silly comments – only to step backwards and titter nervously when one of the lions grunted menacingly. Behind the crowd, other groups, uninterested in these goings on, were barbecuing meat and talking loudly, while everywhere small children scurried about, playing hide and seek or shouting out to one another. At the height of the barbecuing activity, smoke, heavily laden with the odours of cooking meat, lay over the camp and the waterhole like a white mist. Meanwhile, at the water's edge, carnivores watched and curiously sniffed the air. Returning to our bungalow at the end of that landmark day, there was one last cameo to be seen and absorbed. As we passed the open door of our neighbours' bungalow, the gathered members of a family were eating their supper. However, at their feet was a jackal, lured inside by offerings of tit-bits from the children, and it scuttled about in the doorway begging for more. Beyond the ray of light from that open door, other, less brave jackals hung about in frenzied frustration.

After four weeks of 'carnival' at Okaukuejo we were ready to move on to Namutoni. We were sad in some ways, for it was an end to the surprises that the waterhole had provided on a daily basis. But too much of a good thing can also eventually numb the mind to the reality that these were living, feeling animals we were watching. So it was also a relief to be gone from the circus atmosphere of tourists cheering as wildlife battled for survival in the arena. The last items to be loaded were the paintings I had completed at Okaukuejo. These were carefully packed in their special place on the roof-rack. Somehow that was the symbolic end to our stay at this amazing place and we found ourselves suddenly very eager to leave.

On the long road to Namutoni the traveller must first pass through the mopane thickets and grasslands that lie close to the southern shore of Etosha. The roads hereabouts are made of white calcrete. Every car leaves a choking white cloud in its wake, and the trees and bushes

Secretarybirds near Salvadora spring.

flanking some of the busier routes are covered in a frosting of calcrete dust. Much of the scenery en route to Namutoni can be monotonous and on the long dreary stretches of road linking the various springs, there is little wildlife to add excitement to the journey. When the open grasslands next to the Etosha Pan are in sight, the journey becomes more bearable, but invariably the road returns to the seemingly lifeless mopane thickets.

It is then that the traveller comes to realize that Etosha is very much a 'waterhole' experience. This is where all the action is to be found, where all the wildlife congregates. Interestingly, there are three distinct types of natural waterholes in Etosha. The most scenically endowed are the 'contact' springs, such as the one at Okondeka. This type of spring arises when erosion lays bare the horizon between the overlying calcrete formations and the underlying clay. The clay is impervious to water and so it collects at that horizon. When enough has collected, it begins to flow along tiny underground streams. Where the calcrete horizon has been removed by erosion at the shoreline fringe, these underground streams emerge as springs. All the springs along the very edge of the shoreline are of the 'contact' variety.

The second type of natural waterhole is the 'Artesian'

Ground squirrels PA.

spring. Here water flows out under Artesian pressure and not under gravitational flow such as occurs at the 'contact' springs. Instead, water percolating down through porous rocks forms large underground reservoirs when it encounters an impermeable horizon. If that horizon is not perfectly level, then the water migrates slowly towards the lowest point. A pressure builds up there, and if there is a weakness in the rocks above this point, water will force its way to the surface as a spring. An interesting characteristic of this type of spring is that there is often a clump of reeds at its centre. Also interesting is the fact that these springs invariably arise on limestone hillocks, which are several metres higher than the surrounding country. Good examples of Artesian waterholes are Namutoni, Aus, and Chudob.

The third kind of spring is the 'water-level' spring, which is similar to the 'contact' spring. 'Water-level' springs also occur at the boundaries between permeable and impermeable layers. This water will flow from various points on that horizon where it intersects the slope of a hill or depression. In Etosha the water table is only a few metres below the surface and so any depressions in the countryside that dip lower than the water table are candidates for this type of spring – but this type of spring is very susceptible to drought. Examples of 'water-level' springs can be found at Ngobib, Groot Okevi and Klein Okevi.

When there is little to watch for on the long roads that connect these oasis, I tend to fall back on that other great pastime of bored travellers – people watching. Why is it that in game reserves and on dusty roads such as these, travellers seem to clump together in herds for protection? The result is the dreaded 'tourist convoy'. Here, two or three cars go game viewing together and instead of spreading out, they sit directly behind the leading car and eat each other's dust. Amazingly, they never seem to mind, and long distances are travelled in this way. Invariably, these are the same inconsiderates who stopped at waterholes and keep their motors running. I am also certain that these are the same types who always camp as close as they can to your own tent – in an empty campsite!

Keeping close to the pan whenever a side road permitted, we returned to the 'real' Etosha about two-thirds of the way to Halali. The mopane thickets recede and the main road is left to the convoy addicts and their

calcrete clouds. A side road took us through the vast yellow grass plains fringing the white, dazzling surface of the pan, and here we came to a waterhole that was positively alive with game and blessed with a viewing-point that was higher than the surrounding country. Looking at the map, we found out that we were at Salvadora. Miraculously, we also had the place to ourselves.

Below us and only a few metres away from our craning necks was the spring. Large pools of water had formed in among the tumbled blocks of calcrete and from these pools a small rivulet of water ran to ground a few metres from the pan. On the grassy plain around us, whinnying zebra herds trotted back and forth as they prepared to approach the water. Springbok, wildebeest and kudu nervously paced the muddied strip just beyond the salty-smelling water. Several ground squirrels ran over from a nearby burrow and sat in the shade of our vehicle. They all looked up at us expectantly and I had the feeling they were waiting to be fed. We sat there for a while, oblivious to all but the scene before us. Then, from the back of the vehicle, Rosemary started rapping urgently on the window between us. Silently mouthing "Rhino," she jabbed her finger to the rear. Looking out and backwards through my own window revealed the startling sight of a large, suspicious rhino only a couple of metres away from our rear bumper! It was a fantastic sight – to be so close to a black rhino during the day and without a wall in the way. Flies buzzed around its ears and its tail swished as it examined us with its head high. After giving a deafening snort, as if to let us know it was there, it then proceeded to walk carefully down the slope to the water. This rhino was an old warrior, for its ears were torn and its hide scarred. It must have wallowed in a pool earlier on and was encrusted with white muddy patches. It was very particular as to where it would drink and, after trying the various pools, it chose one in the rocks just below our vehicle. A Kori Bustard was quietly drinking on the opposite bank and for a while these two shared the same pool. Such was the peace of the scene that it was hard to remind ourselves that these are both gravely threatened species.

'Threatened' and 'endangered' are overused words these days and our sensitivities are being slowly numbed by continuing doses of bad news. A tranquil scene such as this made it easy to dismiss the alarmists' warnings, but the threat is real. The bustard family of birds, for example, has a distribution that covers Asia, the Middle East, Europe and Africa, and there are 22 species altogether. But everywhere it is threatened, and only in southern Africa are there strongholds of some of the species. The Houbara Bustard has the widest distribution of all, extending from North Africa to Mongolia. Yet, in recent years it has almost been wiped out by the activities of Arab falconers. For two thousand years falconry has been a traditional sport in Arabia, but the oil-fuelled enrichment of this area has led to a vast upswing in the activities of sport falconers. Whereas previously these falconers consisted of small groups of men with one or two falcons, now parties are often made up of several wealthy sportsmen, 400 falcons and hundreds of camp followers. Bags of a hundred bustards in a day were normal. The Houbara quickly disappeared from the Middle East, and then the sportsmen turned their attention to North Africa and Pakistan. The Houbara has now been virtually eradicated from these areas as well.

This wanton greed touched me personally in my years in Botswana. In the early 1980s I noticed a drastic decline in the Black Korhaan populations of a favourite area of mine in the Makgadikgadi. Later, I found out that they were being trapped and shipped to the Middle East, where they were used as live bait in the training of falcons. Frustrated with the poor sport among the decimated Houbara populations, these same sportsmen are now looking covetously at the bustards of East Africa, and when they are finished with those, they will cast their eyes at southern Africa. For the present the Kori Bustard seems to be safe in its southern African strongholds, but the warning signs are there.

If the Kori Bustard is considered 'vulnerable' then the state of Africa's black rhinos must almost be a lost cause. The figures are nearly beyond belief. Twenty years ago in Kenya there were twenty thousand rhinos roaming in the bush. Of these only four hundred remain, most of them on private land. In the Central African Republic, there were 3000 rhinos in 1980 and now the species is extinct there. Three years ago the Zambezi Valley was refuge to 1200 hundred rhinos, but now there are fewer than 400 left. It is extinct both in Angola and Uganda. In the Cameroons there may be twenty, while in the Sudan it is gone forever. This tale of woe seems never-ending. How is it that we are so clever that we can, at the cost of billions of dollars, put a man on the moon and yet be incapable of halting the staggering decline of this animal? How is it that we are able to build such a miraculous piece of machinery as a Jumbo Jet in which, far above the planet's surface, passengers, entertained by films and music, are whisked to another continent? And yet, we are unable to halt the destruction of the last numbers of a species.

In Namibia the story of the black rhino is just as sad, but Etosha is probably now the best place in Africa to see them. When all the various deproclamations of the original Etosha had taken place, the wildlife of the Kaokoveld was decimated by both the local people and some immoral elements in the South African army. During this troubled period, 43 rhinos were translocated from the upper Ugab River and central Damaraland to the Etosha National Park. These and the few rhinos native to Etosha flourished and the situation is that there are now over 300 in the park. When the translocation were complete, they had left behind over 150 rhinos in Kaokoland and a hundred in Damaraland. The slaughter in the Kaokoveld continued unabated, and in 1982 there were only ten left in Kaokoland and 40 in Damaraland. Uncharacteristically, this story has had a happy ending and the Kaokoveld population has been on the increase since Garth Owen-Smith's innovative system of auxiliary game guards was established in the 1980s.

In 1989, however, as an added protection against an upsurge of poaching, dehorning was carried out in some of the more vulnerable populations. This drastic measure

Kori Bustard at a contact spring on Etosha Pan.   P. A

involved darting the rhino and sawing off its horns as close to the base as possible. The theory was that a poacher would not risk his life or his freedom for so little return. This is, however, a very controversial exercise. Two American researchers claim that in fact the horn regrows at the rate of nine centimetres annually, but this is the *total* figure for both horns, and their studies were conducted on adolescent animals whose regeneration is known to be more vigorous. They also maintain that all the calves of these dehorned rhinos have been killed by predators – the assumption being that the weaponless mothers were unable to defend their young. The local NGOs involved at ground level in monitoring all the rhinos in Damaraland have, however, rejected this and say they have documentary evidence that the calves are thriving. Meanwhile, the most telling fact is that since 1991 only one rhino has been poached.

We lunched that day at Halali. This camp is about halfway to Namutoni and is probably the least interesting of the three camps in the park. Nevertheless, we were glad of the shady car park while we waited for the heat of the day to subside. This part of the day is the bane of travel in Africa. Wildlife is most active in the early mornings and late evenings, which leaves a long period between nine in the morning and four in the afternoon when there is literally nothing to be seen. Indeed, only "mad dogs and Englishmen" venture out in those midday hours. So one sits and waits, in essentially the suburban surroundings of a

camp, swatting flies with a magazine and looking endlessly at the clock for salvation. We had indeed been spoilt by Okaukuejo! Finally, my watch showed four o'clock and we set off again towards the distant Namutoni.

Late afternoon is the best time of day in Africa. The sun drops low in the sky and the scenery is bathed in the evening light. Even the mopane thickets start to look attractive. At a small fountain called Springbokfontein, Clarissa glimpsed something in the bush and asked me to pull over.

"Look, over there at that clump of grass – is that a cheetah?"

As we coasted to a halt, a cheetah stood up and moved off very deliberately across the plain. In the next few minutes we sighted another cheetah creeping through the distant field of grass. They were hunting – and we were being treated to a perfect view of the stalk! Beyond them, several springbok grazed out in the open scrub of a flat plain. When the larger cheetah had wiggled close enough, it burst from cover, accelerating spectacularly as it went. Even before we realized what was happening, it was over. Panting hard, the unsuccessful cheetahs retired to a nearby bush. In the distance alarmed herds of zebra whinnied and snorted. Beyond them, mirages danced over the white horizon of Etosha Pan.

Long before you get to Namutoni, you can see the fort. In that flat terrain its white towers stand out conspicuously. Even from a distance it looks like a fort and of course its locality has a history, which goes back to a time long before any German set foot on the shores of the Namib coast. There is a fountain here and the Ovambos had kept cattle on the grassy plains surrounding it for more than 300 years before Andersson and Galton passed by in the 1850s. After that, a few traders and hunters followed in their footsteps, but it was not until thirty years later that a hardy band of trekkers settled here for a while. They were here for a few months and the grave of one of their number can be seen at Rietfontein Pan, half-way between Okaukuejo and Namutoni. These were the 'Thirstland Trekkers'. Their journey to Etosha and their travels beyond are a classic story of adventure and hardship.

The Thirstland or Dorsland Trekkers were refugees from the spreading rule of the British in the Transvaal. They set forth from there in two parties, the first leaving in 1875. This was led by Gert Alberts, and in a year they had travelled up the Boteti River and beyond Ghanzi. Here the trekkers settled at a small spring called Rietfontein (not to be confused with the Rietfontein in Etosha), just inside the present-day boundary of Namibia.

The first party had dwindled to about fifteen families by the time the second group of trekkers set off in 1877. This was a very much larger party and started with 128 wagons.

Travelling up the Boteti, they lost huge numbers of oxen to drought and suffered terribly in the process. Messengers were sent to Alberts at Rietfontein, asking for help and oxen. Alberts responded by sending them 180 oxen to make up their losses and then met them at a drift near Chief Sebitoane's capital at Lake Ngami. By this time, 37 of the trekkers had died and 86 wagons been abandoned along the route. The larger party then began to break up, and Alberts returned to Rietfontein with a few of the families, while the remainder started up the western side of the Okavango swamps under the leadership of Greyling and Van Rensburg. Later on Alberts and his followers joined them and the united party set off towards the Okavango River. Along the way Greyling and four families disappeared on a hunting expedition and were never heard of again.

By 1879 they had trekked up through what is now known as Bushmanland and then followed the Okavango River to the Omuramba Namungundu. Here they met Axel Eriksson, a trader, and together they trekked south-west across the fossil dunefields of the Kalahari sandveld to reach Etosha and Namutoni. Their stay here at Rietfontein spring was short, however, and, during the few months that they were on the southern shore of Etosha, they realized that the water supplies were insufficient for them to settle permanently. During this time Alberts and seven others made a reconnaissance of the Kaokoveld all the way to the Atlantic as described in the last chapter. By May they were back in the Namutoni area and, with the whole party, moved south along the pan and into the Kaokoveld. Eventually, they settled for a year or so at Sesfontein.

During that year Alberts explored the Kunene, while the majority of his party stayed at Sesfontein, hunting in the surrounding valleys, tending gardens next to the springs, and keeping cattle on the abundant pastures of the vale. Meanwhile, news of their trials and tribulations had slowly filtered back to the Cape and a relief operation was set in motion. A schooner was chartered and R. Haybittle, a trader based in Walvis, was hired to take supplies to them. When the *Swallow* berthed in Walvis in late 1879, Haybittle went to Sesfontein to inform the trekkers that he had supplies for them and also to let them know that there was free passage back to the Cape for any who wished to return. He found them thriving, however, and counted 352 settlers, 70 wagons and 600 cattle. No one

At Salvadora, another 'contact' type of spring on the southern shore of Etosha Pan, impressive gatherings of plains game, as well as rarer animals such as the black rhino, come to drink from the pools that issue forth from beneath the tumbled boulders of a thick calcrete outcrop.

was interested in returning to the Cape. Eventually, the Trekkers moved northwards again and, by 1881, were established on the central plateaux of Angola. Some of them were unsuccessful in farming there and planned to return to the Transvaal, but when an entrepreneur, W. W. Jordan, got wind of this, he bought a vast stretch of land from the Ovambo king. This undefined piece of land extended from the Etosha Pan for an unspecified distance to the east and included the area of present-day Grootfontein and Otavi. He divided it into 6000-acre farms and offered it to the returning Thirstland Trekkers. This offer was taken up in 1884 by twenty-five families returning from Humpata in Angola, and the area came to be known as Upingtonia. This was a doomed affair, however, as the Damaras considered the land that the Ovambos had sold to be theirs in the first place. Jordan found himself isolated and unable to obtain supplies from Walvis, as all routes from there had, by necessity, to pass through Damaraland. Furious, he unsuccessfully petitioned for the protection of the Cape. Somehow the farmers struggled along, but one by one the settlers departed. The first stirrings of the German influence in Damaraland was just starting to be felt at this time. When the German Acting Commissioner went to Upingtonia in 1886, he found that Jordan and some of the farmers were hunting elephants on the fringes of Etosha and that there were only ten families left in the Grootfontein area. Jordan was killed by the Ovambos that year, and the remaining families placed themselves under German protection. By 1887 the dream was over, and the last of the settlers abandoned their farms after repeated attacks from the Damaras.

In the coming years the Germans strengthened their grip on the area and steps were taken to protect the wildlife as early as 1892, when regulations were drawn up. In 1896-97, when the rinderpest epidemic moved down from central Africa to reach Damaraland, huge numbers of wild animals died. In order to control the movement of cattle and to prevent healthy stock from coming into contact with infected wild game, control posts were established at Okaukuejo's waterhole, at Rietfontein (where the Trekkers had camped), and at the spring at Namutoni. Later, when the rinderpest emergency was over, these places became police posts. Thus the early forerunners of the present-day camps at Okaukuejo and Namutoni were born.

The Thirstland Trekker graves at Rietfontein.

The Halali camp is situated at the base of a hill which in that era served as a heliographic station between Okaukuejo and Namutoni. A clay-brick fort was constructed at Namutoni, but this was destroyed in 1904 when it was attacked by Ovambo warriors. A new one was built later on that year, but in 1907 the game reserve of Etosha was proclaimed and in subsequent years Namutoni became progressively unimportant as it lay within the boundaries of the game reserve. The fort became dilapidated, but in 1951 it was restored to its former glory as a national monument.

Today Namutoni is a fort in name only – it has no function other than being a curiosity, but it is also a reminder of the days before 1907 when this fort

above – Namutoni fort, inside the large camp at Namutoni. Left – There are splendid views of the surrounding country from the watchtower. below – View of the fort from within its walls. P.A.

Opposite
The dark plume of smoke from a distant bushfire disturbs thirsty animals on their way to drink from a waterhole. Away from the grassy plains that surround the Etosha Pan, the scenery of the Etosha National Park is uniformly stark, reminding you that, although this is neither the Namib nor the Kalahari, you are still in a desert environment.

represented the furthest reach of the German empire in Damaraland. Beyond, to the north, lay the truculent Ovambo nation. Herein lies a clue to the real reason why a game reserve was proclaimed on the southern fringes of the Etosha Pan: the political expediency of a buffer zone between German-controlled Damaraland and Ovamboland was the real midwife of the National Park that we see today. Namutoni fort is a vivid reminder of this, but now it is just part of a large tourist complex that is known as Namutoni Camp.

We stayed only a few nights at Namutoni. There is no doubt that this is a comfortable place, but it lacks the excitement that haunts Okaukuejo and its waterhole, where something was always happening. At Namutoni they have tried to emulate this by floodlighting the spring at night, but it has none of the relaxed atmosphere of the other place. Indeed, Namutoni seemed rather dull after a month at Okaukuejo, and during the long hours in the middle of the day, with nothing to look at, our minds started turning to Ngamiland and the Okavango. Sitting by the pool in the heat of the midday sun, Clarissa had looked up at one of the nearby palms.

"You know," she had said as it rustled in the wind, "I think that I'd like to see a few forests of those!"

"And some swamps and rivers with lots of running water", Rosemary had added, remembering the green marshes of the Okavango.

"It's time to move on!"

So, had my prejudices about organized places such as Etosha proved to be true? The answer is yes, but with qualifications. Yes, this is a place that has truly been tamed by man – the bureaucrats and scientists do not want adventurers here. The wilderness has been replaced by a farm. No matter how loudly its administrators would splutter and disagree with me, they also know that there is no wilderness here. But, on the other hand, it is possibly one of the best places in Africa to see wild animals in such abundance and at such close and intimate quarters – and so easily. For the photographer, it is a dream come true. For the artist, it abounds with opportunities to get abundant material for paintings. For the tourist, it is the whole African experience in a nutshell. Would I ever go back there? Of course!

P.A.

CHAPTER FOUR

SECRET HAVENS
OF THE OKAVANGO

In August the skies above these southern deserts are clear and blue. The cold nights of winter start to warm up and ahead lie the driest months of the year – the drought season. These portents of the passing days were a constant reminder that there was still a long way to go on our desert odyssey, and only a few months before the rains commenced. The Okavango beckoned.

After leaving Etosha we returned to Windhoek and spent the night there in an attractive campsite set in a picturesque location in the Daan Viljoen Nature Reserve. Here there was a bizarre disturbance of our slumbers in the early hours of dawn, when a stampede of wildebeest passed between the tents and caravans. As the sun rose, however, we found ourselves refreshed and in fine fettle for the long journey ahead.

Windhoek is a modern city and, like all capitals constructed in the interior of Africa in recent times, modern architecture dominates. However, this small city has far more atmosphere and ambience than its soul sisters on the continent – Harare, Gaborone, or Nairobi. Even though it is set in the arid environment of highlands between the Namib and Kalahari deserts, green lawns and gardens filled with colourful blooms abound. That morning we shopped for supplies in one of the modern supermarkets in the city centre and were late in starting for Botswana – so late, in

The old abandoned pole bridge at Ngabekka. These rough but sturdily constructed mopane pole bridges are found so commonly in the Okavango wherever vehicle tracks have penetrated that they have become a very characteristic part of Ngamiland scenery.

145

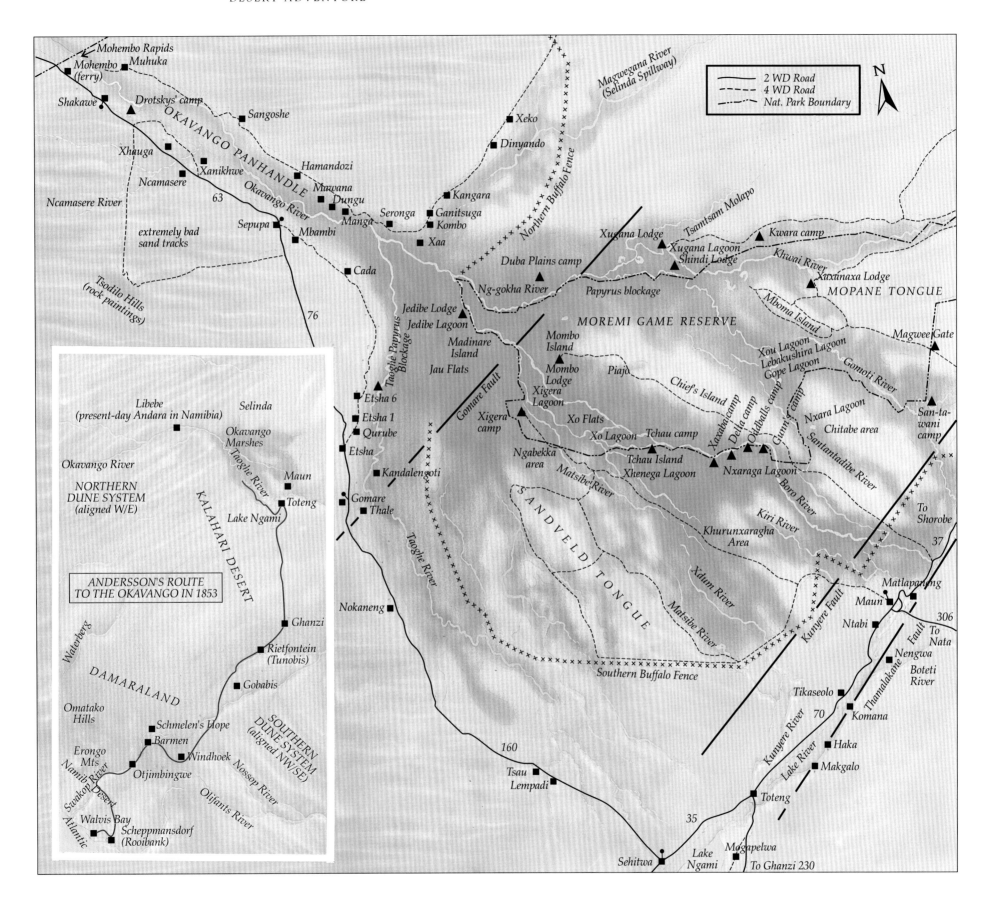

Mohembo Rapids
Mohembo (ferry)
Muhuka
Shakawe
Drotskys' camp
Sangoshe
Xhauga
Hamandozi
Ncamasere
Xanikhwe
Mawana
Dungu
OKAVANGO PANHANDLE
Ncamasere River
63
Okavango River
Sepupa
Manga
Mbambi
Seronga
Ganitsuga
Kombo
Xaa
Kangara
Xeko
Dinyando
Northern Buffalo Fence
Magwegana River (Selinda Spillway)

2 WD Road
4 WD Road
Nat. Park Boundary

N

extremely bad sand tracks
76
Cada
Xugana Lodge
Xugana Lagoon
Shindi Lodge
Kwara camp
Tsamtsam Molapo
Khwai River
Xaxanaxa Lodge
MOPANE TONGUE

Tsodilo Hills (rock paintings)
Duba Plains camp
Ng-gokha River
Papyrus blockage
MOREMI GAME RESERVE
Mboma Island
Magwee Gate

Jedibe Lodge
Jedibe Lagoon
Madinare Island
Jau Flats
Taoghe Papyrus Blockage
Mombo Island
Mombo Lodge
Piajo
Xou Lagoon
Lebakushira Lagoon
Gope Lagoon
Gomoti River

Etsha 6
Etsha 1
Qurube
Etsha
Gomare Fault
Xigera Lagoon
Xigera camp
Chief's Island
Xo Flats
Xo Lagoon
Tchau camp
Xaxabai camp
Della camp
Oddballs camp
Gunn's camp
Nxara Lagoon
Chitabe area
San-ta-wani camp

Libebe (present-day Andara in Namibia)
Selinda
Okavango Marshes
Taoghe River
Okavango River
Lake Ngami
NORTHERN DUNE SYSTEM (aligned W/E)
Maun
Toteng
Kandalengoti
Gomare
Thale
Ngabekka area
Matsibe River
Tchau Island
Xhenega Lagoon
Nxaraga Lagoon
Santantadibe River
Boro River
To Shorobe

KALAHARI DESERT
SANDVELD TONGUE
Kiri River
Khurunxaragha Area
Xdum River
Matsibe River
Kunyere Fault
37
Matlapaneng
Maun

ANDERSSON'S ROUTE TO THE OKAVANGO IN 1853
Nokaneng
Southern Buffalo Fence
Ntabi
306
To Nata

Waterberg
DAMARALAND
Ghanzi
Rietfontein (Tunobis)
Gobabis
Nengwa
Boteti River
Tikaseolo
Komana
Kunyere River
70
Thamalakane Fault
Haka

Omatako Hills
Schmelen's Hope
Barmen
Windhoek
Nossop River
SOUTHERN DUNE SYSTEM (aligned NW/SE)
Makgalo
Lake River

Erongo Mts
Swakop River
Otjimbingwe
Olijants River
160
Tsau
Lempadi
35
Toteng

Namib Desert
Walvis Bay
Scheppmansdorf (Rooibank)
Atlantic
Sehitwa
Lake Ngami
Mogapelwa
To Ghanzi 230

fact, that we were only halfway to the border by three o'clock that afternoon.

A little later and outside Gobabis, a town near the border, we saw a sign indicating a campsite nearby. Evening was approaching and soon it would be time to find a place to spend the night. Softened by the luxury of our lodgings in Etosha, we decided that a campsite and a hot shower in an ablution block was preferable to our original plan of camping in the bush just across the border in Botswana. Try as we would, however, we could find no further trace of the actual site of this travellers' haven, so with the sun slipping ever lower in the sky, we made a dash for the border at Mamuno. Here we arrived a minute before closing time and soon afterwards found ourselves driving off down the sandy track to Ghanzi.

A few kilometres inside the Botswana border we pulled well off the road and made camp for the night. Relaxing around a cheery campfire that night, I extricated the road map from my map box and made an interesting discovery. According to the map, we were only a few kilometres from the tiny Namibian settlement of Rietfontein, the very same Rietfontein where the Thirstland Trekkers under Jan Alberts had stayed for a few months in 1876. Interested now and having connected a story from the distant past with a nearby locality, I pulled out another of my map collection – a German military map from 1908. Peering hard at it in the dim light of a torch, I searched for Rietfontein and found it, discovering also that the German cartographers had noted in brackets that it had an alternative name: Tunobis. This rang a bell in my mind, for Tunobis fountain was the farthest east that Galton and Andersson had reached on their travels together. Without knowing it, they had journeyed to within fourteen days of Lake Ngami's shoreline.

Ever since Livingstone had discovered the location of Lake Ngami in 1849, the possibility of a route there from the west coast was a prize ripe for the taking by some adventurous traveller. Andersson had, of course, thought much about this and, after Galton's return home, he pondered the possibility of blazing that route. There was much at stake, for these were heady times: in the nineteenth century, both in England and on the Continent, the adventures of explorers in central Africa were followed with the same enthusiasm as were the Apollo moon landings by the world in the twentieth.

Andersson returned to the Cape one and a half years after Galton had set sail from Walvis bound for England. Once there, he outfitted himself for an attempt on the Ngami route, and in January 1853, Andersson arrived back at Walvis Bay and made his way inland. Leaving his wagons at Rehoboth in April, he proceeded into the Kalahari Desert. Two weeks later he had crossed the Nossop River to the south of present-day Gobabis and journeyed to Tunobis, which had been as far east as he and Galton travelled in 1851. Beyond, lay the route to Ngamiland and fame for Andersson. This time his goal was a known entity, a lake of vast extent. There would be no repeat of the disappointments that he and Galton had experienced at Omanbonde.

He pressed on into uncharted territory, aided, it must be added, by a Griqua guide who had already been to Ngami along Livingstone's route and had recently been to within a few days of the lake by the same route that Andersson now wished to explore. They had also been informed by Bushmen that the route along the bed of the Otjombinde River (known on present-day maps as the Rietfontein or Buitsivango River) would take them in the direction of the lake and that there were several fountains along the way. By the end of June, the party had arrived at the important springs at Ghanzi.

"Ghanze," wrote Andersson, "according to the interpretation of my Griqua, signifies very large, and yet very small. . . . The very large means that, from the moisture in the ground, there is an indication of much water, whilst the real quantity is trifling. Ghanze is a peculiar and dreary-looking place, consisting of an extensive hollow, with innumerable stones scattered over its surface. . . . The whole is hemmed in with thorn-coppices, intersected by numerous foot-paths, the work of those huge creatures, the elephant and the rhinoceros."

Indeed, in the few days that Andersson and his party were at Ghanzi, they shot numerous rhino, both black and white, for the pot.

They left Ghanzi at the end of June and moved ever eastward. One day, short of water, Andersson had gone ahead to look for supplies of the essential substance. Soon he found a rocky hollow similar to the one at Ghanzi. Elephants had trampled the ground around it and so he felt assured that, somewhere, water was to be found nearby.

Eventually, he discovered a narrow crevice in the calcrete where birds were flitting in and out. Running over to the spot, he peered in and detected a glimmering at the bottom of the darkened crevice. Taking it for granted that this was water, he leapt into the hole and greedily gulped down several mouthfuls of the liquid.

"I was too eager", he wrote, "to be able to distinguish its taste; but, having somewhat slaked my burning thirst, my palate resumed its function, and I thought that I had never experienced so abominable a flavour. Imagine my horror, when taking a small portion in the hollow of my hand and holding it up to the light, I found that I had been drinking blood, mixed with the refuse of some wild animal!"

Later, when Andersson had recovered from the nauseous after-effects of this discovery, the mystery was cleared up. A zebra had scented the same source of water as Andersson and had fallen in the crevice, where it was found by some Bushmen and killed where it lay.

Late in July and after many adventures, they found themselves crossing a series of ridges and from the top of one of these, Andersson had his first glimpse of the fabled lake.

"In an instant I was with the men. There, indeed, at no very great distance, lay spread before me an immense sheet of water, only bounded by the horizon – the object of my ambition for years, for which I had abandoned home and friends, and risked my life."

This must have been an emotional moment for Andersson, who had to dismount and lean against a tree for support until his excitement had subsided. The coming days were an anticlimax, however, for the lake proved to be neither as large nor as attractive as he had been led to believe. It had in fact shrunk since being seen by Livingstone and would continue to shrink in the coming decades, and on that, more later. Skirting the southern shore, they took several days to reach the capital of Ngamiland where Letsholathebe, the chief of the Batawana, held court. This place, known as Toteng even to this day, was situated on the Lake River that issued from the eastern end of the lake. Of course, this was known territory. Andersson, however, later persuaded Letsholathebe to let him travel up the Taoghe River, the source of Ngami's water, and thus had the honour of being the first westerner to penetrate what we all now know as the Okavango swamps.

C.A.

The next day we carried on towards Maun, following in Andersson's footsteps. This road, which passes the modern-day settlement of Ghanzi, traverses the same monotonous countryside through which Andersson had struggled so many years ago. It is on the northern fringe of the Kalahari and so there are few trees, those that thrive being of the scrubby, stunted variety of acacia. Calcrete outcrops are the norm in this undulating countryside So, too, is the white dust that bedevils any road built on this stuff. As the route is well used, a white snowy pall lies over the strips of country flanking the road. This hostile region, the Thirstland that defeated so many hardy travellers in the past, is slowly being tamed by man and there are farms here now. But, despite this, the wildlife of the region persists. Farmers are always complaining of cattle losses to marauding lions, and packs of African wild dogs are regular stock-killers. The rhinos and the elephants are long since gone, however, and, in time, even the lions will be but a distant memory.

Ghanzi has had a long and chequered history since Andersson passed by. In 1874 the six families led by Hendrik van Zyl became the first of the white settlers to brave these dry wastes. While he was here, Van Zyl was said to have built a double-storey house, filled with antique French furniture, and had a staff of over a hundred servants. His downfall came, however, when he aided the Thirstland Trekkers who passed this way in the late 1870s, thereby causing Letsholathebe, the chief of the Batawana, who lived near lake Ngami, to become suspicious. His attack on Van Zyl with 400 warriors was repulsed, but some of the Hottentots that were in Van Zyl's employ were killed and they turned on him, forcing him to flee to Damaraland.

Later on, in 1898, when Cecil John Rhodes had perceived the expansionist policies of the Germans in Damaraland as a threat to his plans for central Africa, Rhodes settled 37 white families in the area surrounding the Ghanzi springs. These were to be a buffer against any possible German expansion into the newly declared Bechuanaland Protectorate (1885). The Dutch origins of these original settlers is still much in evidence today, and for the small community of white people here the lingua franca is still Afrikaans. Indeed, one of the busy shops in Ghanzi recalls the past in its evocative name – the 'Hollandia Cash Store'.

By lunchtime we were past the tiny town of Ghanzi, and here the engine again started to play its mischievous tricks on us. For the first time in several weeks, the engine suddenly died and we coasted silently to a halt. I felt a sudden, overpowering desire to take my spade and batter the vehicle like a mad person, but after having walked up the road and calmed myself down, I returned to the vehicle and set about the daunting task of trying to solve the problem. No one spoke as I pulled out my toolbox from behind the seat, and went through the motions of searching for a problem that had also evaded the detection of the smarmy mechanic at Swakopmund. The hard ridges of corrugations, like small fossilized waves on the dirt road, are the bane of this route and easily the equal of those encountered on some of Namibia's worst roads. These corrugations seemed always to be at their worst when the engine had played its tricks in the past and so I racked my brain to discover what the connection would be: as always, dirt in the tank or in the carburettor seemed to be the most obvious answer. There followed an hour of work under the bonnet, while I logically tried to eliminate the possible causes of its infuriatingly intermittent fault. The carburettor was totally dismantled and float levels adjusted, fuel lines checked and jets cleaned – but no dirt was to be found. However, when the last bolt was tightened and the starter tried, the engine roared into life again. And so the journey went on: whenever the road became corrugated or there was heavy going through drifts of sand – the engine faltered and died. Thus we slowly proceeded towards our destination in fits and starts.

As evening approached we were passing the silent wastes of Lake Ngami's dry bed. Then, crossing the river at Toteng, Letsholathebe's old capital, we made the final run down a pleasant, forested tar road to Maun. Finally, at seven o'clock, our headlights picked out the gates of Chris and Karen MacIntyre's home on the banks of the Thamalakane River. As we struggled with their gate latch, unsteady after a day of being bumped and jolted by the Ghanzi road, Chris came out to see what was going on. Grinning hugely, his voice boomed out for all the district to hear, "How are ya? Late as usual I see!"

It is always nice to be expected and even nicer to be welcomed into a friendly house after a long and frustrating day. Chris and Karen were old friends from the days when I had lived permanently in Botswana, and I was establishing my reputation as a wilderness artist. As I was developing my career, Chris, Karen and another friend of mine, Colin Bell, had been establishing their extremely successful safari operation in northern Botswana. The three of them then operated their fledgling mobile safari business in the same areas where I was camping and painting and so we had got to know each other very well in an era when the names of the only other people operating in the whole of Botswana could be counted on one hand. In the years since those heady days of the early 80s much had changed. I had established myself as an international artist, handled by the best galleries in the world, had had a book and several prints published, and numerous exhibitions behind me. Likewise, their safari operation was transformed into huge concern with a worldwide reputation for excellence. Whether they liked it or not, Chris and Karen had become fast-lane executives, and found themselves spending less and less time in the bush and more time behind a desk as their company grew by leaps and bounds.

Botswana had changed as well. As we had supper that night, Chris and Karen filled me in on what had happened in the few years I had been away. In the twelve or so years since I had first arrived in Botswana (in the late 70s), more than seventy-five per cent of the wildlife had been eradicated by drought, poaching and veterinary fences. During that period my own experience of Botswana had, from choice, been confined to certain remote areas in the Chobe district where a vast array of wildlife was to be seen. I had shunned the Okavango deliberately in favour of the empty tracts of the Ngwezumba in the Chobe National Park. Now, the wild nature of my favourite areas had suffered a decline in the face of surging tourism. Poaching had also taken a heavy toll. Finally, I found myself looking towards the Okavango as a place where I might relive some of that elusive wilderness freedom. So, on this desert odyssey, I felt myself to be back home and about to discover a treasure that I had ignored in the past.

Outside, the Thamalakane glinted in the light of a full moon and the night was full of the sounds of Africa. Choruses of frogs croaked in the

149

reeds, a hippo snorted now and then, and in the distance tribal drums throbbed a beat which spoke directly to my crocodile brain. On the opposite bank, silvery palms rustled in the night-time breeze, tantalizing the mind with hints of secret places to be found beyond the horizon in the Okavango.

The miracle of the Okavango is that this vast marshland exists at all in the midst of the northern Kalahari Desert. This is an entity whose existence depends on an amazing geological balancing act. Also, purely coincidentally, the evolution of the Okavango and the emergence of mankind occurred simultaneously, which underlines how young a system it really is. If the planet's age is represented by a length of string a kilometre long, the system we now know as the Okavango swamps only began to emerge within that last half-metre of the piece of string.

That half-metre of string very roughly represents a period of the last three million years, at the beginning of which the Okavango swamps did not exist. Instead, the large proto-river that would eventually be known as the

Part of a very much larger herd, a small group of buffalo fords an open expanse of water between two islands. This remote and inaccessible part of the Okavango provides refuge for some of the largest herds of buffalo remaining in Botswana.

Opposite
Buffalo graze on the grassy fringes of islands set in the lush expanses of the permanent swamp. This area, known as the Jau flats, is host to some of the largest concentrations of game in the Okavango.

151

Okavango, wandered slowly westwards through undulating countryside which sloped very gradually to the south-east. It is not known whether this early Okavango had an outlet to the sea at this time, but the indications are that it fed a vast lake where the Makgadikgadi pans now exist. Elsewhere in Africa during this era, ape-men, the precursors to Stone Age man, were evolving rapidly.

By two million years ago and at the beginning of the Stone Age, compression and tensional forces in the crust of the African continent started to create fractures and faulting. Slowly, these forces, which would eventually shape the Great Rift Valley's extent, came to bear on the continent. As a result of this and as a distant offshoot to the events forming the Rift Valley, several fault lines fractured the crust in the area now occupied by the Okavango swamps, cutting across the path of that ancient proto-river. While this was happening, humanoids were already busy making and perfecting tools in the Olduvai area of Tanzania. Meanwhile, all around them, other mammals were also rapidly evolving and animals that we would recognize today began to appear. For example, it was at about this time that the giraffe emerged in the form we are now familiar with. Others such as the fearsome sabre-toothed cats were in their decline and would soon become extinct.

By one million years ago, the forces in the crustal plates that had started the formation of the Rift Valley continued to build up. The East African Rift Valley deepened and its floor was racked with extensive vulcanism. Far to the south, smaller movements were taking place, and the Okavango swamps began to form. Following a slight subsidence of the crust between the Gomare, Kunyere and Thamalakane faults, the underlying structure shaping the present-day Okavango gradually became etched on the terrain of the region. The movements were tiny: an almost imperceptible tilting of the flat terrain in such a way that it disrupted the proto-river, levelling its surroundings so perfectly that it was forced to spread out over a vast area. The odds against this fortuitous accident of nature happening at all are so huge, and the successful balancing act of the system so delicate, that to the thinking person it has an eerie, 'planned' feel about it.

As the Okavango swamps continued to evolve, so did life itself. The brain of the hominids increased in size and speech developed. Divergences and evolutionary radiations caused the African bovids (the hollow-horned ruminants), to increase to more than seventy species, and the climate began to undergo rapid cyclic changes.

Half a million years ago the Okavango as we know it today was almost fully formed and a complex delta of rivers had evolved in the vast area between the faults. All the while, the downward movement of the land in between the faults continued to develop. Slowly, the basin between the two faults began to fill with a bed of white and brown sands, brought into the system by the source river and by wind during the periodic arid epochs. The depth of these sandy deposits increased from one hundred metres near the Thamalakane fault to nearly three hundred metres towards the apex of the swamps. To a very small degree, the slightly higher land on the north-eastern side of the Kunyere fault acted as a dam wall, and here the swampland ended. The rivers and streams coalesced to carve routes through the slightly higher ground between the Kunyere and Thamalakane fault lines. The final fifteen kilometres of the Boro River is a good example of this. The higher land on the south-western side of the Thamalakane fault, however, was a much more formidable barrier. Every river was forced to turn here, abruptly changing direction to form one large river parallel to the fault. Thus was born the Thamalakane River. Thirty kilometres south-east of where the Boro joins the Thamalakane, the latter breaches this last barrier and then abruptly changes direction so that the waters of the Okavango flow again, as the Boteti River, towards the Makgadikgadi pans. As these formative events were taking place, *Homo erectus* had evolved in East Africa, discovered the use of fire, and was starting to spread into Eurasia. Most, but not all, of the animals we know today had already emerged at this point, although the bushbuck, for example, had still to evolve to its present state.

One hundred thousand years ago there was a worldwide drop in temperature. For the next ninety thousand years the earth would be in the grip of an ice age during the Pleistocene epoch, which would gouge out the Great Lakes from the Canadian Shield. The sea levels would drop and a vast land bridge would form between Asia and the Americas, and across this, man would enter the New World. The tropical rainforests of Zaïre virtually disappeared and the Kalahari Desert expanded to form the Mega-Kalahari. Relics of this era are still discernible today, with dune patterns being visible in the topography of southern Zaïre, an area that now has more than 2000 millimetres of rain annually. The characteristic parallel dunefields surrounding the Okavango were also formed in this era. Interestingly, two separate dune systems occur in the vicinity of the Okavango, each with a different orientation, which suggests that circulation patterns during the period varied radically over time. Sandy deposits, known by geologists as the Kalahari Beds, extended over the entire catchment of the Okavango River – and it ceased to flow for long periods during the peak of the Mega-Kalahari's influence. Humankind was also expanding and this invasion, together with changes in climate, would adversely affect the wildlife of the continent so that a decline in the number of mammal species began to take place – a decline well-documented in the fossil record. The antilopine antelopes of Africa were reduced from twenty-five to twelve species. The pigs declined from twelve to four species.

Twelve thousand years ago the climate warmed up, became wetter, and the glaciers of the higher latitudes and altitudes receded. The Okavango swamps, active again, swelled in size and at various times covered an extent far greater than that of today. Where Ngami is now situated there was a huge lake (larger than anything that Livingstone would see) and a vast swamp extended north of the Mogohelo River into the Mababe Depression. The earliest human inhabitants of the Okavango had already arrived by this time, and the present-day San or river Bushmen are the descendants of those people.

Between 250 and 150 years ago the Okavango was again starting to shrink in size. However, the swamps that covered the Mababe Depression were still extensive, and it was over these waterways that the next wave of human settlers arrived. In the 1750s, these new settlers, the Bayei peoples of the Barotse flats in central Africa, were forced to flee westwards to escape the expanding and hostile Lozi empire of King Ngombela. Arriving via the Chobe, Savuti, Mababe and Thamalakane river route, the Bayei were the first Bantu-speaking immigrants, and it was they who introduced the mekoro, or dugout, to the Okavango. Originally settling in the area around Toteng, they would later spread throughout the delta. Another group of that same migration from the north-east, the Hambukushu peoples from the Katima Mulilo area of the Zambezi, also

fled from their homeland for the same reasons as the Bayei. They were, however, an agricultural people who had no use for mekoros, and instead searched out a new homeland similar to their own. They moved directly eastward to the Kwando Valley and then to the Andara area on the Okavango River.

Other groups came from a different direction. One hundred and seventy years ago an offshoot of the Bangwato nation, which became known as the Batawana, travelled across the Kalahari Desert. Their leader, Tawana, had quarrelled with Kgama I, the Bangwato heir. After a war that ended in stalemate, Tawana and his followers moved to Ngamiland where they established themselves in the Kwebe Hills to the south of Lake Ngami. Later they moved to Toteng and, from 1847 to 1874, Letsholathebe I was their king. Meanwhile, Portuguese slavers began to penetrate as far inland from the Atlantic as the Okavango and Zambezi rivers. The Hambukushu were thus forced to move southwards into the Shakawe and Seronga areas of the Okavango swamps. Finally, one hundred and fifty years ago, white-skinned people began to penetrate the northern Kalahari from the south and, in 1849, David Livingstone 'discovered' Lake Ngami.

Over several days following our arrival from Namibia we tried to plan our movements for the coming months, but the incentive to dally was strong. By day, the green lawn outside, shady trees overhead, and the cool waters of the Thamalakane did nothing to prompt serious plan-making. At night, it was the same, for the company was too convivial and our hosts too welcoming to contemplate such matters. As the days passed, however, reality became impossible to ignore – there were but a couple months left before the onset of the first showers of the rainy season.

And then there was the little matter of our now thoroughly disgraced vehicle. It was deposited at one of the garages in Maun, and after yet another discussion with yet another mechanic, I was promised that the problem would be found and rectified. This time I was told that there had been similar problems with other Hiluxes of the same year, all related to some inadequately insulated wiring in the distributor. Naïve fool that I was, I believed him!

At this stage in the journey, Clarissa was due to go back to South Africa for a few weeks, to attend an anthropological conference and to work at her thesis on a computer.

The mekoro, the ubiquitous watercraft of the Okavango was introduced to the region by the Bayei in the 17 ths. Above. – A reedcutter loads up his mekoro with reeds from the Boro River. P.A.

In the meantime, while Clarissa was away, Rosemary and I decided that we would go to the Okavango panhandle in search of the birding opportunities that Karen and Chris assured me were to be found there in abundance. Through Chris, we also arranged that when Clarissa returned four weeks later, we would meet her in Maun and then fly into the north-western part of the swamps. There, in the Jau region of the permanent swamp, we would undertake a series of adventurous mekoro journeys through the wildest remaining parts of the Okavango, areas far removed from the tourist-oriented operations based on the middle reaches of the Boro River.

I had long known that the Okavango River, in particular the panhandle of the Okavango swamps, was a birder's paradise. This part of the Okavango is also far off the beaten track and blessed with splendid scenery and atmosphere. The Okavango, with its reedbeds, sandbanks, riverbanks and riverine forests, provides the habitat for vast numbers of a great variety of birds. I was particularly interested in Carmine and other bee-eaters as well as African Skimmers. Karen, knowing of my plans, had been unequivocal in her advice.

"You should camp at Drotskys", she instructed us. "Remember Jan and Eileen Drotsky? They used to have a garage in Maun in the early days?"

"Of course!"

"Well, they now have a camp to the south of Shakawe. Get them on the radio and find out if the Carmines are nesting there yet!"

This I did, and a little while later had a reply from Eileen, who remembered me. The Skimmers and Carmines were indeed nesting and the message ended off with a heart-warming invitation to come and stay with them for a few weeks.

A few days later Clarissa left by air for South Africa. Then, as the sound of the departing aircraft faded into the distance, I drove over to the premises of the Drotskys' agent to see if there was anything we could take up to Shakawe for them. Twenty minutes later we departed Maun for Shakawe, the springs of the vehicle creaking under the additional load of many boxes of vegetables and frozen meat, the latter item already beginning to defrost in the morning sunshine.

We retraced our steps to Toteng and, an hour later, taking the Sehitwa road, skirted the northern side of Ngami's old shoreline. There is nothing here now – no glittering sheet of water extending to the horizon, just a vast flat plain that becomes muddy in the rainy season and is slowly being colonized by bush. Scrawny cattle forage here in numbers far beyond the carrying capacity of the land. If Chief Letsholathebe were to return to his kingdom today, he would find a ravaged land, no lake and no wildlife. We sped on past this sorry relic, shaking our heads at the fuss that had been made over its very existence in the London of the 1850s. There are many ghosts lurking here – ghosts of people, wildlife and rivers.

Somewhere along the road and near Sehitwa, I knew we should cross the ancient bed of the Taoghe River where it once used to flow fast and deep into the lake, but every trace of its existence is gone. This was the river that Andersson had used to explore the Okavango, but now the active rivercourse of the Taoghe only exists further north. Soon after Andersson was here the river's upper course, which was the main feeder of the vast lake that Livingstone had seen, became blocked by papyrus beds: in the end the river literally choked to death, and with it went Lake Ngami – such is the delicate balance of nature in this system. The long-vanished watercourse must be crossed on that short stretch of road near Sehitwa, but nothing remains – no sandbanks, no empty channels, nothing except a flat expanse of thorn-scrub and acacias. Scanning this arid landscape from our speeding vehicle, I found it hard to imagine what it must have been like in those far-flung days when an unknown Okavango lay before Andersson.

On Andersson's arrival in Toteng he visited Letsholathebe and, in the course of the interview, asked him for information about the interior, the swamp land reputed to exist to the north of the lake, and the source of its waters. He inquired about Libebe, an important town reputed to exist far to the north and deep in the unexplored hinterland of marshes and rivers (this is present-day Andara in Namibia). Letsholathebe was not forthcoming and replied, "I know nothing at all".

Piqued at this, Andersson went back to his camp. A few days later, however, Letsholathebe relented and gave Andersson the men and dugouts needed for the journey that he wanted to make to Libebe.

They had first to cross the lake to reach the mouth of the Taoghe River.

A Marsh Sandpiper on a Shakawe sandbank.

"After about an hour's paddling, the broad expanse of the Lake lay before me, glittering in all the beauty and softness produced by reflection of the warm rays of a tropical sun. It was indeed a luxury, after so much travelling in the burning desert, to be able at last to float upon

'The glassy, cool, translucent wave;' . . .

"As I felt the cool breeze fanning my cheeks, new life seemed to stir within me. It was not . . . until the third day that we reached the chief entrance of the mouth of the Teoge (for here the river spreads out into several branches), where there is a bar. The water was so low on it that although the stream was fast rising at the time [August], we were forced to draw the canoes across it by main force. . . . For the first few days' journey, the country presented a rather dreary and monotonous appearance, being frequently flooded for many miles; thus converting the land on both sides into extensive reedy marshes, only occasionally relieved by a pleasant group of the date and the fan-palm. The banks were in many places so low, that when bivouacking on shore, we often slept in the water. Even where the banks rose a few feet above the water, they were entirely undermined by the stream; and if a stick was thrust through, water immediately appeared in the hole. Fuel was exceedingly scarce, and could only be purchased from the natives (thinly scattered along its banks) who not infrequently brought it from a great distance.

When the level of the Okavango River starts to drop in September, sandbanks appear and African Skimmers use these as their nesting sites. It is during this nesting season that the skimmers are most visible, 'skimming' the water in formation and calling to one another in high, fluting whistles.

155

"On the fourth day, the landscape assumed a more pleasing aspect; the banks of the river became higher, and were richly covered with a rank vegetation. There was the fan-palm, the date, the black-stemmed mimosa, the wild and wide-spreading sycamore, the elegant and dark-foliaged moshoma, and a variety of other beautiful, often to me new, trees; many yielding an abundance of fruit . . . The arboreal scenery, indeed, in some places exceeds in beauty anything that I have ever seen. I could have spent days under the shade of some of these ornamental trees resounding at times with the wild notes of birds, whilst in the distance might be seen herds of the finest of the antelope tribe.

"Animal life was almost on a par with the exuberant vegetation. Rhinoceroses, hippopotami, buffaloes, sassabys, hartebeests, pallahs, reed-bucks, leches, &c., were constantly seen; and every day some game animal was shot. Thus I was able to support our large and hungry party, now consisting of fifty or sixty individuals.

"One fine afternoon, we came to the place where the tracks of buffaloes were unusually numerous; and, having hitherto seen little of that animal, I determined to halt for a day or two, in the hope of not only getting better acquainted with it, but of having good sport. . . .

"The first night I passed at a 'skärm', was a failure in respect of game. . . . A small herd of these animals, however, came within range of Timbo, whom I had placed in ambush some little way from me; but, as usual, he missed, and they all went off unhurt."

When he returned to the camp the following morning he found his followers hungry, so that, together with some of them, he returned to the bush and brought down some impala and a kudu. Immediately after bringing the meat back to camp, Andersson, keen to bag his first buffalo, went out again.

"At last, we came to the skirts of a dense thicket; and, peering amongst the bushes, I presently espied several dark objects on the ground, which at once struck me must be buffaloes. Placing my finger on my lips . . . and pointing in the direction of the dark objects, I whispered the word 'onja', meaning buffaloe. Not the presence of his Satanic Majesty could have caused greater consternation amongst my followers; for no sooner was the magic word uttered, than one and all of them wheeled about and made a headlong retreat. One of the men was carrying a heavy

rifle of mine, and wishing to get possession of it, I followed in their footsteps. But this made bad worse; for seeing me also running, and thinking the enemy was at their heels, they redoubled their pace; nor did they stop until at a most respectful distance from the thicket. It was really absurd to see us thus endeavouring to outrun each other.

"Having, at length, overtaken the men, and secured my rifle, I returned to the spot whence I had first observed the suspicious objects. . . . For a moment, I fancied I must have been in error, and that what I had taken for animals, were neither more nor less than huge stones. However, . . . at the report of the gun, up sprung to their feet, four magnificent male buffaloes; and after tossing their heads proudly, and sniffing the air for a moment, they broke cover in good style, and, to all appearance, unhurt. I never saw them again.

"Following leisurely on their tracks, in order to ascertain whether any of the beasts were hurt, a herd of buffaloes – at least two hundred in number – suddenly rushed past us with the violence of a tornado, breaking down and crashing everything that opposed their headlong career; and raising so great a cloud of dust as nearly to conceal their dark forms from view. . . .

"On the ninth day after we had entered the Teoge, we left the principal channel and passed into the Omoroanga (little river) Vavarra. This rivulet is merely one of those small branches of the main stream (formed by its overflowing its banks) so frequently met with, and which usually rejoin it after a day or two. The Omoroanga Vavarra is only navigable with canoes when the Teoge is at its greatest height, and even then the navigation is of the most intricate description. The boatmen, many of whom were born and bred in the neighbourhood, constantly lose their way. We passed two nights on the Omoroanga, during which we were exposed to much inconvenience and hardship.

"Lecholetebe had placed two canoes at my disposal; but the rascally boatmen had by this time so filled them with their own things that no place was left for me. The consequence was, as the country was one succession of swamps, lakes, rivulets and quagmires, I found myself early and late immersed in water, sometimes swimming, at others wading up to my neck. Indeed, from the time I left my camp on the Zouga, to my return to it, a period of about a month, I scarcely knew what it was to have a dry thread about me. The only time I could partially dry my clothes was at night along the bivouac-fire; but then I had to lie down wet. It would have been ruinous to any constitution not previously inured to hardships of all kinds.

"But I was compensated for what I lost in comfort by the beauty of the surrounding scenery. . . .

"At length and after about twelve days voyaging, we reached a large village where the great chief of the Bayeye [Bayei] resided. This was a charming spot, and one to which the most skilful artist would have had some difficulty in doing justice. Located on a small island, about two hundred feet long, by one hundred feet in breadth, standing in the midst of a beautiful group of elegant fan-palms, and some gigantic wild fruit trees. At the foot of the werft, in a semicircle, the clear transparent Teoge wound its meandering course. On every side, as far as the eye could reach, lay stretched a sea of fresh water, in many places concealed from sight by a covering of reeds and rushes of every shade and hue; whilst numerous islands, spread over its surface, and adorned with rich vegetation, gave the whole an indescribably beautiful appearance. This was particularly the case at sunrise and sunset, when the luxuriant vegetation received additional charms by the brilliant, but softened, rays of a tropical sun.

"I had been given to understand by Lecholetebe that the chief at whose werft I had now arrived, was to have provided me with other men and boats. To save time, as also in accordance with the men's own wishes, I sent my principal guide and others to inform the chieftain of my coming, requesting him to get everything ready; but on reaching the place, the following day, I found, to my utter astonishment, that he, with all his people, had set out that very morning to hunt the sea-cow [hippopotamus]; and no one could, or rather would, inform me when the great man was likely to return.

"It now occurred to me that I was deceived; and my suspicions at once fell upon Lecholetebe. Still, hoping I might be mistaken, I waited patiently for several days, but to no purpose . . . I felt excessively mortified at being thus basely duped, and at once called on the only man left in the place, who, I was informed, was the chief's brother, and ordered him to tell me, without prevarication, the real state of the case. As I had suspected, Lecholetebe was at the bottom of the affair. The man declared that he had no orders to furnish me with men and boats, but that, if I

insisted on proceeding, he was to give a guide to the next tribe, whence I was to find my way to Libebe as well as I could, well knowing that such an arrangement was quite incompatible with my designs. . . .

"Finding remonstrances unavailing, I had no alternative but to retrace my steps; and, accordingly, I requested the temporary chief to prepare the canoes to convey me back to the lake. . . .

"After about a week's stay at the Bayeye werft, I was once more launched on the Teoge, and only regretted that my course did not lie to the north instead of to the south. My departure afforded fresh proof of the rascality of the Bayeye. As previously mentioned, according to the injunctions of Lecholetebe, I was to have two canoes at my disposal; but, on the day in question, the natives unceremoniously deposited me on a raft composed solely of reeds! When I first saw the unshapely mass, I could not help smiling; and it was not until I had set my people the example that they ventured to embark. . . .

"Though I was at first much disconcerted at the appearance of our very primitive looking craft, I soon got accustomed to it, and it proved far more comfortable than might have been supposed. It was much safer, moreover, than our own canoes, one or two of which we obtained shortly after our departure. No efforts were made to steer or

The permanent swamps of the north-western part of the Okavango, and the numerous islands that occur there, are best visited by mekoro. This is the only way that this region and the wildlife that inhabits it can be properly appreciated for what it is – a fabulous wilderness where adventure can still be experienced.

propel the raft, which was left entirely to the stream. As soon as we were caught by some projecting reed-bed – and this was of frequent occurrence – the raft immediately swung around and thus disengaged itself; but when we came in contact with trees overhanging the river, we were more inconvenienced; for before we could get clear of them, ourselves and baggage were at times nearly swept into the water. In this manner, nevertheless, and without serious accident, we accomplished about one hundred and fifty miles in nine days, entirely by the force of the current, which rarely exceeds two miles an hour."

On his return to Toteng, Andersson's exploration of the Okavango came to an end and he made his way back to Walvis Bay.

Cool water, flowing streams and green reedbanks – this was indeed hard to imagine as we sped along the road towards Sehitwa. In their place were scrawny bushes, dustdevils and herds of goats. At Sehitwa we veered northward and sped on towards the distant Shakawe, past villages and herds of cattle huddled in the shade of huge, leafy trees. A few hours later the road approached the river at Seronga and here the Okavango tantalized us with glimpses of a blue river and vast, green floodplain. Eventually, four hours later, we reached the turn off to the Drotskys' camp. At the end of a short sandy track we came to the boundary of their property.

Once inside the gate, we were in a different world. Outside, there had been few large trees and the bush consisted of scrubby thorn trees, most of which sheltered hordes of omnivorous goats from the harsh sun. Inside, in sharp contrast, a cool, shady gloom prevailed and thick walls of dense vegetation closed in over the track ahead. Huge trees jostled for elbow room and a cacophony of bird calls filtered down from the high canopy of the forest. Squirrels darted from almost under the wheels and a bushbuck, surprised as it browsed a track-side morsel, barked and bounded out of sight.

Soon we came to the buildings of the lodge and parked next to a battered-looking Landrover. As we stretched our legs and admired the expanses of watered lawn, Eileen Drotsky came out of a nearby office. Walking over, this attractive, tanned woman recognized us and smiled dazzlingly.

"Hi there, it's nice to see you again after all these years." Seeing the overflowing boxes of her supplies inside my

vehicle, she stopped me unloading. "Leave that, my staff will see to it. Come inside and have some tea."

So, as her staff unloaded the vehicle of its defrosted cargo, we went inside and drank cup after cup of tea. A little later, Jan came in and joined us. A quietly spoken man, Jan's mild-mannered way belies a gritty determination. Although I had met him briefly on several occasions before when they were living in Maun, in the coming weeks I came to know him well. For one thing, I found out that he was a direct descendant of one of the Thirstland Trekkers and that one of his ancestors was buried at Rietfontein (the Rietfontein close to the Ghanzi road and near where we had camped on our first night after crossing the border from Namibia). Also, that he had grown up on the actual Ghanzi farm where the historic springs were to be found.

Later on that afternoon Eileen had taken us over to the campsite and I had selected a beautiful spot under the dense shade of the leafy riverine forest.

"When you have put up your camp, you must come

over and join us for dinner", she had said and then added, as if to underline our welcome, "I hope that this isn't going to be a short visit, is it?"

We stayed for four weeks, during which time I discovered that the Panhandle is an artist's paradise.

The Okavango River at Shakawe is wide and deep, with a swift current, so that the mekoros plying its waters keep close to the edge. It meanders through a vast sea of papyrus contained by banks that are many kilometres apart. Most of the human habitation occurs where the loops of the meanders touch the high banks. At these points villages would appear, with their attendant fleets of mekoros, and herds of watering cattle constantly coming down to drink. After flowing swiftly and carving a high, forested bank, the river would then turn away and follow a winding course through the green sea to the other bank, several kilometres away. In the papyrus beds between these loops sitatunga are common although seldom seen. The river itself is still

host to numerous hippos, although an increase in the human populations at Shakawe and Seronga, together with rising boat traffic on the river, is now threatening these huge mammals. Buffalo and elephant are also occasional visitors to these impenetrable, soggy refuges. In August and September when the river starts to drop, numerous sandbars form and these quickly become the favourite nesting and resting places of many interesting and rare species of birds.

One of the birds that I particularly wanted to paint and photograph was the African Skimmer. The skimmer, which is closely related to gulls and terns, has developed several unique physical and behavioural features. One is the cat-like vertical pupils of their eyes, while another is the graceful and eye-catching way in which they feed. Flying close to the surface of the water, they drag their lower elongated bill through the water, scooping up small fish in this slender, flexible extension. They are beautiful

A leopard feeds on an impala that it killed the day before. In the Okavango leopards are very common, and their calls are often heard at night by campers.

159

The most graceful birds to be found in the Okavango Panhandle are African Skimmers. These birds, which nest on the sandbanks exposed at the end of the dry season, are superb flyers, and their feeding technique of scooping the water with their beak while on the wing is a delight to watch.

Right
An African Skimmer nest site and chick after the bow-wave of a passing powerboat has washed over it. This singular hazard, brought on by increasing river traffic as the region develops, may eventually result in the disappearance of the skimmer from the Panhandle.

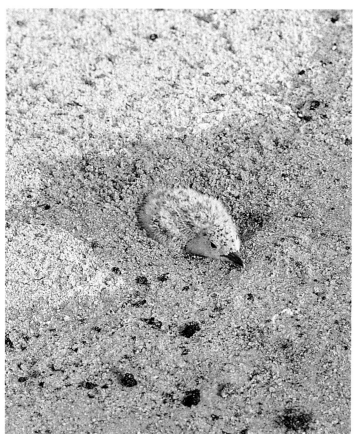

to watch and often fish like this in pairs or groups, skimming gracefully in formation over the mirrored surface of the Okavango with their long bills slicing the water, and uttering high, fluting calls.

Both up and down stream from the Drotskys' place there were several sandbanks on which the skimmers were nesting, and for several days following our arrival I photographed and sketched them as they went about their daily business of survival. Considering the small number of sandbanks that are available to them – and the fact that there are numerous monitor lizards, water mongooses, otters, storks and hordes of raptors waiting to prey on them – it is amazing that any of the nestlings survive. An added hazard are the cattle and hippo that often wander about on the sandbanks and take their toll of the young birds, while fishermen from the nearby villages are not above using the nestlings as live bait. But these are ancient hazards which the skimmers have managed to surmount and still thrive. However, sitting quietly in the crude blind that I had made in the reeds near one of these sandbanks, I became aware of a new threat facing them. Several skimmers were dotted about on the sand and sitting on nests when a powerboat came round the far bend of the river and, without slackening its speed, zoomed past and out of sight round the next bend. Thirty seconds later the bow wave hit the sandbank and surged across the surface like a miniature *tsunami* or tidal wave. The skimmers, flushed from their nests, flew up and called in alarm as the nests momentarily disappeared under water. Other, smaller surges of water followed and only as the noise of the motorboat's engine was fading into the distance, did the little waves die away. I walked over to have a quick look at the nests and was relieved to find that the nestlings, although wet through, were all alive. This, however, happened several times in one day. Jan later told me that it was a considerable problem and that, although the lodges and safari operators were careful to slow down when they passed the sandbanks, uninformed or indifferent inhabitants of Shakawe or Seronga were becoming a serious threat to the skimmers of the Okavango River.

These sandbanks were also host to numerous other flocks of waterbirds. Sometimes Jan would drop what he was doing and take me far downstream to show me some special area or a secret island. We would pass sandbanks that were covered in huge flocks of Openbilled Storks and Whitefaced Whistling Ducks. We would see Longtoed, Blacksmith and Wattled Plovers mingling together on sandbars where there were also huge crocodiles basking in the sun. Once, when Jan had realized that I had never seen a Pel's Fishing Owl, he took me to a small island not far from the camp. This owl is very special: one of the largest of that group of birds, it is unusual in that its prey is fish which it hunts for in the black of night.

"We'll see one here," he confidently informed me as he guided the boat in through a narrow channel to the bank, ". . . with a little luck".

We had then criss-crossed the densely forested island, backwards and forwards, pushing our way through massive palm thickets and crawling under low branches. Jan, his face upturned towards the canopy, had searched tirelessly for the sight of a Pel's flitting away. This, it seems, is the trick to this difficult game: the Pel's flushes, you watch to see where it alights, and then creep close for a glimpse of the suspicious bird. After about an hour of this hard going and with no sign of the elusive owl, Rosemary retreated to the boat. For another hour, I silently followed Jan, my camera at the ready, straining my eyes in the gloom to catch the telltale glimpse of a fleeing bird. Eventually, we

A midday break on a submerged sandbank of the Okavango river. A few minutes later, on the small forested island opposite us Jan showed us our first Pel's Fishing Owl.   P.A.

had returned to the boat unsuccessful and Jan, piqued at his failure, vowed to show me one that very afternoon.

True to his word, later on that afternoon we found ourselves on another island upstream from the camp. This tiny island had a small open clearing at its centre. Our luck was in, for after walking slowly through the forest for a few minutes, a Pel's flushed from a dense, leafy tree overhead. Looking back at me to see if I had observed the departing blur, Jan beckoned me and we cautiously moved on to where it had settled. Silently, we crept up as close as we dared, wary of flushing it again. In the tree above, the large owl was sitting calmly on a branch, examining our approach intently. Almost as we arrived, it flew off, leaving me with a fleeting impression of this secretive bird.

The Pel's Fishing Owl is arguably the most beautiful of all the owls. It has an attractive face and is coloured a rich rufous tawny, barred with black, its covering of feathers appearing bulky, more like the mane of a lion. Its large, liquid eyes and beak seem softer, less vicious than those of other owls. It is also very different in several ways. All other owls rely on silent flight to surprise their prey, and their feathers have evolved to facilitate this. As the Pel's prey is underwater and deaf to what is going on above the

Any sighting of the Pel's Fishing Owl is to be treasured because, once located after a long stalk and much patience, this elusive and secretive bird rarely sits still for long.

Pel's Fishing Owl.   P.A

162

surface, this owl has no need to fly silently, and indeed it does not. Likewise, other owls rely heavily on their hearing to locate their meals on the darkened floor of the forest. The Pel's relies instead on sight to locate its prey in the murky, night-time waters – hence the huge, limpid eyes that dominate its face.

"Do you want some flying pictures?" Jan had whispered at me when our quarry had flapped out of sight. "Go across to the other side of the clearing and wait."

I scurried off to the other side of the nearby clearing and, sure enough, a few minutes later, the owl, disturbed again by Jan, came winging my way. Framed against the backdrop of a dense forest, the Pel's leisurely flapped over and past me to the opposite fringe – providing me with an unparalleled view of its large size and exquisite markings.

Eileen had insisted that we eat with them in the lodge. Rosemary, however, preferring her own tiny meals, usually left me to do the socializing. These dinners were spreads of the standard expected by international guests, and a month later, I found that I had put on weight and grown very used to delicious three-course meals!

The guests at the table varied from night to night. They were all either very keen sport fishermen or world-travelled birdwatchers, equipped with photographic equipment that would have made a professional's mouth water. Often the birders were very interested in the fact that I was an artist. Luckily, I was just able to hold my own in the esoteric bird arguments that raged back and forth across the table, and also to talk knowledgeably about Alaska, Botswana, history and art. It was just as well that I had my own areas of expertise as most of these birders were professional people at the peak of their respective professions. People such as these can, and usually will, debate anything. This is especially so around a roaring camp-fire and with the drinks flowing under the stars of an African night. Also, many of them knew me by name from my previous book and from my international reputation as a wildlife artist. If I was at home with the birders, I was, however, an outsider among the sport fishermen, and on nights when these Nimrods were in the majority, I would retire early.

Such was the turnover among the guests that I often found myself telling the same stories night after night, and after a while I began to realize how difficult it must be for guides to remain fresh and enthusiastic for months at a time. One night, tired with my own stories, I had been less than forthcoming when Eileen had introduced me to the group of British birders at the table. The next day when Jan, Eileen and I were sitting in the bar, cooling off in the midday heat, Eileen had taken me to task for being so quiet the evening before.

"You were really boring last night, Paul", she had said as she got herself a drink from the deep freeze. Jan laughed goodnaturedly at this. Such is the open nature of this couple that it was impossible for me to take offence. In fact she was right, and I could not help but smile in agreement.

Jan was busy building a huge extension to the lodge and the beginnings of this were starting to take shape on the riverbank in front of the bar. A large raised platform was topped by a magnificent, soaring, thatched roof, which was supported on massive pillars of solid wood. Its floor was planked throughout. When planning the project Jan had decided that, rather than buying the necessary timber from Maun, he would mill it all himself. Obtaining the logs locally, he had then dumped the massive trunks into the river in front of his plot where they had seasoned in the water for a few months. Behind his workshop, in the meantime, he had built his own sawmill to cut the timber to the sizes that he required. This sawmill, which I was later to examine for myself, had been assembled from bits and pieces of machinery that he found lying around in his workshop yard. Indeed, establishments such as these always have fascinating workshops, and invariably there are piles of worn-out machinery, bits of engines, cannibalized Landrovers and innumerable items of old camping gear. From this rich source, Jan had created a wonderful Heath Robinson contraption consisting of an old engine, bits of girder and railway-line, belts, gears and – the only purpose-bought item I could make out – a circular saw blade. With this splendid item of mechanical artwork he had cut his own flooring planks, hundreds of them, and also the solid support columns. The determination involved in doing this all on his own shows that the spirit of the Thirstland Trekkers still lives on in Shakawe!

Downstream from the lodge, the Okavango had carved a steep vertical bank which was much favoured by the Carmine Bee-eaters as a nesting site. Hundreds of Carmines, the most spectacular of the species with their bright rose-red plumage, had excavated their nests deep into the steep wall of the bank. I spent many days at this idyllic spot, seated on the overhang above, trying to sketch

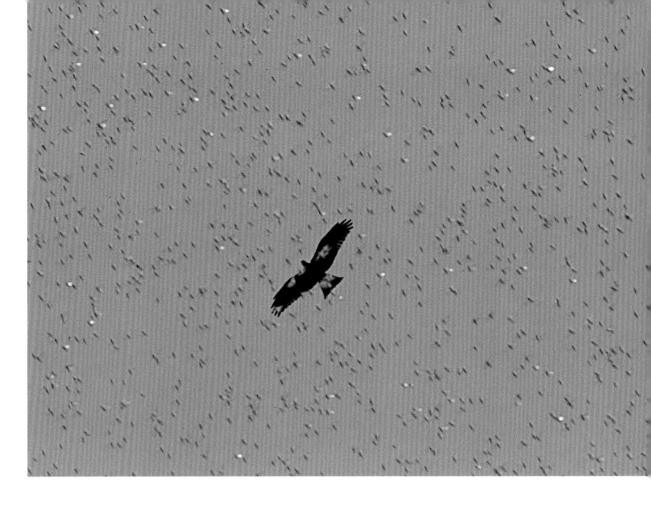

the essence of these birds in the rapid blur of their flight. They were quite content to alight on the branch on which I was perched and, as long as I kept quite still, they would soar and flutter, oblivious to my presence. Sensory overload can easily take place when enveloped by the denizens of a Carmine colony. Hundreds of red, day-glow blurs confuse the eye with the unending restless movement typical of these colonies. Simultaneously, the din of their combined calls drowns all other sounds of the bush in a melodic symphony of twittering.

In front of the campsite and below the deep shade of the riverine forest, a tiny stream hugged the narrow space between the steep banks and the sea of papyrus beyond. This stream ran crystal clear over a bed of coarse white sand and, about a hundred metres downstream of the last camping place, it formed a small secretive pool. Hemmed in by the papyrus and the forested riverbank, it was almost invisible from the single and rarely used path nearby. The perfect nature of its natural design had often roused my curiosity and every time I slid down a narrow cleft in the bank for a better look, I disturbed many secretive birds. On one such day, when I had a frustratingly short glimpse of a

One morning a strange dark 'cloud' floated over the papyrus from the north and as it approached a great whirring of small wings could be heard: a locust swarm was on its way, closely tracked by many varieties of raptors. When the swarm passed overhead, the sun was visibly darkened.

Purple Gallinule, I decided that the location was worthy of a hide. When I talked to Jan about this, he had led me to some storerooms and, after much rooting around under piles of dusty equipment, he had unearthed a collapsible hide that had been used and left behind by a German film-maker. I staggered back to the pool with my new-found toy, erected it in the shade of an overhanging bush, and then left it, intending to return the next morning before the sun was up. For the next ten days I did exactly that and, as the days passed, I was treated to a secret onlooker's views of a tiny cosmos which I had never imagined could be so vibrant and full of interest. In the first hour of that first morning, I squirmed uncomfortably in the confined space, wondering whether I would be able to stand another hour in the hide. By the third day, however, I knew all the players on this tiny stage, and long before dawn I would leap out of bed, breakfast quickly and then rush along to the hide before first light, positively relishing the idea of spending the entire day in the stuffy hide.

The first hour would always be the least interesting. Then, as the first rays of the morning sun brushed the tops of the trees, a trio of Malachite Kingfishers would dart in from somewhere upstream. Their tiny whistling call was the signal that the pool was coming alive. Two of these Malachite Kingfishers were nearly fledged offspring that were actually bigger than the adults. There would be the faint hint of tiny, whirring wings and, suddenly, with movements almost too fast for the eye to follow, three iridescent blue-coloured birds would materialize on their favourite perch. The chicks would chirp plaintively and flutter as the older bird dived off the perch. There would be a dainty splash and a second later the parent would be back on the perch with a silver fish in its bill, only to be harassed by the outsize offspring as they begged to be fed.

Even as this was going on, other birds would start to emerge from the papyrus forest on the other side of the pool. Secretive and cautious, Moorhens crept cautiously from the tangled beds. At first there would be only one daring individual, but as the minutes wore on it would be joined by another. Soon the cold, damp shoreline of the little pool was alive with the black-coloured birds as they wandered to and fro, pecking at morsels in the muddy fringe. Occasionally, they would all freeze and stare momentarily upward as a Greenbacked Heron flew in over the papyrus. Settling on a partially submerged stump,

it would extend its neck and then freeze in that position for minutes at a time as it played its patient waiting game.

By mid-morning the pool was teeming with birds. Giant Kingfishers lurked on the higher perches, while groups of twittering Pied Kingfishers would sometimes invade the quiet solitude of the shady pool with their noisy aerial ballets. Purple Gallinules, splendidly iridescent in the pools of light, moved out from the flattened vegetation on the opposite fringe, always suspicious and seemingly aware that something was not quite right on my side of the pool. Little Bitterns skulked about under the dank vegetation, never coming out into the light, behaving more like rodents than birds. Paradise Flycatchers, Woodland Kingfishers and Plumcoloured Starlings were all regular visitors to this private Garden of Eden.

As the sun rose higher, other denizens of this tiny universe began to move about. Numerous small, thin, green snakes would issue silently from the rank vegetation and criss-cross the pool all morning, endlessly patrolling its fringes. Once an ominously large, black snake slithered out of the forest and disappeared into the papyrus nearby. There were other reptiles here as well – monitor lizards. Every day these large beasts would treat me to dramatic episodes that I would have expected to experience on the open plains of the Serengeti rather than on the grassy fringe of a tiny pool. These big lizards were capable of creeping through the dense vegetation to within a metre of a Moorhen wandering about at the water's edge. Long minutes would then elapse as the bird, unaware of its presence, moved closer. Then the monitor's dark, scaly head would rise slowly from the grass, and, with its tongue flicking out, it would inch forward. After half an hour of this, during which I endured as much tension as I had watching the lions at Okaukuejo, the climax would come. There would be a violent lunge and then a splash, followed by the calls of the various birds as they flew off in panic. Occasionally, the monitor was lucky and it would waddle noisily off into the papyrus with a bird in its mouth.

Loud cracking noises in the papyrus would indicate the presence of something much larger moving around in the reeds – yet just out of sight. These were sitatunga and they would sometimes push their way through the reeds, move daintily into the open and then browse on the shrubbery along the water's edge. Much to my chagrin, it was only

Opposite
Both down and upstream of the Drotskys' camp there were numerous Carmine Bee-eater colonies.

165

Shakawe residents trapping fish with baskets in the shallows of the Okavango.

the does that would show themselves. Bushbuck, too, were frequent visitors in the late afternoon, as was a Little Banded Goshawk that would flutter down to one particular corner of the pool. Here it would sit patiently and then, extending its wings, strut the last metre to the water's edge to drink. The outspread wings, back-lit by the afternoon sun, were every bit as representative of aggression as the eagle on a Roman legionary's standard. The late afternoons was also the favourite time of vervet monkeys and baboons. The latter were never fooled by my hide, for they would sit cheekily on the surrounding branches and stare at me as though the walls of the hide were transparent. I would stare back through my little slit and communicate with them by bobbing my head up and down. Their reply was to mimic me and a frenzy of head-bobbing would follow, which I would end by thrusting my head into the open and snarling loudly. At that point the baboons usually vanished.

On the tenth morning my hide days were abruptly brought to an end! I was sitting in the hide, carefully cleaning the front element of my $5000 lens during a hiatus in the activities of the now very familiar surroundings of the pool. Insidiously, an unfamiliar noise broke through my concentration, and I found myself listening intently to a rustling of leaves above and behind me on the steep bank on which the hide was anchored. Twisting around and looking out of the slit behind me, I caught sight of an enormous black snake sliding down and into the hide. Time seemed to stand still as I launched myself forward, demolishing the hide in the process. Flinging my precious lens aside, I was aware only of a thrashing at my feet, and half a second later, or so it seemed in my frantic haste, I was some twenty metres away and on top of the bank, my heart beating wildly. Yet I looked back just in time to see a black mamba lunging away from the hide in the opposite direction – presumably just as frightened as I. Later on in the afternoon I returned and repaired the demolished hide, but somehow its claustrophobic confines seemed too much like a trap and I never used it again.

An interesting diversion from my birdwatching activities occurred halfway through our stay at Shakawe. Jan and Eileen decided to do a supply run for petrol and groceries for the camp. The nearest shop was a cooperative general store at a village called Etsha 6, just an hour's drive

back along the road to Maun. However, near Etsha was a safari camp that they were considering buying, and when I expressed an interest in going with them to Etsha, they decided to make a short detour and visit the safari camp as well. Set off the main road from Sehitwa, Etsha 6 lies about a hundred kilometres south of Shakawe. It has an unusual history in that it represents the final chapter for one group of people, the Hambukushu, one of several groups that migrated into Ngamiland in the 1750s. Originally from the Katima Mulilo area, the Hambukushu people were forced to flee to the Kwando Valley by the invading Lozi. The Lozi continued to persecute them, however, and they moved further westward to the area around Andara on the Okavango River and settled there. Between the 1850s and the 1890s Portuguese slave trading again forced many of them southward, to the Shakawe area. The most recent migration of the Hambukushu peoples who remained behind in Angola occurred in the 1970s, when the Portuguese colonial wars were at their height, and a new wave of immigrants flooded southwards across the border into Botswana where they were welcomed as refugees and settled in the vacant lands surrounding Etsha. Etsha 6 is the 'capital' of these new immigrants. What would King Ngombela have thought had he known that the Hambukushu of Katima would only find their new homeland some two hundred years after he had expelled them from the Zambezi Valley?

Like most days on safari it was an early start from the Drotskys' camp and, an hour later, as we approached Etsha, the rising sun was well up, and every hint of coolness gone. While Jan and Eileen did their shopping in the single co-operative store at Etsha, I was free to wander. The whole place reminded me very much of what Maun had looked like in the late 70s, although on a much smaller scale. The store itself was run by a Welshman, Malcolm Thomas, and his management style was renowned throughout Ngamiland for its success. Business was thriving and this was borne out by the crowds queuing up at the counters and the wildly disparate goods in his storeroom – ranging from outboard motors to saddles and camping gear. The back of Jan's Landrover soon started to fill and, when it was packed solid with supplies of soft drinks and groceries, Jan filled up the six 200-litre drums on the trailer with petrol and then we were ready to leave. The safari camp that they were considering buying, lay directly eastward of

Etsha and it was in this direction that Jan guided the now heavily laden vehicle and trailer. Taking a small, sandy track, we soon found ourselves lurching and grinding over picturesque floodplains and past islands of palm trees.

This side of the Okavango is heavily populated and the effects of cattle and goats are readily visible on the countryside. However, it still has that Okavango magic, for the scenery is that typical mix of forested islands and open molapos and watercourses. Even if man has taken it back from the wildlife, no fences or brick buildings have been erected here, and all the little villages are of traditional materials and design. The rough track we were following was very sandy and on occasion the heavily loaded Landrover shuddered and sagged. As we neared the vicinity of the camp, the countryside became greener and in the distance open patches of water could be seen. Here and there small, perfect channels of flowing water meandered across the road. Birds, too, were everywhere and some huge flocks of Meyer's Parrots flew up as we passed. Soon we were approaching the camp and as we crossed the last grass-covered plain, a herd of lechwe watched our progress suspiciously.

The camp, situated in an idyllic setting on a large lagoon, had been mothballed by the previous owners and it showed. Tents were in need of repair, walkways were clogged with leaves, and there was a general air of decay. Jan and Eileen wandered around checking this and that, talking of their plans for its renovation and all the while chatting to the caretaker. I followed in their wake, trying, unsuccessfully, to fend off the affectionate head butts of the camp's very lonely cat. After a short tour of the camp's facilities, we left on our return journey, the cab of the Landrover full of talk of their plans for the place. Jan, however, keen to see some part of the surrounding country, took a different route back. So began my education in what a grossly overloaded Landrover (pulling a trailer holding six full drums of petrol) is capable of doing.

The track chosen by Jan quickly petered out as we struck out northwards along the edge of the floodplains. As we skirted the edges of densely forested islands and avoided the wet molapos, our surroundings became gradually wetter and greener. Shortcuts over the larger islands meant threading winding paths through almost impenetrable thickets of forest, with thorny branches whipping and scraping along the doors and windows. With great aplomb,

Jan would approach open stretches of water across our path, calmly change down and slowly splash and gurgle his way across to the next dry island. The vehicle seemed to take it all in its stride, albeit with occasional patches where the engine would labour as the mud tried to halt our passage. Finally, after a couple of hours, one of these boggy stretches succeeded, and both the vehicle and its trailer sank to the level of their chassis in the soft mud. There then followed an hour of unloading the vehicles, extricating the vehicle and trailer from the mud, and then reloading them again on the drier land ahead. This was no mean task, as anyone who has ever tried to manhandle a full 200-litre drum of petrol across boggy ground will tell you. The engine of the Landrover had now begun to boil repeatedly and it was allowed to cool for a while before we set off again. Half an hour later the whole process had to be repeated, except that we now found ourselves stuck in a drift of deep, loose sand on the edge of a large village. Naturally, the inhabitants of this village turned out en masse to watch as we struggled to extricate ourselves. Again, we unloaded all the drums of petrol and rolled them up the track to firmer ground. Then we tried to free the Landrover and trailer. This deceptively simple task took an hour of work and only with the help of some of the villagers, were we able to proceed again. When we finally reached the main road to Shakawe, Jan and Eileen were mortified to find themselves out of cigarettes and with a long drive ahead of them. Jan stopped at many roadside stalls along the way before he could find one that sold cigarettes. At all the unsuccessful stops, the person behind the counter had sported a badge of sorts pinned to his shirt: a silver star set on a green ribbon.

"What are those badges?" I had asked Jan when he had received yet another shake of the head to his inquiry.

"They're Zionists. There are lots of them around here. They don't either drink or smoke and so their stalls don't sell those items!"

That night I staggered into camp, sunburnt, tired and with my feet and hands cut to ribbons – but with a fresh appreciation of yet another aspect of a day in the life of a camp manager.

By late August it was time to return to Maun. Clarissa would soon be arriving from South Africa and then we would depart on the next stage of our odyssey – exploring two little-known corners of the Okavango swamps by

Greenbacked heron P.A.

mekoro. I had good reason to be satisfied with my progress so far. Indeed, Shakawe had exceeded my wildest hopes and provided me with an excess of material for my projected bird paintings. I now had six fat sketchbooks filled with studies of skimmers, bee-eaters, kingfishers and goshawks, as well as many reference photographs. It was time to move on. Typically hospitable, Eileen seemed quite put out when I told her of our planned departure.

"But you've only been here a month", was her reply.

Back in Maun I set about organizing the next stage of our travels. What I wanted to do was two mekoro journeys through some of the last wild bits of the Okavango. I was not interested in the regular routes or areas used by virtually all the operators for their mekoro trips. Rather, I wanted to go to two specific areas in the northern, permanent swamps where I would see no one else and where there was also plenty of big game such as lion, elephant, and buffalo. I wanted to hire two mekoros with polers and, taking only the very basic camping necessities and food, to island hop in the last truly wild area of wilderness left in Botswana. I knew 'where' I wanted to go – that much was certain. The 'how' was the big question.

One evening I tentatively broached the subject with Chris. Realizing what I wanted and seeing a way to expedite some of the problems, we worked out a plan and an itinerary that would benefit from the infrastructure of Wilderness Safaris. Typically, Chris became very exuberant and soon I was being swept along on the wave of his enthusiasm as he regaled me with stories of his own trips in the areas I had mentioned. Tales of vast herds of buffalo and of close calls with hippos followed. His best story was of a lucky observation of a sitatunga kill in progress. While on a remote mekoro camping trip a few years back, he and his clients had been astounded to see a sitatunga, which they had managed to approach, suddenly be taken by a huge crocodile. After a short struggle, the sitatunga was pulled below the surface. Then, while submerged in the crystal-clear water, they could see the crocodile begin swimming with its prize in their direction, its path about to take it underneath their mekoros. Realizing this, Chris grabbed the pole from the poler and thrust it into the water and in front of the crocodile, bringing it to a halt beneath them. Through the transparent water they had a perfect view of it and of the dying sitatunga. What struck Chris most was that he had seen the open eye of the

sitatunga change from alive to dead as he watched its struggles subside. All the while a thin stream of saliva, blood and little bits of bone was issuing from the mouth of the stymied crocodile.

The next morning I went along with Chris Mac. to see Chris Kruger, the energetic and very capable general manager of all the Wilderness lodges in the delta. Always smiling and optimistic, Chris Kruger was in his office in town. Here, too, I bumped into Alistair Rankin, an affable bush type whom I had previously met when he was managing Mombo Lodge, a camp on the northern tip of Chief's Island. The office buzzed with frenetic activity. Trucks were being loaded with supplies, phones answered, radio calls taken, and guests in transit collected from the airport. In the midst of a conversation, someone would come to the door and Chris Kruger would have to rush off to sort something out. Half an hour later he would be back, thinking hard about something and apologetic for the interruptions. "Man, every day is a crisis here. Anyway, where were we?" Then someone else would come to the door and he would be off again.

Nevertheless, I somehow managed to pin down these busy people for a while, and before the morning was out, I had succeeded in organizing what I wanted to do. I would fly to Jedibe village near one of their lodges in the northern Okavango and hire polers and mekoros there for my first journey. This would take me into the area adjacent to Madinare Island in the Jau area of the permanent swamps. The second journey would be undertaken later, but it would involve hiring polers and mekoros at Tchau further down the Boro River, and spending a week travelling from island to island northwards, then over the Xo flats to the Ngabekka area, and finally to the camp at Xigera, which had just been taken over by Wilderness Safaris. Alistair, who was the moving force behind the establishment of Tchau camp, had looked with interest at the map when I told him what I wanted to do. "Hmm, that could be quite a nice trip", he said. "You must let me know how it turns out!"

Suddenly everything seemed to come together. The research notes and dotted lines that I had drawn on my detailed maps of the Okavango over the years now began to represent something more than possible future journeys. Odd snippets of information gleaned from a hundred conversations in Maun were now about to coalesce into

Painted Snipe   P. A.

Opposite
A Crested Francolin pair scavenging on the ground beneath the thick bush of the kind that fringes most Okavango islands. In these shadowy places there was always the constant movement of many different species of birds as they scratched about among fallen twigs and leaves for grubs and seeds.

Paul Augustinus

the basis of journeys that we were shortly to make.

Once back at the Wilderness plot I got to work sorting out all the equipment and supplies that I would need. Soon the lawn in front of Chris and Karen's house was littered with the equipment I planned to take. As I became stricter with myself, the pile gradually diminished in size. The journeys would have to be made using a minimum of equipment because of the restrictions of what we could carry with us in the aircraft we had chartered. Additionally, there were limits on the space available in two mekoros that had also to hold the food and bedding of the polers. Nevertheless, my final selection still seemed rather large. Yet, we were not taking mattresses or pillows. There would be no chairs or tables, and our tent was an ultra-light dome tent. Food would be our normal 'balanced diet', and there would only be enough for the seven days that each trip would last. Clothes would be limited to a couple of shorts and shirts each and a jersey and trousers for the mornings. My folding easel, four canvases (which were inconveniently large) and the necessary art materials would be bulky, but there was nothing that could be done about that. There was also a lot of photographic and video equipment, and a tripod, to say nothing of a cooler bag for the film and tape. I began to wonder whether a second plane might be needed? Examining this bulky pile of equipment and supplies, Rosemary decided that she would sit this one out in Maun, and simplify things generally.

A few days later found me waving delightedly to Clarissa as she stepped off her plane from Johannesburg. It was good to see her sunny smile again and yet I had arranged things so finely that we had little time to talk. Less than half an hour later – and once Clarissa had exchanged her business suit for khaki shorts and shirt – we were busily loading up our chartered aircraft with our food and equipment, not a little excited about the prospect of the coming days.

Journeys into the Okavango always start with a flight and this is a fitting way to get to grips with the vastness of this wonderful place. Also, it is a fine way to see with your own eyes the fault lines so instrumental in the formation of the Okavango swamps. The first few minutes of the journey takes you across the barren stretch of mopane that lies between Maun and the first patches of the Okavango wetlands. This dry bit of land is the barrier against which the marshes end, and it was created by the slightly higher

land between the Kunyere and Thamalakane faults. Indeed, this stage of the flight is where, from the wonderful vantage-point of a high-flying aircraft, you can see the faults themselves, defined by the Thamalakane River in the case of the Thamalakane fault, and the ruler-edged start of the swamps in the case of the Kunyere fault. This abrupt line, where the mopane ends, is where you come to the Okavango proper. Beyond, the green waterways and myriad islands stretch away towards every horizon. Looking downwards at the palm-covered islands as they slide past the windows, you are immediately struck by the fact that there is water everywhere. Seemingly dry fields of yellow grass reveal themselves to be waterlogged when the sun glints sharply back at you. Little cameos of wildlife scenes rush past, tantalizing in their briefness, and are replaced immediately by another and yet another. Buffalo herds lying up in the shade of the island trees, lone elephants foraging in dense papyrus beds, glimpses of sitatungas browsing the open molapos – these are the scenes that flash past.

A hundred kilometres from Maun the scenery becomes progressively wetter, the islands smaller and the lagoons larger. The open spaces of inundated reedbeds become larger and more defined. This is the region of the permanent swamp where the Okavango always has water and where the molapos are always flooded. The islands here are permanent and not temporarily isolated patches of higher ground. This is also the area where few people go and where a lot of wildlife exists in splendid isolation.

Our pilot finally reported that we were approaching Jedibe and as we descended, a tiny airstrip seemed to float into view from behind a belt of trees. Landing at this place is an experience in itself, for the strip is not only tiny, it is flanked by flooded molapos on one side and a village on the other – both only a few metres away from the runway. It is also very short and ends in a dense clump of trees. After touchdown on the bumpy surface, the pilot has to brake hard and the overall sensation is of a roller-coaster ride. This is indeed a fitting way to arrive in a place such as this. Yet, as the engine dies and relative silence reigns, you become immediately aware of the noises of the village, the nearest huts of which are close to the aircraft parking place. Grazing nearby in the flooded molapos are hordes of cattle and these have displaced the wildlife from the vicinity of the village, but both the cattle and the village

Opposite
A male sitatunga makes its leisurely way through the shallows to a dry island in the middle of a vast, flooded molapo. Although not regularly seen because of the nature of the terrain they inhabit, they are common in the Okavango.

171

are an anomaly in this remote wilderness. Only ten minutes away down the Boro River is Jedibe Lodge, and beyond lies the vastness of the northern swamps.

At Jedibe we were greeted by Alistair Rankin, whom I had met at the office in Maun when making the arrangements for the trip. A permanently cheerful individual, Alistair is of the same exuberant school of story-telling as Chris Mac. He is also of the school that regards all problems as 'no problem'.

That night we heard of Alistair's latest escapade. The meat ration for the staff at Mombo Lodge comes from Jedibe where a cow is bought from the village and slaughtered. The meat is then flown to Mombo on a specially arranged charter flight. The previous week the cow slated to be that week's ration had vanished. By the time it had been found and slaughtered, the scheduled plane had departed and the staff at Mombo had been up in arms when the promised rations had not arrived. To Alistair this was simply a case of 'no problem'. He borrowed a behemoth of a mekoro from a hunting camp at Madinare, far downstream on the Boro, loaded it with the meat and persuaded some polers to help him transport it to Mombo via water on a route that few people had ever taken – let alone in such an outsized mekoro. In a race against time, for the meat was not refrigerated, he and the polers pushed, pulled and, when the water became too shallow, carried the mekoro and its stinking load. This went on for the whole day, all the while making slow headway towards Chief's Island. Eventually, night fell and they had still not reached their destination. The success of a good story is 'all in the telling' and here Alistair excelled, with vivid descriptions of mutinies by his polers, marauding hyenas attracted by the smell of meat, ominous lion roars in the dark and other such incidents. It must be remembered that the entire area between Madinare and Mombo is lion country *par excellence* and this, too, was uppermost in their minds, especially considering their cargo! Eventually, they arrived, worn out but victorious, late that night, having finally seen the lights of the lodge in the far distance. Needless to say, the guests at both lodges were enraptured by this tale of derring-do.

The next morning after breakfast, we started stacking our equipment near the landing and here Alistair introduced us to our polers, John and Isaac – our companions for the next week. Meetings such as these are always strange encounters. John and Isaac undoubtedly looked us over, sizing us up. We shook hands, there was some polite conversation, and the mekoros were packed. The preliminaries over, we settled into the mekoros, myself with John and Clarissa with Isaac, and then set off under the envious gaze of several of the guests.

Travel by mekoro requires patience: you do not get anywhere at speed; rather, like the tortoise, you proceed slowly and deliberately. The first part of the journey was down the Boro River in the main channel and then, after a couple of hours, John crossed to the other side followed by Isaac, and we entered a small, swiftly flowing channel that meandered through a maze of densely forested islets. After an hour or so, this narrowed down to a tiny stream into which the mekoros barely fitted. There was much reversing and pushing as the bends became tighter. Now and then we would emerge into open, flooded molapos and the pace would quicken. Indeed, this was the pattern that would repeat itself in the coming days and weeks: endless pushing and negotiating of narrow, claustrophobic channels was interspersed with faster, more pleasant sections in the open molapos. Occasionally, over the tops of the swaying papyrus heads, we would get passing glimpses of densely forested islands. Lack of visibility is often the rule for the idle passenger, whose reclining position is only centimetres above the water-line, while, the poler of course, stands and sees everything and thus has a vastly different view of the surroundings.

In that first day we moved south and east of Jedibe, attempting to get as far as possible into an area which I understood was more open and the islands larger. Here, I had been told there were many buffalo and elephant as well as sitatunga. As the day passed, the reed and papyrus beds retreated, leaving us in a chain of long, winding islands separated by molapos, and narrow but unclogged streams of flowing water. From a sitting position the view opened out and soon we were slipping silently past islands that were not the dense jungles of previous hours. Rather, they were open islands covered by tall *Phoenix* and *Hyphaene* palms, as well as the occasional acacias. Every bend in the stream we were following revealed secluded white sand beaches that were fringed with short green grass – every one an idyllic camping place. The tracks and signs of big game were everywhere. Buffalo dung was particularly common, and not a square inch of dry land was unsullied

Opposite
Left: Departure by mekoro is always an exciting moment. The dugouts are packed, equipment stowed in every conceivable place, and, finally, it is time to push off and head out into a wilderness of the kind of which adventurers' dreams are made.

Right: In the northern reaches of the Jau flats Clarissa and I, together with our polers, John and Isaac, head off into a wonderland of islands inhabited by buffalo, leopard, elephant, and thousands of lechwe. This mode of travel is decidedly relaxing when crossing the open expanses of water, but hot and claustrophobic when hemmed in by the narrow channels for hours at a time.

by the tracks of those and many other animals. Lechwe herds stared as we approached and then splashed off through the water. Twice, sitatunga, from their hiding places in the patches of papyrus, barked and then bolted deeper out of sight. As the mekoros forced their way along narrow channels, Pied Kingfishers rose, protesting, from their overhanging perches, cormorants ducked below the surface and Pygmy Geese took off from the water, their fluted alarm whistles a symphony of delight for the ear. There was also the light, rhythmical splash of the poles as John and Isaac propelled us through this natural wonderland. Each splash was followed by a thrust of speed, then a few seconds of coasting, and a small splash as the pole entered the water again, to be followed by another rush of speed. And so it went all day long. At times it was hard to stay awake for the rhythm of the splashes and the rocking of the mekoro were almost hypnotic in their regularity.

In these many long hours of the first part of our journey, we got to know John and Isaac better. They relaxed, and their stiff, reserved demeanour gradually disappeared as the day wore on. The silver Judaic star that John wore on his shirt at all times identified him as a Zionist. Dapper and articulate, he could tell a good story. He was also capable of identifying every bird, as well as giving the scientific

names of many of them. Of the two, he was the older and more experienced. The opposite of John, who tended to have a rather serious side at times, Isaac sported a permanent smile and was always ready for a laugh. He had already tried to escape the limited opportunities of Jedibe village and had travelled to Gaborone in search of work. Unsuccessful in this, he had returned to look for employment in the tourist industry. In reality, this meant seasonal, back-breaking work as a poler for people such as ourselves. John, too, was obviously hopeful of eventually being more than just a poler. During the following days, whenever we rested in the shade of a dense acacia during the hottest hours, John would pull from his bag a textbook and a writing pad and work on some lessons. It was a strange thought that at one end of the mekoro was usually a person who thought he was in paradise, while at the other was somebody who had been trapped there since birth and was desperately trying to find paradise somewhere else. Such are the realities of the Okavango!

Late that afternoon John decided that we had gone far enough and we beached on the nearest island. I had no complaints about this, for I had long since given up trying to decide where would be the best place to camp. Every island we had passed during the afternoon was, without exception, a perfectly stunning camping site. And so it was with this one. As Clarissa and I stretched our legs and unloaded our equipment, John and Isaac went off and inspected the rest of the densely forested island, presumably looking to see if there were any buffalo around. Then, taking the mekoros around to a slightly different part of the shoreline, they proceeded to cut a head-high tunnel through a dense belt of palm scrub. This led to a tiny clearing, which was backed by a splendid, palm-fringed pan, and it was here that they set about clearing a place for the fire and our tent. This done, they took their own bags and made their beds right by the fire, next to the trunk of the giant fig under which we were camped.

With a fire blazing merrily away, the sun slipped slowly below the horizon. As darkness pressed in on the tiny island Clarissa and I moved ever closer to the fire. John and Isaac chattered between themselves and put a three-legged pot on the fire to cook their food. There was a momentary silence from them as we got out our two tins – and without heating them, ate the contents with one spoon. This we followed with cup after cup of tea as John told us stories about growing up in the Okavango. In the distance hippos snorted and cavorted in one of the deeper channels. Then, as the light breeze dropped, the mosquitos descended in a whining mist. Saying our goodnights we retreated to our tent, slapping at our ankles and legs, to settle in for what turned out to be an uncomfortable night of disturbed dreams.

The next morning Clarissa and I awoke to the distant sound of an elephant trumpeting. Looking out of our tent, we could see that dawn was breaking and that at last the night was over. Nursing a root-shaped depression in my chest, I staggered out of the tent and over to the fire. Here, John and Isaac were already boiling water for tea. In the coolness of the morning, the freshness of the pristine wilderness was almost a physical sensation. The life-force of the natural earth seemed to shout its presence out loud. Heuglin's Robins whistled and warbled gustily from the nearby bushes, millions of frogs sang forth from the nearby reedbeds, and in the distance hyenas whooped at the rising sun. Dewdrops trembled on every bush and blade of grass. Everything seemed fresh and new, reborn with a vitality that would soon be wilted by the midday solar blaze.

"The elephants were on the next island last night", said John as he brought some hot water over to where I was making my tea. "Did you hear them eating from the branches?"

"Nope", I replied, thinking more of the aches and pains I had developed during the night's tossing and turning on the bare earth.

There was a slight mist curling over the water, but by the time we had breakfasted, taken down the tent and packed the dugouts for departure, it had started to lift. White and tenuous, wisps of this mist obscured parts of our island refuge creating an air of mystery. Suddenly, adding to the eerie mood, a sawing, grunting call echoed through the trees. Clarissa, half into one of the mekoros, stood up. "Goodness, that's a leopard", she declared only to be silenced by John. He held his finger to his mouth and we listened again as the call echoed about the island, startlingly close.

"Is it on this island?" I asked John, but he shook his head and pointed to the island nearest to us.

As we pushed off from the island, the sun's first glint appeared on the horizon. Dew, clinging to the reeds, sparkled like a billion diamonds in its first rays. At first the

dewdrops that festooned everything were attractive to look at in their brilliance, but they quickly became a curse as we entered a belt of reeds and narrow papyrus-fringed channels. As we pushed through these, we, the passengers, were showered repeatedly with the dew as we brushed past. In a few minutes we were as wet as if we had stepped into a cold shower. We were also covered in hordes of spiders similarly displaced from the passing vegetation. At any one time there could be literally a hundred spiders of several different varieties on our legs, inside our shirts, or on the floor of the dugout. I squirmed interminably that morning, but by the end of the week I was oblivious to their presence.

During the long journey down a maze of such channels and across open molapos, I explained to John what I wanted to achieve on the trip – namely, I wanted good photographic material of sitatunga bulls and, if possible, to be in a position so that I could sketch them rapidly. Also, I wanted to see buffalo in these permanent swamp conditions and, if there was time, to do an oil sketch or two on some of the more interesting islands. I added to this that I would pay each of them twenty Pula for every male sitatunga that they got me close enough either to photograph or to sketch.

Although common on all of the larger islands, and often heard at night, a chance sighting such as this – a leopard crossing the shallow water between islands – is invariably the highlight of any Okavango journey.

Opposite
A Slaty Egret, oblivious to the proximity of our mekoros, hunts in the shallows with its characteristic technique of using half-unfurled wings to confuse or deceive its prey by shadowing the water.

By late afternoon that day we had arrived at our destination: a series of very large islands separated by narrow streams and adjacent to a complex network of papyrus beds and small, flooded molapos. Beaching on one of the islands, we threw out the equipment and, after another 'tunnel' had been cut through to a small protected clearing, made camp. Here there was a vast mahogany tree and beyond, at the centre of the island, the usual small clearing that was surrounded by dense palm scrub. By the time the tent was up, the bedding unrolled, and the art and photo equipment stored safely inside, evening was setting in fast on our picturesque location. On one side, through a small patch of acacia forest, the white salty plain at the centre of the island was starkly visible in the deepening gloom. In the other direction, beyond the beached dugouts and the narrow molapo, was another, larger island bristling with a forest of *Hyphaene* palms and elegant *Acacia tortilis* trees. Crouched by the fire, mugs of tea in our hands, both Clarissa and I were in complete agreement that this was truly paradise. We ate our usual supper, had more cups of tea, and listened to the sounds of a night-time wilderness. From every quarter hippos were snorting and grunting and a cacophony of noise came from the frogs in the reedbeds. From the centre of the island, Crowned Plovers called

plaintively to one another. Later on we retired, noticing that both John and Isaac had again made their beds very close to the fire.

At midnight an angry, deafening snort rolled through the camp like a peal of thunder. In our little dome tent, Clarissa and I sat bolt upright – instantly awake from a troubled sleep of vivid, coloured dreams. For a few panicky seconds we struggled unsuccessfully to find the torch, which had rolled away from its usual place. There was an element of slapstick comedy here as we each tussled with disparate pieces of strange equipment, I receiving an elbow-jab in the face from Clarissa, and she a bruise on the leg as I scrabbled over her to get to the door. Just then, my fingers closed on the familiar shape of the errant torch. With my heart beating fast and not a little confused, I was about to call out to John when another snort of similar volume cut me short. With the last wisps of sleepiness now gone, I knew that a hippo was in the camp and a feeling of being trapped swept over me. The desire to tear at the zip and look out to see what was happening was almost irresistible, but Clarissa's two hands gripped my arm, and although it was pitch dark, her fright communicated itself to me. Somehow I stayed put. Suddenly, there was a scuffling noise from the direction of the fire, followed by running, and someone started breathing deeply right next to the wall of our tent – on the opposite side from where the snorts had come. Time seemed to stand still in the ensuing silence, but after a few seconds there was a third explosive snort succeeded by a splintering crash as the hippo dramatically charged off through the bushes. Seconds later, a gargantuan splash in the nearby molapo indicated that the dangerous moment had passed.

Poking my head out of the doorway and shining my torch about, I could see Isaac hiding on the opposite side of our tent. What protection he had thought that our flimsy tent would afford him, heaven only knows. Grinning hugely, he moved back to the fire, and from the tree above, John's voice wafted down to me.

"Paul, are you O.K.?"

Isaac began hurriedly to pile the fire's dying embers high with new fuel as John slid down the tree. There were gales of laughter from them as they relived the incident. As we joined them by the fire, John pulled me over to where he had made his bed and showed me a trail of hippo spoor leading right up to where his blankets lay.

As we glided silently along channels of crystal-clear water that flowed strongly over white sand bottoms or beneath dense patches of riverine forest, the pristine nature of our surroundings brought only one thing to mind – the Garden of Eden.

"See this", he had said, pointing first to where his head had rested and then to the spoor imprint about twenty centimetres away. "When the hippo wakes me up, I see him leaning right over me. I leap away and then I climb that tree very fast."

There were more peals of laughter, John and Isaac almost bent double from the hilarity of the situation as they acted out and recounted what, to us, had seemed rather a startling encounter. After a while, we went back to the tent and tried to resume our sleep. At the fireside John and Isaac chattered long and loud, far into the early hours of the morning, and every now and then they would break into long bouts of almost hysterical laughter.

Dawn came too soon, and, as it was Clarissa's turn to make the tea, it was she who had to stagger blearily out of the tent. A few minutes later a steaming cup of the brew was thrust through the door.

"You know, Paul, we were really lucky last night. You've got to see what that hippo did to the bushes!"

Later I examined for myself how the huge beast had punched a perfect hippo-shaped tunnel through a thick clump of brittle palm scrub – and only a couple of metres away from our tent!

"See what I mean?" she declared, grinning hugely. "Just like in the cartoons!"

John, keen to be off in search of sitatunga, seemed to have already put the incident from his mind, but Isaac had not: as we trooped down to the mekoros, he pointed out the dinosaur-like tracks that the running hippo had left embedded deep in the mud.

That morning there was no chatter between Isaac and John as we silently glided along. The hippo was forgotten and they had their sights firmly fixed on the rewards I had offered them for choice sightings of male sitatungas. This was stealthy stuff! Sitting at water level, we could not know what was going on. After creeping along in this furtive manner for what seemed like hours, the two Nimrods suddenly became agitated and a flurry of hand signals was exchanged. Finally, John braced the dugout with his pole and whispered to me to stand up. This I did and there, a few metres away, was a beautiful male sitatunga. It was staring hard in my direction, caught in the middle of a nibble as it were – for there was a papyrus plant in its mouth. It uttered a light 'woof' and flared its nostrils. I had begun to raise my camera, but it bolted off in long,

Clarissa, John and Isaac around the fire early on in the evening that the hippo decided to rampage through our camp.

Suddenly there was a scuffling noise from the direction of the fire.

177

In search of the sitatunga one must travel by mekoro down narrow, papyrus-choked channels. Silence, patience and much time is needed, for they are skittish animals that bolt at the slightest suspicion. Disappointment is often the reward for a morning's exertion, but, when your luck is in, the sight of a magnificent male always makes the effort worthwhile.

splashing jumps, barking loudly in alarm. Behind me, John hissed in frustration and I sat down again, cursing my slowness! And so the morning passed.

During the long hot, hours of the middle of the day, we rested under shady acacias on a small jungly island. Isaac slept, John was busy writing, and Clarissa leant up against an anthill and read. How I envied her ability to relax under these circumstances. It was infuriating to me that she could appear so comfortable leaning up against an anthill, casually waving away flies, oblivious to the ants crawling across her feet, and totally engrossed in the pages of a good book.

These were the hours of the day that I disliked the most while on safari. Little happens after nine or ten in the morning and it remains that way till three in the afternoon. These are the wasted, unproductive hours when the only sensible thing to do is swat tsetse-flies and follow the shade round a tree. Usually one is so uncomfortable that work is impossible, so instead one just sits and waits, and waits . . .

My impatience soon got the better of me, however,

and I wandered off around the island with my sketchbook and found a garden of aloes which were in flower. The flowering plants of this incongruous 'garden' were alive with Bronzed Hummingbirds, all intent on the nectar held within the ruby-red blossoms. These I attempted to sketch, but the swarms of stinging tsetse-flies that settled on my legs soon relegated my efforts to that of an exercise of futile madness. The sketchpad was returned unceremoniously to my carry bag, the blank pages unsullied by my pencil.

That afternoon John was more successful and we saw three sitatunga bulls. Unfortunately, all of them spooked before I could bring my lens to bear on any of them, and we returned to the camp, tired, scratched and dirty.

The next day produced similar results, but on the day after that we were lucky. Coming round a bend in a fast-flowing channel, we were presented with the splendid view of a spectacular bull browsing the papyrus – and blissfully unaware of our presence! I got my photographs and even then it continued to feed, as we slowly drifted ever closer. Finally, when we were only metres away, it sensed something was amiss and froze, its ears swivelling this way and that. Gradually, it turned its head and when it noticed us, its reaction was instantaneous. Barking gruffly and loudly, it splashed hurriedly away into the protective depths of the papyrus.

We started back along the channels towards camp rather satisfied at the outcome of the day's proceedings. Soon after this we were negotiating a huge reedbed when John pointed out to me an island in the distance. Just visible over the tops of the reeds, the luxuriant foliage of this particular island was speckled with white dots.

"Cattle Egrets! There are buffalo over there", said John. "The egrets follow them." He put his finger to his mouth. "Quiet now!"

Searching around he found a small channel leading towards the island and, after swinging the mekoro about, he started punting along its course. As we got closer the egrets began to fly down from the trees and into the reeds. Our dugouts 'swished' along through the tiny channel, while ahead of us the distinctive bellows and bleats of buffalo grew louder. We could clearly hear the sound of large animals on the move and there was much cracking and rustling as they headed slowly towards us through the dense reeds.

Multitudes of spiders covered my legs and arms, clouds of midges hovered irritatingly about my head, and the shallow waters swirled with fingerlings and tadpoles. We were surrounded by a tangled, verdant jungle of reeds which was alive with birds, and a short distance away, a hundred, massive wild animals moved slowly by. These sensations were heightened by the feeling of vulnerability when three of them scented us. With heads held high and wet noses glistening in the sun, they fixed our position with a steely stare. Then, almost as one, they turned and splashed thunderously off through the greenery.

That evening we returned to the camp, tired and dirty as usual, but happy, and very satisfied with the day's proceedings. The next day we would have to break camp and head back to Jedibe. I had many photographs of sitatunga and my sketchbooks were full of studies of the islands. While Clarissa went down to the mekoros for a wash in the river, I worked out the arrangements for the following day with John. The plan was to travel as fast and as far as possible. Then, camping close to Jedibe, we would easily make the airstrip in time for our ten o'clock flight back to Maun.

The next day was indeed a long one. Up early, we packed quickly and spent the whole day retracing our route along the myriad waterways. The welcome cool of the evening found us camped three hours away from Jedibe and busy making preparations for yet another early departure on the following day.

Sitting around the fire that night John, Isaac and I tallied the number of male sitatungas

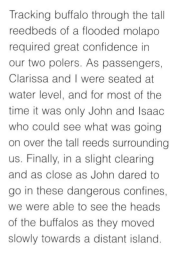
Tracking buffalo through the tall reedbeds of a flooded molapo required great confidence in our two polers. As passengers, Clarissa and I were seated at water level, and for most of the time it was only John and Isaac who could see what was going on over the tall reeds surrounding us. Finally, in a slight clearing and as close as John dared to go in these dangerous confines, we were able to see the heads of the buffalos as they moved slowly towards a distant island.

"They are crossing to another island", John hissed at me. "Do you want to go closer?"

It was the photographer in me that nodded in reply, and so we moved onwards and closer, John struggling to push the mekoro through shallow water and chest-high reeds. Behind me, Isaac followed reluctantly, muttering to himself and shaking his head. Finally, we were within twenty metres of the buffalo as they slowly negotiated the flooded reedbeds. The sensation of being enveloped by the rampant power of nature was almost a physical one.

179

that I had managed to photograph and the figure came to five, which meant a hundred Pulas each for their efforts. In a moment of weakness, I decided to pay them their bonus there and then, rather than waiting till we touched the shore at Jedibe – and I did so, much to their delight. Up till that point they had been busy cooking their evening meal and their three-legged pot was on the fire, next to our kettle. However, the pot and its contents were not touched that night. Instead, a pack of cards was produced from somewhere and for the rest of the evening their usually cheerful chatter was transformed into the muted talk of gamblers. Soon all the money lay in a pile at Isaac's feet. Flush with money, the expression on Isaac's face was exactly the opposite as that of John's thunderous visage. A little while later, however, the situation had changed: the two hundred Pulas had accumulated at John's feet and he was sporting a huge smile. And so it went, back and forth, all night long. Clarissa and I eventually fell asleep in our tent to the sound of cards being shuffled and dealt, and the groans of the loser at the end of each hand played.

When Clarissa got up to make the tea in the morning, she found them still at it, beds rolled up, and their supper untouched in the pot. We breakfasted and packed up our gear. Unfortunately, John seemed to be the current loser and, with the time of our flight looming ever closer, Clarissa and I soon realized that we would have to move things along and pack the mekoros ourselves – which we did. Even then, they seemed reluctant to call a halt to the game and it was only when we had started to break up the fire, and shovel the ashes into the nearby molapo that reason returned. John, presumably disgusted at his losses, threw down the cards, gathered up his bedding and carried it down to the mekoro, barking orders at Isaac to bring the rest of the things. Clarissa and I just smiled knowingly at one another. It seemed that Isaac had broken a cardinal rule – that of fleecing his superior at cards.

The journey back to Jedibe was a fast one, with John and Isaac poling us along hurriedly for we were late. At first our stalwart companions poled in silence, but a couple of hours later they were chattering away, the card game forgotten, and we were delivered to Jedibe with time to spare. When the plane had been packed and we were about to board, they came over, smiling broadly as usual, to shake our hands.

"If you come back again, you must ask for John", declared that stalwart.

"And Isaac also", added his fellow poler.

"I'll do that", I said truthfully, meaning every word of it. And so we parted.

After take-off, the first few minutes of the flight were over the flooded Jau terrain through which we had travelled in the previous days. Looking down at the gem-like islands, and clear streams which slipped steadily past below us, I experienced the curious sensation of being very small and insignificant: the Okavango was so vast that, in a week's travel, we had seen but a tiny, trifling corner of this pristine cosmos. There was, however, none of the sadness that usual accompanies such return flights to Maun: we were about to undertake the next stage of our Okavango exploration – a mekoro journey from Tchau to Ngabekka and Xigera, through some of the best game country left in the Okavango swamps.

The middle of August saw us in the air again. After landing at Xaxaba airfield, an hour's boat ride took us northwards along the Boro to Tchau on the edge of the Ramosanyani flats. Northwards of this is a huge area bounded by the dry land of Chief's Island to the east and the Sandveld Tongue to the west. In the centre, lie the Xo flats and the various channels of the Boro. Most of the area had been hunted until recently, but even so this is a region in which much wildlife is still to be found. This whole area is rarely visited and the scenery is amazingly varied. On the eastern side of the Xo flats there are open plains, in complete contrast to the dense, thorn thicket bush and palms of the islands in the Ngabekka region. And at Xigera, huge islands with spectacular *Hyphaene* forests abut directly against flooded scenery where the only dry land is lawn-fringed termite mounds.

At Tchau camp we transferred our equipment from the boat directly into the two awaiting mekoros and it was here that we met our two new polers, Jimmy and Olay. Again, I felt that we were being sized up by our companions of the coming week. Jimmy, slight of build, turned out to be rather a serious individual. He never laughed and only occasionally smiled, but his bushcraft was amazing, and his eyesight unbelievable. Olay was the joker of the pair and, although his English was limited, he was the chatty one. Both of them also had extraordinary

P.A.

Opposite
On cold July mornings, damp white mists blanket the channels of the Okavango, transforming them into mysterious, silent places. Every papyrus head is adorned with hundreds of dewdrops that glitter like diamonds, and among them birds flit about in the gloom. Calling loudly, a Pied Kingfisher, disturbed by the passage of our mekoro, flies on in search of another, more private, perch overlooking the channel.

stamina, for they would pole their dugouts from dawn to dusk and then become impatient when we insisted on resting for an hour on an island at midday!

We went far on that first day. Jimmy and Olay poled the mekoros hard and fast up the Boro for a while, and then struck off through the floodplains. Vastly different from the places we had been with John and Isaac in Jau, they were much more open and, instead of streams, floodwaters seemed to be moving in sheets across wide, plains-like scenery. This was not permanent swampland; rather, it was seasonally inundated and the waters of the Okavango were only now pushing in to the grasslands. Before the floods started, huge fires had raged and the *Phoenix* palms that clung to the shoreline of every termite mound were now blackened and burnt. Consequently, lechwe herds were everywhere, attracted by the green shoots that were pushing up through the shallow water.

Travel by mekoro in this type of terrain is very restful. You can see far into the distance and watch the lechwe or birdlife at your leisure. There are no reeds or papyrus stems to brush past your face and deposit a crop of spiders in your lap. There is always a cool breeze and, what with the gently rocking movement of the mekoro and the swish of the water as it gurgles past, there was the eternal problem of trying to stay awake.

By late afternoon we were approaching an island that John referred to as Makokalwan, or so its name sounded to me. In the distance a large sinuous island with splendid shade trees cut across our path, and it was on the grass-covered shore of this beautiful landfall that Jimmy and Olay beached the mekoros.

A more idyllic setting would be hard to imagine. We were in fact at the very end of a vast peninsula, surrounded by an immense floodplain of short, green and yellow grasses, interspersed with sheets of shallow water reflecting the blue of the sky. In among the trees of a tiny patch of forest we made our camp on a carpet of green lawn, which had been closely cropped by the numerous lechwe. A giant anthill dominated the centre of the island, and this Clarissa and I climbed and were then able to see herds of lechwe, zebra, some giraffes, and a lone elephant on the plains around us.

Before the sun had set, we had erected our tent and stowed the equipment inside. Once night had fallen, we were sitting by the fire 'preparing' our supper when Clarissa drew my attention to the humming noises all about us: it was mosquito time, and they descended on us in their millions. Soon the itchy effects of these busy insects were felt on our arms and legs, clouds of them enveloping us as we swatted at them constantly. Without saying a word, Jimmy nonchalantly picked up a ball of elephant dung from a neat pile at his feet. He lit one side of it from the fire, and it began to smoulder, a thick aromatic cloud

issuing forth. Then he walked over to us, set it next to Clarissa so that the smoke enveloped her, and proceeded to do the same for me. To our astonishment, the mosquitoes vanished entirely! Only then did I notice that both Jimmy and Olay had smouldering balls of dung set about them. Strangely, the smoke did not make us cough as much as one would have expected, and its aromatic smell made it far from repulsive. And that is how it would be for the following nights after sunset: Clarissa and I would simply light up balls of elephant dung like true professionals. Indeed, the first thing we looked for at a new campsite was not firewood, but elephant dung!

That night I told Jimmy that for the next couple of days I did not want to go anywhere. Rather, I would stay put and do some oil paintings of the island and its scenery. He just nodded. Later on we went to bed, but before doing so we took our boxes of food and put them into the tent. This meant that the inside of the tiny tent became rather crowded, with the supplies taking up valuable leg room.

Unlike John and Isaac, who had always bedded down in the open (and whom we had never seen using dung as an insect repellent), Jimmy and Olay slept in a small pup tent and I wondered what was the reason for this. In addition, they left their food supplies outside. Indeed, they had festooned a nearby bush with strands of raw meat and I felt compelled to ask if they were not worried about hyenas stealing their supplies?

"No problem with hyenas here", was Jimmy's reply. He was, however, very careful to tell me to keep my zips closed at night, for lions were common in the area. And how right he was – all night long, both Clarissa and I were disturbed by the calls of lions reverberating across the flats. In the early hours of the morning the calls grew very much closer, and it seemed for a while that they would pass close by or even *through* the camp! Fortunately, dawn intervened and with that the lion calls stopped. It was during the night that I realized another reason why Jimmy and Olay had left their supplies outside their pup tent. They did this for the same reason that backpackers in Alaskan grizzly-bear country stashed their food a hundred metres away: they did not want a bear – or in our case, a lion – coming into the tent after food!

My intentions were that for the first three days I would

Lechwe on an Okavango island.   P.A.

paint and sketch the camp's glorious surroundings. Field painting under these conditions is a tortuous exercise at the best of times, yet to me it is a form of homage to the great explorer-artists of Africa, artists such as Thomas Baines and Wilhelm Kuhnert. Wildlife art in the last few decades has become a genre dominated by mainly stay-at-home artists, who occasionally visit Africa – and then only for a couple of weeks as guided tourists based in lodges. Even my own long experience in the Botswana bush, spent living in wild, remote places for years at a time and actually painting for my living from a small tent, did not compare with the difficulties that Baines or Kuhnert had endured in pursuit of their art. I felt that there was a principle at stake here: I had to be able to say I had done it the real way – without four-wheel-drive vehicles or powered boats as transport.

The first day of this exercise found me preparing to paint and, as I was pulling the wrapping off one of the canvases, I began to appreciate the problems involved. The surface of the canvas had been damaged – presumably in transit in the mekoro – so that I had to spend an hour restretching another piece of undamaged canvas onto the stretcher pieces. Then, when I had chosen a suitable scene and lugged all my equipment to the spot, other irritations arose. Setting up the easel, I placed my new canvas on it, but a gust of wind promptly blew over the whole lot and when I tried to erect it again, I found that one of the easel's legs had snapped off. Another hour passed while I repaired this and, once the epoxy glue had dried, I finally managed to get started again.

With a flourish of my brush I commenced painting in the sky. As I proceeded, midges and flies began to settle on the wet paint faster than I could remove them: the cerulean blue pigment seemed to attract them like bees to honey. Halfway through the day another gust blew the easel over again, and bits of grass and dung joined the midges on the canvas.

When they had seen me set up the canvas and start painting, Jimmy and Olay came and stood right behind me. Ten minutes later, instead of leaving, they sat down, closer, and watched my every move for the rest of the day. When I was finished, the three of us simultaneously stood back to look at the results. From beneath a layer of dust, midges, dung and grass, a glistening painting had emerged. At a distance, the organic 'extras' were not obvious and the painting did not look too bad. Behind me, my faithful critics were studying it as well, and Olay finally spoke out.

"That is beautiful", he exclaimed. I was flattered, but he somewhat spoilt it by going on to ask. "Could you do that on a T-shirt?" Then, unceremoniously, another gust of wind knocked over the easel and canvas for the third time, and more organic material was added to the composition as the painting flopped face down in the grass.

The following morning my 'field art' endeavours continued apace. As if on cue, a buffalo walked past the island and for the rest of the day I worked on a small cameo scene of that moment – Jimmy and Olay continuing to be hugely entertained by my efforts. On the third day I had completed my last painting, a largish campfire scene with the moonlit flats in the background. This canvas then joined the other two where they lay outside our tent, drying, and collecting more midges!

That afternoon, following closely in Jimmy's and Olay's footsteps, we went out on a long walk. We had not gone more than a hundred metres along the peninsula when a small, drab bird started to flutter and twitter in the branches of a tree ahead of us.

"You see the honeyguide? It wants us to follow it", declared Olay.

I nodded back at him. I knew all about the bird's reputation and its supposed relationship with honey-gathering humans, but I was sceptical. The Greater Honeyguide was reputed to be able to lead humans to honey, but I had never spoken to anyone who had seen it for themselves. As far as I was concerned, it was a nice story, but a myth, and that is how I treated Olay's statement. As we walked further and further along the peninsula, however, the little bird persisted, staying a little way in front of us. When we were about a kilometre from the camp, the peninsula widened, and became fringed with dense stands of sausage and mahogany trees. There was the spoor of buffalo everywhere in the gloomy stillness of this dank forest – and yet still the honeyguide fluttered along in front of us.

Further on we came to the usual, open clearing to be found in the middle of islands such as these. Here, in the white chalky earth, we found the fresh spoor of lions.

"Last night! These were the ones we heard last night", declared Olay as he followed in their tracks.

Naturally, the honeyguide was still in front of us as we

entered the forested fringe on the other side. Something started to nibble at the back of my mind and I decided to ask Jimmy how it was that the honeyguide was always exactly in front of us.

"Because we are following it", was his matter-of-fact reply.

And on we went, getting farther and farther away from camp, the evening sun softening the harshness of the landscape with its yellow rays. Once, as we walked slowly along a bushy path, a bushbuck male flushed from almost underfoot, startling us all. Soon after that a small herd of lechwe thundered past, spooked by something unseen up ahead yet oblivious to our presence. Then the forested patch of land narrowed and petered out, and we found ourselves in another open patch of wetland. We were about to cross this when both Jimmy and Olay stopped and turned to look back along the way we had come.

"See, the honeyguide is behind us now", said Jimmy. We turned, and there indeed sat the honeyguide, twittering and fluttering its wings as it perched in a bush a few scant metres away from where we stood.

"We must go back", he continued. "We have passed the honey."

With a fair amount of scepticism, Clarissa and I followed as Jimmy and Olay retraced their steps a short

Repairs to the easel and the care of my painting equipment were executed under conditions of great inconvenience. At the same time, however, I was beginning to appreciate how the great adventurer-artists of 150 years ago, when Africa was truly a wild place, must have struggled in similar fashion.

After following the honeyguide for a considerable distance, we came upon our goal – a tree with the hive in it. Jimmy calms the bees with smoke from a ball of smouldering elephant dung.

Our reward for having followed the honeyguide: wild honey that was completely different from any that I had tasted before.

A honeyguide begs for attention. P.A

way. They then started examining the nearby trees. A minute later they had located a huge hive in a hollow tree, and at the precise moment of their discovery, the honeyguide fell silent for the first time in the two hours we had been walking.

Jimmy and Olay became very business-like and quickly collected some balls of elephant dung which were lit without further ado. They puffed away at these until clouds of the familiar aromatic smoke poured forth.

"My goodness, they're going to smoke the bees",

exclaimed Clarissa, her eyes wide at the prospect of the honey that was about to be harvested. My own scepticism lay in tatters in the face of what we had seen. Indeed, there are some things that have to be seen with your own eyes if they are to be believed, and this was one of them. Thinking hard, I could find no flaw in the sequence of events leading up to the scene in front of us. There was no doubt about it: the honeyguide had led us to the honey. The myth had become reality.

With a smoking ball of dung in his hand, Jimmy then advanced on the hive, which was conveniently within reach of a low branch. Bees buzzed angrily about his head as he thrust the smouldering dung into the hollow trunk, but within a few seconds they had calmed down. Reaching deeper inside, he pulled at something and a second later his prize came to light. In his hand was a large chunk of honeycomb, glistening in the sun. With the honey oozing between his fingers, he handed this comb to Olay, who passed him another ball of smoking dung. More smoke was blown into the hole and more honeycomb retrieved until, at last, a few minutes later, a sizeable pile lay at our feet.

When Jimmy had jumped down from the tree, we moved off to a nearby patch of grass and there we feasted on the golden honeycombs. It was quite unlike any honey I had ever tasted – there was an acrid tang to its sweetness – yet its taste fitted the surroundings, for this was wild honey and we were enjoying the privilege of tasting the very essence of the wilderness around us. This was also one of the few occasions when Jimmy actually smiled broadly. "Mmm, *very nice*", was all he had to say as he tucked in.

Finally, the time of day forced us to set off home for the sun was dropping ever lower in the sky. The bulk of the honey remained uneaten and Jimmy put most of this in a bag to take back with him, but at least one-third of what remained was left in a little pile on a nearby tree trunk. "That belongs to the honeyguide", explained Olay when I queried this. "It is payment for his work!"

The next day we packed up and set off for the Ngabekka area on the other side of the Xo flats. Little did we realize what a marathon this would be. As the attractive scenery of Makokalwan island disappeared behind us, the water became shallower – so shallow in fact that we were required to disembark and follow as the mekoros were pushed through ankle-deep water for long distances.

Then came the Xo flats. The less said about this green hell the better. For hours we toiled along, surrounded by towering *Phragmites* reeds, and slowly frying in the midday sun. Luckily for us we were used to the spiders by then, and I was unperturbed even to see them busily at work spinning their webs between my blackened feet.

Five hours on into the journey Clarissa declared that she needed to heed the call of nature. When a tiny platform of crushed reeds appeared round the next bend, she insisted that we halt. "It'll have to do."

A few minutes later, we were on our way again, and I asked Jimmy what had made the neat little floating platform.

"It's a crocodile's bed", was his laconic reply.

Our toils in this claustrophobic maze continued for another hour, and then, after turning into and retreating from several dead ends, we were finally free. The monotonous, rustling forest of *Phragmites* reeds thinned out and gradually vanished behind us. The day wore on and yet Jimmy and Olay poled effortlessly onward. Soon we found ourselves entering the Ngabekka region. Here, strongly flowing channels bisected the deep molapos and long, thin islands began to replace the smaller ones of the Xo flats. Finally, at three o'clock, as we were paddling silently along a channel between two large bodies of land, we encountered some elephants crossing over to a palm-covered islet. Putting on a burst of acceleration so that we could catch them up before they disappeared, Jimmy and Olay treated us to the exhilarating sensation of speed as we rushed headlong through the shallows. Just as the elephants reached the forest fringe, we ground to a halt on the sand. Only metres away, the elephants dallied among the palms and bushes, unaware of our close proximity.

As an individual who has seen and watched countless elephants over the last decade, I was surprised to find myself looking at these individuals as though they were the first I had ever seen. There were even goose bumps on my arms and legs. In order to cross paths with these elephants we had travelled long and far, through pristine wilderness, in a craft whose design and manufacture had not changed in a thousand years. Between my knees lay my artist's easel and, behind me, the canvases poked uncomfortably into the small of my back. I felt transported backwards in time as though in a time warp, for this was exactly how Baines would have done it. Yes, indeed – this was the real way to encounter elephant. It was a delight to sit there, silently watching those grey ghosts and realize that we were in ankle-deep water – with nothing between us and them. Then, one by one, the elephants scented us and moved rapidly off into the forest beyond.

By four o'clock we were finally looking for somewhere to camp. Jimmy and Olay were adamant that we had to find a small island surrounded by open water.

"Hai! The lions around here are bad ones", muttered Olay.

Finally, they settled on a tiny island and we grounded on its narrow shore. After eight solid hours in the mekoros, both Clarissa and I were stiff and burnt, and a cup of tea was all that we craved. A quick examination of the island, however, revealed that it was rather too claustrophobic a place for me. The forest occupied every square metre of dry ground and there was only one tiny place suitable for the tents. Worse, there would be no view of the surroundings. Much to Clarissa's disgust, I told Jimmy that I felt we could find a better, more aesthetically pleasing island nearby. Looking about, I pointed out a slightly larger one about three hundred metres away.

"Okay", shrugged Jimmy and so we climbed back into the dugouts and set off again. When we had landed on my 'selection' and walked about a bit, it became obvious that it was not an island at all, but was connected to the nearby land by a narrow causeway of grass. Frustrated, and with Clarissa glowering at me, we turned to leave.

When we were back at the mekoros and preparing to set off to another nearby prospect, Jimmy noticed something in the far distance and, calling Olay over, he pointed out several specks on the distant shore. After much discussion they turned and informed us that the specks were lions.

As soon as they saw us the lions became agitated but returned to feed at their buffalo kill. P.A.

Jimmy strode through the shallow water towards the lions.
P.A

Opposite
Elephants are found on most
of the larger islands in the
permanent swampy areas of
the Jau flats. Not so numerous
as in some areas to the north
of the Okavango, their presence
requires that caution be
exercised when walking in
the dense undergrowth of island
thickets. In those places,
unexpected and very close
encounters are always possible!

Painting with oils in the wilds:
the materials, equipment, and
conditions are no different from
those of Baines's day.

"They have a kill in the water", Jimmy informed us nonchalantly. Almost before I could stop myself, I asked them if we could get closer so that I could take some video footage. Ten minutes later we were paddling in single file across the knee-deep water towards the now-recognizable shapes of the lions. They had made a buffalo kill in the shallows, and five of them were busy on its carcass. Luckily, there was a small termite mound about thirty metres from the kill and, using this for cover, we silently covered the last hundred metres.

When we reached the anthill Jimmy and Olay scrambled out of the mekoros, beckoning us to follow them. "Very quiet now", hissed Jimmy as we crept over the top of the mound.

There, only thirty metres away, were the lions and their kill. They were very aware of us and, as their tails twitched in irritation, five pairs of eyes stared hard and menacingly in our direction. Suddenly, Jimmy and Olay dropped all attempts at stealth and waded boldly out into the water, which I was alarmed to note was only ankle deep, towards

the lions. One of the lions grunted angrily and two of the younger ones abandoned the kill, running off into the grass nearby. With a low snarl, another of the lions sat up and looked threateningly at us. In fine fettle now, Jimmy strode even further out into the open and started loudly berating the lions in his mother tongue. Olay joined him in this with gusto. There were more grunts from the lion rampant and then it settled back on the kill, determined not to bolt. Jimmy and Olay fell silent, not wishing to push our collective luck too far, for we were not hungry hunter-gatherers on the prowl for food. I knew that the Bushman of old sometimes chased off lions from their kills in order to scavenge the meat, but, as I stood there, so close to those lions in the shallow water, I gained a new insight into what it must have meant to undertake such a deed. Eventually, turning our backs on the lions, we returned to the dugouts. After marvelling at the bizarre nature of what we had just witnessed and delighted that I had managed to video most of it, I found that I was rather relieved to be retreating. Clarissa was in agreement with me as we crept back to the dugouts.

Our camp at Ngabekka on an island far from any shore. This was our second choice of a camping site that day – after our first one had been found to be already occupied by a pride of lions on a buffalo kill.

We were still in need of a campsite and so we crossed to the far side of the immense molapo and searched there for a while. Fortunately, next to a patch of reeds was a small island that exactly suited Jimmy's requirements. What a day it had been! We had slogged through shallows on foot, sat for eight hours in a dugout, seen elephants and then lions and been burnt red by the merciless sun. After all the camping things had been unloaded, our tent set up and the bedding laid out, it was two weary travellers who collapsed by the fire that evening. Of course, Jimmy and Olay were as perky as they had been at dawn. As we sat savouring our sundowner cup of tea, the two of them paddled over to the nearby shore to collect wood and the essential dollops of elephant dung. Even when the mekoros were full of these essential supplies, they dallied, walking along the shore and checking the spoor trails. Two Nimrods in their quest for game, not even the impending disappearance of the sun

seemed to dampen their enthusiasm by a single notch. As they paddled slowly back to camp, the haunting sounds of the song they were singing carried clearly across the water to our ears.

"What were you looking for over there?" I asked Olay when they had unloaded their cargo. He shrugged.

"The ground is my book. I read it to see what it tells me."

That night was the evening of the harvest moon. So, as the sun set on one side of the island, the moon rose on the other. The yellow moon ascended, full and luminous into the red, half-light of evening. Even then Mother Nature had not finished with us. As the red sky faded and the moon rose higher to become a dazzling orb in the sky, hippos emerged from the nearby patch of reeds. Slowly spreading out, they began to feed on the grass sedge of the water surrounding the island. By nine o'clock that night we could take no more, however, and staggered off to bed,

190

leaving Jimmy and Olay still watching the hippos. Even then as our heads touched the pillows, there was one final touch to the day – a lion started roaring in the distance and soon there were choruses of them roaring from every quadrant of the compass.

We camped two days on the island and went for long walks in the nearby forests. One morning we came across the fresh tracks of lions following a herd of buffalo, and for an hour we tracked this spoor, surprising a solitary hyena, which presumably had a similar goal. Only Jimmy and Olay were disappointed when the tracks eventually led into a molapo too deep for us to cross. Another afternoon we found a large herd of buffalo and watched as hundreds of them filed along a wooded peninsula. Back on the island I sketched and painted, or watched otters as they effortlessly hunted the shallows around our grassy shoreline.

On our final afternoon we went out in the mekoros and around a bend in one of the nearby streams we surprised a sitatunga out in the open. Incredibly, it watched us approach and stood transfixed as we floated towards it.

Finally, it realized what we were and bolted off through the shallows towards some nearby thickets.

Our journey was sadly coming to an end and we knew it. We savoured the last night with the gusto and intensity of a traveller who knows that his dream holiday is coming to a close. That night we watched the moon rise as if it were the last we would ever see. In the distance lions started to grunt and we listened, enraptured. Nearby, a leopard coughed loudly as it patrolled the shoreline. All around us, hippos filled the cool night air with the sound of their sonorous snorts and grunts.

All too soon, the final morning arrived, and we packed our things into the mekoro for the last time. A long journey brought us to Xigera where we said our goodbyes to Jimmy and Olay. Our plane arrived, we packed our things inside and then, all of a sudden, there was nothing more to do but go.

Later, as we flew over the green expanses of Ngabekka, Clarissa and I found ourselves looking longingly downwards at the idyllic islands passing rapidly beneath us. It had truly been a memorable adventure.

Paul Augustinus

Chapter Five

THE NORTHERN FRINGES
OF THE KALAHARI

After the excitement and adventure of the mekoro trips, the preparations for the final stage of our odyssey seemed rather tame in comparison: packing camping equipment and supplies into that organic work of art called the mekoro is infinitely more challenging and satisfying than throwing the same items into the back of a Toyota 4x4 pick-up. None the less it was time for us to be on our way, for ahead of us was game country supreme!

First we planned to head for Moremi, then up to Savuti and thereafter to the Chobe River via the Ngwezumba Valley. This would take us through a tiny part of what must be southern Africa's finest piece of sandveld wilderness – well, relative wilderness would be more accurate, for things have been changing fast here, tourism being the driving force behind many of the changes. Ngamiland and the Chobe district will, however, always retain something of the original wilderness flavour, for here the soft sands of the Kalahari will forever dictate that a four-wheel-drive vehicle is a necessary item: mass tourism of the kind that afflicts Etosha will never be possible.

The dry season was well advanced and the skies which had been so clear in the previous months were now tinged with a hazy purple. It was the season of fires, so that little black specks of soot rained continually out of the sky – the debris of bush-fires hundreds of kilometres away. In the

Opposite
Heralding the onset of the rainy season, storm clouds gather over the open plains of the Mababe flats.

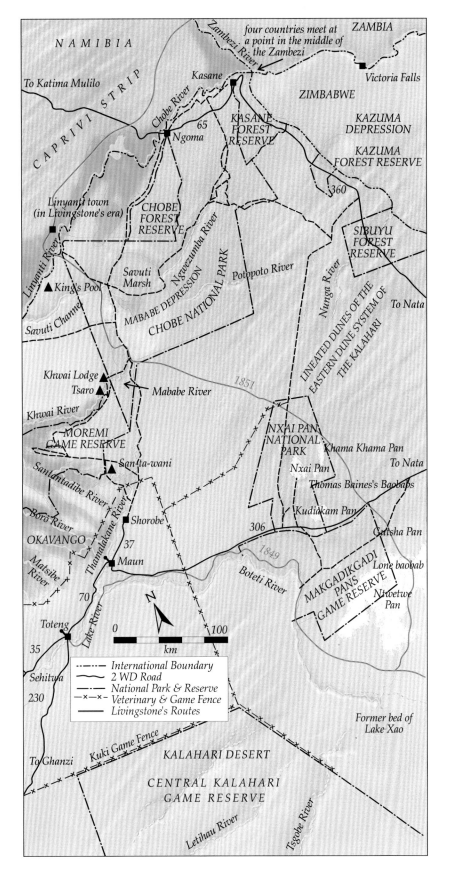

coming weeks, the dawns and sunsets would be increasingly obscured by the smoky hazes of these bush-fires. So, too, would the first short rains of the wet season soon be upon on us, for in the skies above there now appeared small, puffy clouds. Breezes stirred the hot air and occasional dust-devils swirled over the barren pastures surrounding Maun.

We were, however, camped on green lawns under deep riverine shade close to the MacIntyre house, and felt a natural reluctance to move on and out into the searing temperatures of the northern bush. Indeed, Karen had urged us to stay on longer. "What's the hurry?" she had said, making it even more difficult for us to drag ourselves away. But ahead lay very familiar country, where I had many of my finest wilderness experiences while living there in the 80s, and I was looking forward to seeing my old haunts again. If anything, this was to be a sentimental journey through old stamping grounds. Although I did not know it then, the coming stage of the journey would show me graphically how fast things can change in just a few years. "You're going to be shocked", was Chris's only comment when I voiced my suspicions about this.

The irritating problem that had afflicted our vehicle all along continued to be a mystery. When I had picked the vehicle up from the garage in Maun, it behaved impeccably (as of course it had when I had sent it in), but, although I longed to believe the latest explanation that its hidden fault was related to some wiring in the distributor, a little voice inside me whispered, "Let's see!" Now that we were about to move on, my confidence in its reliability had reached rock bottom, especially as I knew only too well the state of the roads ahead. So, just to satisfy my own curiosity, I dismantled and reassembled both the carburettor and distributor just one more time, after which there were no more excuses to detain us from leaving.

The tent was taken up from the lawn and packed away in the vehicle, along with our mattresses, sleeping-bags, tables, chairs and cooking equipment. Tools and spare parts were checked, and all my canvases from the mekoro trips were packed in their usual place on the roof-rack. These canvases were by now very bedraggled, but had dried at last, with all the insects, bits of grass and mud now permanently welded onto the surface. When I had started to pick off these bits of artistic 'jetsam' from the canvases, Rosemary had watched disapprovingly. "Leave them on", she advised. "They're the best bits, and they give the paintings a really good, authentic feel." Accordingly, the wilderness 'jetsam' stayed in place!

Meanwhile our preparations continued apace. The afternoon before our impending departure was spent buying the food and petrol that we would need for the coming six weeks. This was definitely not the chore that it had once been. There were many new supermarkets in Maun, and we wandered about one of these, slack-jawed like country yokels, marvelling at the massive selection of foodstuffs on offer! Having purchased our requirements, including several daring new variations on our 'balanced diet', we then went along to a newly opened fast-food restaurant to have a sandwich and tea. This, of all things in this most African of locales, was an American-style establishment, done out in a country and western décor. Here, we were told, was where it all happened in Maun nowadays. It was here, too, that I glimpsed, in among the hordes of khaki-clad guides and tourist parties, some familiar faces from the past. However, the people whom I had once known as one-man, happy-go-lucky safari operators, more interested in where the next party was being held, had become transformed into tourist tsars. Riding the crest of the tourism wave, they were now, one and all, tycoons, fat-cats and prosperous – the big shots! Inside the airconditioned restaurant there were many pilots, guides and staff associated with safari operations both new and old, and it soon became obvious that some things just never change – for among new and old alike, inflated egos were displayed like badges of honour.

Egos are nothing new to Ngamiland. In the past the region to the north and east of Maun has been the stage for many the epic adventures experienced by the ultimate egotists of their day – the explorers. It was the grossly inflated stories of a mythical lake called Ngami in the northern reaches of the Kalahari which fuelled the determination of the first western adventurers to explore the region. A combination of circumstance and luck ordained that Livingstone, a relative newcomer to Africa, would be the first to reach the shores of that "great lake" in 1849. Although he was accompanied by three other men (Oswell, Wilson and Murray), it was his expedition and so the 'prize' was his. The prize turned out to be rather an anticlimax, and no sooner had Livingstone arrived than he quickly found an

excuse to penetrate further northwards into the interior. His next goal was to pay a visit to a great chief, Sebitoane, who lived on the banks of the Linyanti, far to the north of Ngami.

Such restless behaviour was characteristic of this enigmatic man. David Livingstone arrived in Africa in 1841 and by 1849, he had already moved his mission station three times – each time deeper into the unexplored interior. Back in Kuruman, at the headquarters of the London Missionary Society in the northern Cape, his elders had begun to complain that he appeared to be more interested in travelling than in spreading the word of God. In the years prior to discovering Lake Ngami and becoming a famous personality back home in England, he had finally settled at Kolobeng. This would be his last mission station, and it was here that he became aware that the Boers of the Transvaal were looking enviously across the Limpopo at the land of the Bangwato. In turn they, too, were very aware of his activities among the Batawana peoples there. Accordingly, they attacked Kolobeng and Livingstone was provided with an iron-clad argument that he could take to the elders in Kuruman: his next station would have to be beyond the reach of the Boers. Naturally, this would be further on in the vast unexplored interior, and Lake Ngami became his next goal. When he finally reached the lake in August 1849, his exploits were reported widely in the newspapers and almost overnight he became a household name.

Of course, once he had reached Ngami, he could not bring himself to settle there. Instead, he found himself looking northwards yet again, and this time the 'prize' would not be a lake but a person – Chief Sebitoane of the Makololo. This great chief, whose name was spoken in hushed tones by the inhabitants of Ngamiland, lived far to the north on the Linyanti River and beyond the scope of Livingstone's 1849 expedition. So Livingstone was forced to return to Kuruman and re-equip himself for that venture.

In April 1851 he set forth from his beleaguered mission station at Kolobeng, again accompanied by his wife and their children. William Cotton Oswell, who had been with him in 1849 to Lake Ngami, would also accompany them on this journey. Oswell was, like Galton, wealthy by birth and thus freed of the need to earn his living, and as such, another of those lucky individuals from that halcyon

Moffat's church at the London Missionary Society mission station at Kuruman.
P.A.

era – the quintessential gentleman-explorer. In this man Livingstone had found a hardy and sympathetic companion and so he was invited to make the journey with them.

In complete contrast, another of the men who had been with Livingstone to Ngami was a rough trader called Wilson. This colourful character, who, for example, travelled with pet lions in his wagon and would later marry one of Lobengula's daughters, was labelled as a scoundrel by the others. He subsequently claimed that it was he who had 'discovered' Ngami, but his claims were rightly rejected by the readers of the day. When he had got wind of Livingstone's plans to go northwards to Linyanti, however, he sensed an opportunity not only to upstage Livingstone, but also to open up a new trade route as well. So he and another trader, Edwards, set off for the Linyanti at the same time. It was to be a race.

At Letlhakane Livingstone's party struck off northwards, away from the Ngami track which he had cut two years previously. Soon they encountered scenery that was radically different from anything they had experienced before – the Makgadikgadi salt-pans. This hostile place is the terminal depositary of the Okavango River. Here, after the waters have wandered through the Okavango swamps and then travelled two hundred kilometres down the Boteti River, the final, salt-laden waters spread out over a white plain almost as large as Switzerland. The origins of this vast system of salt-pans are, however, not that simple. There is ample evidence that in the past there was a lake here and that the evaporative cycles necessary for such an extensive salt deposit were enhanced by greater inflows from the Boteti and Nata rivers. What remains is a very forbidding place. There is no water or shade out on these dazzling plains, and so they have to be crossed as quickly as possible.

On 29 May the Livingstone party found itself nearing the opposite shore of the Ntwetwe salt-pan, and steered towards a huge baobab that was visible from a considerable distance. Once they were off the pan and under the shade of that baobab, they rested for a while. The broad virgin expanse of its imposing trunk was too much of a temptation for Oswell and Livingstone, who both carved their names on its bark. This idle act was the start of a tradition that would be repeated by hunters and traders in the following decades whenever they passed this place.

Ten kilometres further on they came to Gutsha Pan and halted for the night. Here, in a rocky clearing, there was a deep depression where a perennial supply of water formed two muddy 'seeps'. Wildlife was plentiful and there was a small Bushman community that lived nearby. Gutsha Pan provided food for their dinner table: they set poisoned stakes near the water's edge to trap the animals as they came in to drink. After the waterless tracts of the Ntwetwe salt-pan, this was a very attractive place. Blessed with shade trees and fringed by tall date-palms, it was the first supply of fresh water that the salt-encrusted travellers encountered after the dazzling salty flats. Naturally, it would become a popular stopping place for the travellers, hunters and traders that followed in Livingstone's footsteps in the coming decades. Close by the pan there was another giant baobab and here, too, that same passing parade would leave names and dates carved deep in its skin.

Beyond Gutsha Pan Oswell and Livingstone had their first taste of the waterless desert that lay between them and the Linyanti swamps. Unwittingly, they had chosen the wrong year for their journey as the whole region was in the grip of a severe drought, so that the waterholes on which their lives would depend were dry. After some days of travel during which a road had to be cut for the wagons, the party found itself with too little water to turn back and

Gutsha Pan, where the first water is to be found after crossing Ntwetwe Pan at its narrowest point, was a favourite stopping point for all the early travellers including Livingstone. Many of them, such as the Green party in 1858, carved their names in the large baobab tree next to the pan during their sojourn at this place. A cross and the date 1859 were also carved on this by one of the members of the Helmore/Price expedition.

Opposite
It is here, on the flat expanses of the Makgadikgadi salt-pans, that the final drops of water from the Okavango are evaporated by the sun and the salts held in solution crystallized out. This is a harsh environment, inhabited only by ostrich, gemsbok and springbok, and one avoided by the early travellers because of its treacherous surface.

no idea of what lay ahead. Providentially, on 7 June, they came to a small chain of pans which still contained a little rainwater. Beyond this their guide, Shobo, began to lead them in circles, seemingly unable to hold a certain course to the north. On the 9th Livingstone wrote: "Shobo wandered and as he followed the paths made by the elephants in passing from one clump of Mohono bush to another, our course was zigzag enough. . . . Not a bird or insect could be seen during three dreary days. As far as the eye could reach it was a vast plain of low thorny scrub. It was perfectly still. On the third day a bird chirped in a bush and the dog began to bark at it."

Two days after leaving the rainwater pans, Shobo vanished and the party was left to its own devices, pushing onwards through the bush in the direction that their erstwhile guide had last been seen. On the morning of the fourth day their supplies of water were finished, but they came upon a game trail with fresh spoor on its path and here the oxen were unyoked. Instinctively, the oxen disappeared, followed by some of their men, in a westerly direction towards the Khwai River. That night the Livingstones were tormented by the thirsty cries of their children, and it was only on the afternoon of the fifth day that some of their men returned with supplies of water from the far-off Khwai.

The next day, once the cattle had been brought back, they set off and presently joined up with the Khwai River at the place where it emptied itself into a "dismal swamp" sixteen kilometres long. They were not to know it then, but they were on the periphery of the Mababe Depression, that vast relic of a vanished lake that had once been more than eighty kilometres long. Fed by both the Linyanti and the Okavango systems, the waters of the Savuti and Khwai rivers have within recent history flooded this basin to the point where mekoro travel was possible from one side to the other. So much so, that in the 1700s, this was one of the routes that the Bayei travelled by mekoro from the Katima Mulilo area on the Zambezi to settle near the Thamalakane River – and thereby introduced the dugout to Ngamiland in the process. Oswell was a diligent map-maker, and on his field map he noted: "Sonta [the Savuti channel] and Mababi [the Khwai River] said to meet in the rains and allow of canoe navigation from one to the other." Even at that stage, however, the process of climatic change that was starving the Mababe was well advanced: the lake-bed had already become a grassy fertile plain abounding with herds of big game. The only remnants of its previous extent were the two swamps at the end of the Khwai and Savuti.

At the Khwai River they came upon a small Bayei village (close to present-day Kudumane), known as Chombo's village, where they were astounded to find Shobo. Even though he was unrepentant for his treacherous deed, Livingstone rehired him and they set off northwards, eventually crossing the Savuti and reaching the Linyanti a few kilometres upstream from the town where Sebitoane, the chief of the Makololo, was waiting to meet them.

In the coming weeks Sebitoane was to ask them, "Have you smoke that sounds in your country?" This was their first hint of a vast cataract on a much larger river that lay within a few days' riding time to the east of Linyanti. The local people did not approach the cataracts, which they had named as Mosi-oa-tunya, literally meaning "The smoke rises", a descriptive term for the towering plume of mist that constantly hangs over the cataract. Since Livingstone's time the name has been incorrectly interpreted to mean "The smoke that thunders".

Two weeks after their arrival, Sebitoane died of pneumonia, and Livingstone's plans to start a mission station among the Makololo seemed set to falter. However, Sebitoane's successor and daughter, Mamochisane, told them that they would be treated as if Sebitoane were alive, so Livingstone was able to continue with his plans. Nearly four weeks later Livingstone and Oswell set off eastward on horseback in search of a less swampy and more healthy site for the proposed mission. It was on that journey that they became the first westerners to lay eyes on the upper Zambezi River. That moment was indeed to be the high point of their journey.

When they returned to the wagons on the Linyanti River they discovered that Wilson and Edwards had belatedly arrived. Satisfied with what they had achieved, they decided to return to Kuruman, for Mary Livingstone was seven months pregnant and the time of her confinement was approaching.

It would be another two years before Livingstone returned to the Linyanti. But when, in 1853, he did return,

he left the wagons under the protection of the new chief, Sekeletu, and travelled on foot to Luanda on the west coast. Six months later, after much hardship and illness, he arrived there a broken man, and it was only at the close of 1854, when he had recovered his strength, that he would retrace his steps to Linyanti. Even then Livingstone could not rest, and he decided that he would follow the Zambezi's course to the Indian Ocean. As a consequence of this, in mid-November 1855, he became the first European to see the cataract which he named the Victoria Falls.

After Livingstone's first journey to the Linyanti in 1851, others soon followed. In 1853 the hunter/trader James Chapman made the same journey, noting in his journals that, because of a meeting he had arranged with the headman of Linyanti town, he "was prevented from visiting the large waterfall of which the natives say the spray makes a large cloud like smoke which can be seen for many miles". If that meeting had not detained him, it

On the fringe of Sua Pan, in the Makgadikgadi, there is an enigmatic and mysterious island of granite that is covered with ancient, gnarled baobabs and the ruins of a people that have long since vanished. The island of Kubu is noted for its remote location, surrounded as it is on three sides by a salt plain that stretches beyond the limits of the horizon.

O.A.

A Bushbuck near the
Victoria Falls.

would have
been Chapman
who would have
been the discoverer of
the spectacular cataract,
and we would now perhaps
know it by another name!
Such are the circumstances on
which history pivots. Then, in
1859, there was the hapless
Helmore/Price missionary expedition,
which disintegrated as much because of bad
luck, illness, and treachery as for Livingstone's
failure to arrive at the crucial moment. Because of
this, it ended in tragedy on the banks of the Linyanti.
Years later the rumours and scandal resulting from this
final disastrous episode in Livingstone's association with
the region were still circulating in the Cape.

By the close of the 1850s the area we now know as
northern Botswana was well in place on the map of Africa.
The last lines had been drawn in on the blank areas and
the madcap days of exploration were nearly over. But not
quite! There were still some other men with big egos
waiting in the wings to make a name for themselves.

One more prize remained, and in 1861 this was
captured by Andersson when he became the first to reach
Ngamiland from the west coast. After this, Livingstone
moved on to other places in Africa. The interest of the
European public, which had avidly devoured accounts of
exploration in Ngamiland, was on the wane and it was
soon forgotten. The region would become a backwater in
the coming colonial era and was destined to remain so
until the end of the 1950s, when the wilderness of the
northern Kalahari would be 'rediscovered' by a new breed
of modern traveller. These new travellers would not be
motivated by God, ivory or trading. Instead, they were
driven by the simple desire to enjoy the unspoilt wilderness
that was to be found there.

The first of these 'lifestyle' adventurers were the Kays.
In 1957, Robert and June Kay arrived in Ngamiland in
their DUKW, a Second World War amphibious landing
craft ideally suited to exploring the Okavango. For the
next few years they roamed about the Delta, and like the
explorers of the previous century, June Kay wrote of their
adventures in her book *Okavango*. This evocative narrative
sparked an interest in a new segment of South African
society that had emerged in the years following the Second
World War. In the post-war boom, people had the money
to buy four-wheel-drive vehicles purely for recreational
use, and the time to use those vehicles on camping
holidays in the 'wilds'. Small numbers of these people
started making the journey, and soon the names
'Okavango' and 'Chobe' were not just places on the map –
they became words that suggested the ultimate in
wilderness experiences.

When Moremi was proclaimed a wildlife reserve in
1963, this marked the dawn of modern tourism in
Botswana. Throughout the following decades, however,
Moremi would remain a place where heavy sand and
flooded roads ensured that it could be accessed only by
those lucky enough to own fully equipped Landrovers.
Beyond Maun, there was nothing – no shops, petrol
stations, or help in the event of a breakdown. Even as late
as the mid 1980s there was a six-hour slog through heavy
drifts of sand to the Maqwee or South Gate and another
few hours of driving to get to Third Bridge or Xakanaxa.

Beyond Moremi, in the Mababe Depression, lay the
Savuti Marsh. Here the Savuti channel had been flowing
strongly since 1957, and the flooded marsh attracted vast
herds of animals during the dry season. This, too, was
'discovered' by these new travellers and it soon became the
logical extension of a visit to Moremi to continue on to
Savuti via the track from Cotsorogha Pan. Beyond Savuti
were the attractions of the Chobe River and the Victoria
Falls. Naturally, the itinerary extended to these places as
well, so that the route from Maun via Moremi and Savuti

to the Chobe River became the chosen path for those early tourists. Today, the circuit is almost exactly the same and has become the basis of Botswana's tourist industry. Amazingly, although rivers and swamps have dried up and great changes in wildlife distribution have taken place within the last two decades, the basic 'essence' that those early travellers enjoyed has survived to this very day.

After Chris and Karen had waved us off and the gate of their property swung shut behind us, I turned left onto the road (now tarred) towards Shorobe village. Half an hour later we were past the village and the tar road ended, only to be replaced by a fine graded track, "Ah, indeed, how things change", I thought to myself as we sped onwards over the splendidly smooth surface.

Soon we were approaching the locality of the old tsetse-fly chamber, a notorious landmark on the old sandy track where vehicles (including the occupants) were doused with insecticide. There now remained only the foundations of this 'gas chamber' in which every traveller of the past two decades had suffered in darkness as an official, inexplicably chanting "One two, one two, one two", proceeded to spray you with some lethal concoction. Extraordinarily, some people have fond memories of this place – regarding it as one of the 'rites of passage'. Presumably it signalled that their long journey was nearly over. In those days, the journey thus far would have taken a couple of hours. There would have been interminable drifts of soft sand and stops to cool down overheating engines. Yet, here we were, travelling smoothly down a graded road at ninety kilometres an hour. Stupidly, something deep down inside me resented the ease at which we were proceeding.

At the site of the old fly chamber, I turned off the graded road and onto the San-ta-wani track. Here, nothing had changed and the winding, little-used track took us through the mopane scrub to the buffalo fence and a gate where a bored veterinary official did his best to wheedle cigarettes out of us. He did not believe that there were no smokers amongst us and examined the vehicle suspiciously, reminding me as he did so of his 'twin' brother on the veterinary gate near Palmwag.

Beyond the gate, we were finally in game country. The track, now degenerating into deep sandy ruts, was flanked by idyllic acacia forests. Signs of animals were abundant.

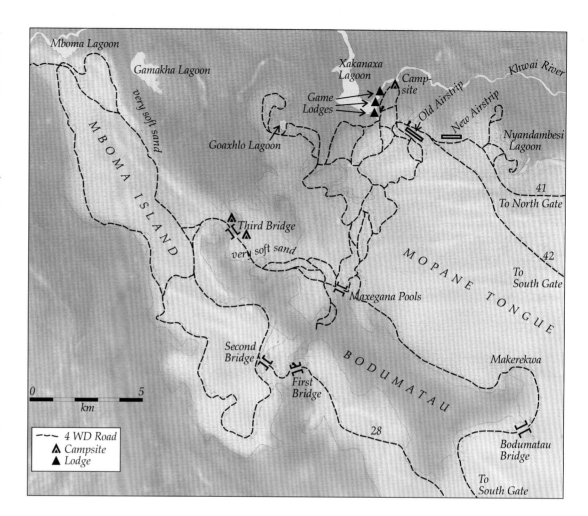

Big dollops of elephant and buffalo dung scattered the route, and the spoor of game had already obliterated the tracks of the last vehicle to pass this way. Trees lay across the road. After an hour, the open molapos of the Maqwee floodplains came into view. In the early eighties this place had been one of my favourite haunts. It was outside the confines of Moremi and thus beyond its rules and regulations. Instead, there was the freedom to camp where you liked and do whatever you wanted.

In the San-ta-wani area the branching channels of the Maqwee River used to penetrate far into the *Acacia tortilis* forests so characteristic of this region. These streams formed wide floodplains of short grass where plains game and lechwe abounded. Prides of lion and wild dogs were also common. Only one safari operator had a small tented camp here, but if the locality of their camp were avoided, it was possible to enjoy an African experience unsullied by the paternal grip of the uniformed bureaucrats. All of the locals from Maun knew of this place and yet it was a rare thing to find anyone else camped there.

As we proceeded down that familiar track and were nearing our destination, I eagerly began to look for the turn-off onto the floodplains, but the green plains failed to materialize, and before I knew it, I had arrived at a deep ditch – the sad relic of a once-flowing river. For a moment or two I was completely flummoxed. Then, seeing the burnt remains of an old pole bridge, I knew where I was. The sad, dry thing in front of us was the Maqwee, a river that I had only ever known as a beautiful, lily-covered waterway. Backtracking, I followed a faint track out onto a weed-choked plain and there I began to see some familiar landmarks. The landscape had undergone a vast change when the water had abandoned the district. Places that I remembered as green plains dotted with animals and laced by clear steams of flowing water, were now a thing of the past. Instead, there remained only hot, open areas of tall, coarse grasses and weeds. Where once there had been lagoons, there were now barren pans, and the streams that had connected these pans were just shallow ditches. Of the wildlife, there was little, but whereas in the past I had never seen a single elephant at San-ta-wani, there were now signs that they were common in the area: every acacia tree and bush showed the diligent attentions of these animals. Wide game paths, all liberally dotted with dung, cut westwards through the area towards the far-off, but still moist areas of the Chitabe region. It was in this direction that we headed once I had had my fill of marvelling at nature's fickle ways. Across the dry bed of the Maqwee we went and along a track through the woodland and towards the Gomoti River floodplain.

This terrain and the track crossing it are the stuff that off-road fanatics crave – meaning, of course, that it was a hellish route. So much so that the seesaw motions of the vehicle where the grey sand was at its softest, proved too much for one of our springs. The vehicle bounced like an unbroken stallion, swaying wildly, and, as Rosemary shouted a protest from the back, there was a violent lurch followed by an ominous crack from the undercarriage. The vehicle sagged to a halt in the middle of the sand drift. Rosemary and Clarissa retreated quickly from the oven-like atmosphere of cab and canopy to the scant shade of a nearby acacia tree while I squirmed my way underneath the vehicle. The flies descended in hordes and, as the sand

trickled into my shirt and trousers, I set about the long process of replacing the broken leaf-spring. Two hours later I was covered in sand and grease, my hands were cut, my head bruised, and I was in a fine rage, for one of the shackle bolts had refused to budge. Knowing the signs all too well, Clarissa and Rosemary kept well away. However, when a cup of tea was thrust wordlessly under the car to where I lay in an exhausted huddle, things seemed to take a turn for the better. An hour later I lowered the high-lift jack and our vehicle was ready to move on, a new leaf successfully installed in place on the spring assembly.

That night we camped on the bed of a recently dried-out river. We should have known better, however, when we saw that the white sand was heavily dotted with elephant spoor. As a result, we were disturbed by the constant passage of elephant along this natural game path and rudely awakened by their startled trumpeting when they winded us. Truly elephants had come to the San-ta-wani!

The next day we returned along the same road and, finding the cut-line of the Moremi boundary, we travelled northwards until we joined the regular track to the Maqwee Gate of Moremi. It was interesting to see that elephants had also made their mark on the rough track of the cut-line: their handiwork lay across the road in many places. Several times we had to slow down and carefully pass large herds that were browsing on either side of the tracks. Even more amazing was the fact that they were as relaxed and as docile as a herd that might be encountered on the banks of the Chobe River. This was a revelation! Indeed, I had long known that elephants were flourishing in the northern reaches of Botswana, but it was a strange thing to see so many of them in a place where for years I had never encountered even one of them.

Once we were through Moremi's entrance gate, we were back in familiar territory. The roads were still as bad as they had been in the past, with long stretches of soft, treacherous sand and the occasional patches of track which were flooded. Herein lies one of the ironies of the 'new' Moremi. This is a National Park that cannot be visited unless you own a four-wheel-drive vehicle – the sandy, flooded tracks dictate that requirement – and yet, in my opinion, rules inappropriate to the type of visitor that comes here are now being applied to the place. One of the most inappropriate of these states that you are no longer allowed to get out of your vehicle. This would seem

On the edge of a broad floodplain in the San-ta-wani area of the Okavango, three kudu males head back to the acacia forests after drinking. The San-ta-wani area has dried out almost completely in the last decade. Where once there were green floodplains, flowing channels and deep lagoons, there are now only dry plains and sandy ditches.

ludicrous in view of the fact that the kind of people who come here in their own vehicles are those who are well able to look after themselves, as they did in the past. So, what has suddenly changed so much to warrant these unnecessary restrictions? Is it that the tiny element of risk involved in visiting these areas is undesirable to the rule-makers and must be eliminated? This is exactly the same as saying that climbing Everest is dangerous, so it should not be allowed. Surely it would be better to try and retain the adventurous atmosphere of the place? People should at least be allowed to alight from their vehicles when no animals are in sight.

This is not to say that all rules are unnecessary: no one would disagree that there should be limitations on driving after dark, indiscriminate off-road driving, or collecting firewood. Ecosystems do need to be protected from disturbance to some extent, but Moremi has long put up with the minor disturbances inflicted on it by visitors. Perhaps Botswana's hard-pressed National Parks staff might concentrate on the infinitely more disturbing events taking place adjacent to Moremi. They have already performed some conservation miracles when compared with the rest of the developing world. Nevertheless, it is well known that Botswana has lost seventy-five per cent of its wildlife in the last decade alone, but none of this can be attributable to non-hunting tourists. Surely the authorities should rather focus on curtailing the excesses of some safari-hunting companies, who, despite their protests to the contrary, have been guilty of many short-sighted deeds in the areas in which they operate. So, too, should they get tough with the citizen hunters, who have been guilty of massive abuse of their traditional rights. In Botswana, a local hunter with a licence for one buffalo will often, instead, over the season, kill dozens on that same licence because he knows that he will get away with it. Because of this, buffalo numbers have declined dramatically everywhere. On the edges of Moremi, where narrow streams form the boundaries, all of the big, maned lions have been shot. There is hardly anywhere in Botswana where the social structure of every lion pride has not been regularly destroyed by this selective elimination of the large males. Most of the boundary rivers are no barrier to the movements of lions (or for that matter, any other animal): in some places a metre of water is all that dictates their fate.

In the case of wild dogs, the visitor who tries to get a closer view of them, does not threaten their future by an occasional bit of off-road driving. The wild dogs are threatened instead by the stock-keepers of adjacent areas into which they invariably wander on their wide-ranging travels. Here, animals which are as rare as the black rhino are shot as vermin, or die of canine distemper from contact with the domestic dogs of the villages. Even within the reserve they are threatened by the very people who claim to be looking after their best interests – the ubiquitous scientists. Wild dogs have their last bastion in Botswana. It is here that they are seen regularly and because of that they have attracted the attention of scientists, who have darted and collared individuals in as many of the packs as they can find. This involves handling the dogs, and there is evidence that this 'handling' by the scientists might be as dangerous to a wild dog as a bullet from an irate stock-keeper. This is possibly borne out by the demise of several packs of wild dogs that were being studied in the Serengeti, allegedly following handling, radio-collaring and inoculation against rabies. Yet, in areas close to the study areas and where Masai pastoralists occurred, packs of unhandled dogs continued to survive.

All of these are, however, but a tiny fraction of the looming problems and far beyond the capacity of a nature lover to change, even of one who feels passionately about the survival of Africa's wildlife and wild places. Like the flies and midges that hover infuriatingly before your eyes, they are just unsettling facts of life that have to be tolerated. Indeed, nature itself comes to the rescue here with its benign beauty which helps one to forget. Gloomy, rebellious thoughts are overcome by the charm of the floodplains and forests, and the deeper one goes into the forests, the harder it becomes to accept that change can ever take place in what appears to be a timeless landscape.

Like the rest of the Okavango, Moremi is an amazingly varied area. Although made up of the same basic palette of trees and sand and water, each part of Moremi has its own unique look. There are the splendidly shady mopane forests of the Khwai River, the lake complexes at Xakanaxa, the acacia and palm forests of Mboma and Chief's Island, and the striking island and pan scenery in the region surrounding the campsite at Third Bridge. It was to this latter spot that we first headed.

Third Bridge is the most popular camping site in

P A.

Little egret

Paul Augustinus

On moonlit nights, lions often use
Third Bridge to cross over
to Mboma island.   P.A.

Moremi and has been for a long time. Indeed, in the 70s when the number of visitors was but a trickle compared with that of today, this was always a crowded place. Two islands are separated by a fast-flowing stream but joined by a pole bridge. The water flows clear and cold over pure white sand – definitely a pleasant place in which to immerse yourself during the midday hours. In fact, this is the main reason for staying at this site, for the tracks hereabouts are truly atrocious, and drives tend to be more memorable for the deafening scream of protesting gearboxes and engines than for sightings of the abundant wildlife. Yet most people steadfastly love Third Bridge because of the delicious swims they can have there – in spite of the specific ban now imposed by the bureaucrats on such 'dangerous' activities.

A few hours after leaving the gate at Maqwee we were near the top of Mboma Island and approaching this 'hallowed' place. Soon we were crossing the last, bare earth plain, and the strip of riverine trees where Third Bridge lay could be seen in the distance. Incredibly, as we passed a small sign heralding our arrival at the campsite, a leopard bolted across the track in front of the vehicle and was gone almost before we had realized what it was. Recovering our composure after this encounter, we moved on. A little further on, past a group of tents, there was a bend in the track and the bridge came into view.

The pole bridges found in these parts are one of the characteristic features of Moremi, and, indeed, of the whole Okavango. Constructed from mopane poles and lashed together with wire, they are, like the mekoro, strikingly aesthetic objects. They rattle mightily as you cross them, the poles creaking and groaning alarmingly as they take the weight of the vehicle. Because they are constructed without plans, there is nothing consistent about them; rather, they take on sculptural forms. Of course, the sandy-bottomed stream that Third Bridge crosses is the great attraction. Consequently, the bridge was covered in the usual crop of scantily clad sun-worshippers, who, because of the narrowness of the bridge, were all obliged to give way to me as I bumped and rattled my way across the length of its span. As I inched past, the disgruntled patrons, some of them barebreasted, seemed reluctant to move.

Once off the bridge, the road continues through the last remaining portion of the campsite (which straddles both

sides of the bridge). Here other 'patrons' of this scenic locale could be seen idly walking and sitting among the tents – the notorious Third Bridge baboons! These baboons are known far and wide for their camp-raiding tactics, and it is the foolish camper who does not leave someone behind to look after their site when they go out for a drive. Stories of these baboons and their exploits abound and each camper usually comes away from this place with one of their very own.

The bridge is also regarded as a convenient and dry crossing point between islands by the lions of the area and the nights are enlivened by their roars as they approach, cross and depart. These lions are very bold and it is not unusual for campers sitting by their fire to notice them stride stealthily past along the track which threads through the campsite – often only metres away from where they sit by their fires!

The campsite seemed rather full, and so we all agreed that it would be more pleasant and less crowded at the campsite at Xakanaxa lagoon. This spot, about an hour's drive along attractive floodplains and island scenery from Third Bridge, is also in some of the best game country to be found in Moremi. So, pressing on past the last tent, we set off again and reached Xakanaxa as the evening set in.

Xakanaxa was, and still is, the most peaceful of the Moremi campsites, but, as we drove through the forested fringe next to the lagoon, some changes became apparent. Where there had once been only a small tented camp, there was now a complex of four lodges and a small roadside shop, while the approach to the campsite was heralded by various 'No entry' and 'Private' signs, as well as advertisements for boat and canoe hire. Nevertheless, Xakanaxa is still an attractive place, and the rambling lodges and their infrastructures did not seem overly intrusive in the context of those dense forests. One of its finer points, which makes it such a pleasant place to camp, is that it has a few grassy patches and abundant leafy shade. An added attraction is the view. Beyond the narrow ring of dry land on which the camp is situated, the flooded reedbeds of the Khwai stretch off to the north. Far away, over waving reeds, the hazy forests of the opposite shore are just visible. In the background the musical grunts of hippos are a constant lullaby, and, together with the many bird calls emanating from the watery domain beyond, there is a sense that one is on the doorstep of abundant life.

The campsite was much as I remembered it and so, naturally, we camped under the same tree I had chosen on my first time here in 1978. It was under that very same tree that I had sold the first painting of my career as a wildlife artist – so this was no ordinary spot for me. The painting, a watercolour of a group of zebras on a plain, is still vividly etched in my memory, as is the person who bought it from me for $50. Of course, this brought out a veritable flood of reminiscences from Rosemary, who was there at the time. Later, after our usual tea-time ritual, Clarissa and I put up the tent in exactly the same position under the tree, framed by low overhanging branches that were exactly as I remembered then. The nail that I had hammered into the tree fourteen years previously was also still there.

Over the next few days game drives revealed other more interesting changes, however. After staying at Xakanaxa for two months in 1978, I had decided that I was not impressed with Moremi, or rather that portion of it. There seemed to be no wildlife there, and so I moved on to Savuti, and eventually to the fantastic game-country of the Ngwezumba Valley. In the intervening years I had only passed quickly through Moremi, en route from San-ta-wani to other, more interesting places. During that first stay, the wooded country west of Xakanaxa had been rather empty of wildlife and not particularly exciting to look at. We saw no cheetah, wild dog or leopards, and only once during the two months saw elephants. That is no longer the case. The subtle forces that have wreaked such startling changes on the face of the Okavango had also been hard at work here. Whereas previously, there had been only one large and attractive lake, there were now dozens of them! These were linked by tiny streams of water that flowed through the forests like irrigation furrows. In other places game paths had been appropriated by the Okavango's tides and now flowed strongly with crystal-clear water. Large, dry plains had been transformed into deeply flooded molapos in the form of lily-covered lagoons. Moreover, big game abounded where once there was little in evidence.

Zebra herds grazed peacefully on the lake-shore fringes. Enveloped mysteriously in dust clouds, massive buffalo herds flowed through the mopane forests. Lechwe, giraffe, wildebeest and impala were amazingly abundant. Every day that we spent at Xakanaxa we saw packs of wild dogs hunting through the molapos. On the best of these days we would also see lion, leopard, cheetah, and a serval – and all

above – Wild dogs hunting through the campsite at North Gate.

left – The notorious thieving baboons found at Third Bridge

below – The flooded glades in the forests near Xakanaxa are home to many lechwe.

before lunch! The serval sighting was something new to me, for in fifteen years I had never seen one of these animals hunting through the grass as we did that day. The serval, which I had spotted only by following the gaze of an obviously agitated lechwe, was totally oblivious to our presence. It proceeded to hunt through the grass in its characteristic way, its two huge ears, like miniature dish-antennae, curved downwards to pick up any sounds in the undergrowth. Then, when it had located its prey, usually a mouse, it would leap, stiff-legged, over the intervening grass and land on its unsuspecting victim. After it had done this three times, it sat down at the water's edge and began to lick its paws as a cat would on the hearth in front of a roaring fire.

After a week at Xakanaxa we drove east along the Khwai to the campsite at the northern entrance to the reserve. Here, next to the pole bridge, is the most recent of Moremi's campsites. On the other side of the Khwai,

which is much diminished in size at this point, there is also a sizeable village, which has grown considerably in recent years. To camp here is to feel as though you are camped within the village itself: the shouted conversations of the inhabitants and the braying of donkeys are as much a backdrop to this place as is the roaring of lions. Alas, there are also other, more unnatural sounds – the din of a radio at full volume, or the monotonous beat of the same record being played over and over again. Yet none of this is too upsetting, and seems to me to be just another part of the African experience.

The Khwai River floodplains are also a good place to see leopards, and their sawing grunts can regularly be heard in the vicinity of the campsite. For those with the will to rouse themselves in the dead of night when one calls nearby, there is invariably the reward of watching a leopard walk past, its eyes burning yellow in the torchlight's beam. The same applies to lions: often under cover of night they

pad through the camp and cross over the bridge to the other side.

If Xakanaxa had changed and become wetter, so, too, had the Khwai floodplains, especially along the portion of the river that winds away in the direction of the Mababe Depression. Here, east of the Mochaba lagoon, the river was deeper and had extended further than I had ever seen it in the past – all the way in fact to the Magwikwe sand ridge, where it finally disappeared into the Kalahari sand, the pulse of the Okavango's seasonal tide still unable to send it over the last hump and out onto the Mababe flats. This was the locality of the vast swamp through which Livingstone had struggled on his journey in 1851 en route to the Linyanti. Yet that swamp has ceased to exist in the fits and starts of the system's dynamics. Thus, the final few kilometres of the Khwai are still dry, a sandy bed whose steep banks speak of a different, wetter era. When you look down and along the final dry stretches of the Khwai's channel bed, it is hard to imagine that in the 1750s, this very ditch was the route along which the first mekoros were introduced to Ngamiland by the Bayei.

Although up and downstream of the campsite, there is much to be seen in the way of wildlife, on the floodplains of the Khwai, the buffalo which were common here ten

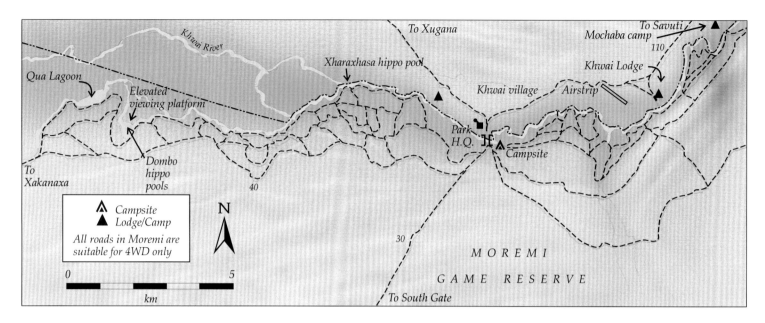

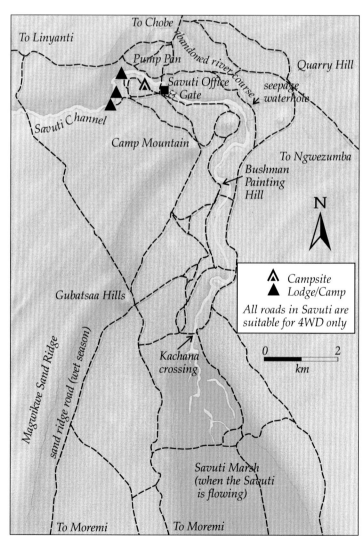

years ago have succumbed to the guns of citizen hunters and poachers, many of whom are said to live in the Khwai village. This is because the diminishing waters of the Khwai form an ineffective boundary between Moremi and the hunting areas beyond. All of the wildlife wanders back and forth across this 'boundary' at will and on a daily basis. Consequently, the big male lions seem absent now, possibly most taken by hunters who rove close by on the other side of the river. This is an area where every pride has its social structure shattered as soon as the dominant (and heavily maned) male lion wanders across to the wrong side of the tiny river. Another silent tragedy follows hard on the death of the dominant male: all of the cubs of its pride are killed by the male which rises to take its place.

The Khwai floodplains are still, however, host to a splendid variety of game. It is here that predators such as wild dog, cheetah and leopard are often seen more regularly than anywhere else. The wide open plains adjacent to the tiny, winding stream are the favourite haunt of cheetah, and, with patience and a pair of binoculars, it is not an impossible feat to see them every day. Roan, sable, kudu, zebra, reedbuck, giraffe and elephants are to be seen as well, making a stay here to be the highlight of many a traveller's adventure. But most who come to Moremi independently discover this place only as they are leaving, and consequently miss out on one of the National Park's most productive areas for viewing predators.

Nine days later we decided to move onwards yet again, bound for Savuti, the next destination marked on our itinerary. Traditionally, for north-bound travellers such as ourselves, after crossing the bridge at the North Gate and leaving Moremi, the goal would be the Savuti marsh in the Mababe Depression.

As the day of our departure dawned, a sharply listing vehicle indicated that there were some chores that I would have to attend to before we set off across the bridge – we had a puncture! Punctures (lots of them) are normal occurrences on any journey in northern Botswana – the spectacular thorns of the abundant acacias see to that! Fixing punctures can be one of the most soul-destroying of exercises, what with the physical work involved, the meticulousness required, and the constant irritations of

flies and insects. My well-used puncture-repair kit was extricated from the piles of equipment in the back, and a canvas tarpaulin laid out on the sand. The offending wheel was removed and the tedious process of fixing it commenced. Needless to say, getting the tyre off the rim is one of the most difficult parts of fixing a puncture: hours of hammering and levering often fail to have any effect. Toes become stubbed, fingers pinched, blisters develop on your hands – and the tyre remains stubbornly attached to the rim. I was well prepared, however, with my most prized possession – a heavy bead-breaker. After just a few blows from this instrument, the tyre literally springs off the rim, and the inner tube is quickly retrieved. However, at every blow there would be a deafening report and this attracted the attention of the inhabitants of the adjacent sites.

Although common throughout the Okavango, leopards are nowhere more visible than along the Khwai River. It is here that patience will eventually reward you with the archetypal sighting of a leopard lounging in a tree.

211

Inevitably, a man from one of them wandered across, his curiosity aroused by my bead-breaker. The man was dressed in regulation khaki, combat boots, belt replete with one of those multi-use penknives, and sported a half-grown beard. He was what some unkind people might refer to as a 'weekend-warrior'. In search of some non-participatory male-bonding, he hung over me irritatingly while I worked. Silly questions followed while I tried to concentrate on the task before me, and I nearly missed finding one of the thorns lodged in the tyre. "What's that thing you are using?" he demanded. "How many punctures have you fixed this trip . . . ?", and so on. When I had finished, my unwanted observer declared that he had a slow puncture and asked to borrow my bead-breaker to see for himself how much easier it made everything. Later, after returning from a clean-up at the ablution block, I discovered that my kindness had been sadly rewarded: the man and his group had packed up and left the campsite – taking my precious bead-breaker with them.

The journey to Savuti is not a long one – a few hours at the most – but it passes through countryside that to the casual observer is unremarkable in every way. Yet this is a terrain that has a fascinating story to tell of its past. Those slight undulations and sandy patches speak volumes to those who know what they are looking at.

For a while, the track skirts some forested country and then clings closely to that last dry portion of the Khwai. This is near where Chombo's village must have been situated and where Livingstone stopped on his way to the Linyanti in 1851. Then the track becomes sandy and soft, and it is here that the driver has to concentrate for a time on not getting stuck. That this has happened to other travellers is evident from the numerous pits in the track, some being of near-epic depths, where others were not so lucky. All of this is as a result of the white, wind-blown sands of the Magwikwe sand ridge. This sand ridge, derived in part from the Kalahari Beds, almost completely encircles the Mababe Depression, but it is more pronounced on the western side. A living relic from the dry epochs of the Stone Age, a time when the climate of the planet was fluctuating wildly, it was almost certainly laid down at the same time that the linear dune patterns of the Mega-Kalahari were being formed.

Livingstone, when he departed from Chombo's village on the Khwai, had been given a choice of two routes to the Linyanti: a faster one to the west of the sand ridge, which would take him through tsetse-fly belts; or a slower one along the sandy spine of the ridge, which was fly-free. His choice of the speedy route would cost him several of his cattle when they later succumbed to the tsetse-fly. The modern route is to the east of the ridge (except during the rainy season when the track on the back of the ridge is used), and soon after crossing the ridge, the road enters the acacia-scrub forests fringing the Mababe flats, were the sandy track becomes firm and flat, and the soil is darker and very silty – the notorious black-cotton soil in the rainy season! Thirty years ago this was still a vast plain, the relict floor of a dried-out lake – hence the nature of the soil. Since Livingstone and Oswell passed this way, however, it has gradually been colonized by mopane and acacia trees. Eventually, as you speed towards Savuti along the smooth surface of the track, the trees thin out and become stunted, and soon there are only short, thorny bushes left. It is here that you come across country such as Livingstone or Selous would have seen. Finally, the Gubatsaa Hills, hazy and blue, appear on the distant horizon. It is at this point that the bushes lining the track fall away and you can see out and across the last true remnants of the Mababe flats: the claustrophobic dustbowl of the previous hour has been left behind and you are enveloped in the grandeur of the classic African plain. Short and sweet grass makes this plain the favoured locality of large herds of plains game, and many wild animals could be seen far out on its unbroken expanse. Near the hills, the yellow grasslands are fringed by forests of huge, stately acacias and, in the shade of these, herds of tsessebe, wildebeest and impala were huddled together in the midday heat. Far out on the plains, giraffe herds, distorted by heat-shimmer mirages, seemed to be suspended in the air above the horizon. Here, Clarissa took over for her turn at driving.

Exactly a minute later, around the next bend and where the acacia forest pressed in close to the winding track, we were brought to a sudden halt by the looming bulk of an enormous elephant bull. Motionless except for the flick of its tail or a long sigh from its flaccid trunk, it refused to acknowledge our presence or move off the track. After a few minutes, my patience had expired.

"These bulls wouldn't hurt a fly. Just push past it!"

Clarissa looked at me quizzically. "You're sure, now?

Roan antelope   P. A.

Remember I don't have your experience at this kind of thing."

At that moment the elephant roused itself, swung around and executed a wonderful charge at the vehicle, which ended a couple of metres away from us in a cloud of dust. Clarissa needed no further encouragement. With a spurt of speed, and accompanied by a loud trumpet, we accelerated past, leaving the elephant posed dramatically like a bronze statue. Slowing down a few metres on, Clarissa let out a laugh. "Wouldn't hurt a fly, eh!"

From here on the elephant herds of the Chobe National Park would dominate every aspect of the coming weeks. What lay ahead was, more than anything else, going to be an elephant experience!

Six hours after leaving Khwai village, we pulled up at the small National Parks office at Savuti, where we bought our camping permits for the next few nights. Savuti had been almost a second home to me in the early eighties, and yet as we drove into the camping site I was staggered by its changed appearance. The demise of the Savuti channel and the disappearance of the Savuti marsh had all happened when I had been there previously, so I knew that there would be no sparkling stream flowing between the channel's banks. But when I had seen it last, patches of the riverbank lawns had survived and in the exposed bed there had been clean white sand. Now all that remained was a nondescript ditch of dirty sand. I found myself shaking my head, incredulous at the power of nature to alter things so quickly.

The campsite looked like an abandoned construction camp. An attempt had obviously been made to fence off the site, but this dubious effort at upgrading what was always a difficult place for a camp, had made things very much worse. Bits of wire fencing trailed everywhere, and there were large gaps where elephants had pushed their way through, regardless of the electrification. In the campsite itself the sandy tracks were still as treacherous as they had always been, and for the first time that day I was forced to engage the low-ratio gearing of my four-wheel drive.

Eventually, after much argument, Clarissa, Rosemary and I finally agreed on which tree we would camp under (not a small decision in the oven-like heat of an October day). By four o'clock we had made camp: the tent was up, the gas cooker lit, and soon we were sipping at our first cup of tea that day since breakfast.

At that moment, when we were relaxed by the tea and with the sun losing some of its mid-day ferocity, a line of stately bull elephants filed by. Completely oblivious to the nearby tents of other campers, they stamped past, heading westward to Lloyd Wilmot's camp, a tented lodge near to the campsite. In the back of the vehicle, Rosemary hardly looked up as they went by, but Clarissa, who had never camped here before, was less blasé. Rocking back in her camp chair, with feet up on one of the jerry cans, she sipped appreciatively at her tea, and as the solemn procession passed by, she shook her head in disbelief.

"What a fantastic sight! This is unbelievable", she declared as one of the bulls stopped to browse on a bush only two metres distant. "Look – there's another lot over there next to those people's tent as well!"

Indeed there was, and behind them, near a tap, another group of elephants was sniffing the damp ground with their trunks. None of this kind of animal movement is unusual for this locality – indeed it is famous for it. Before the Savuti dried up, the campsite was regularly visited by elephants and the hippo from the channel. There was even a small group of buffalo that would enter the camp at night to graze in between the tents, undeterred by the revelries of the campers. When the channel eventually died, however, the buffalo were all killed by lions (several in the

The vast plain of the Savuti marsh. P.A.

213

were installed, and new ablution blocks built, but the elephants continued to win this water 'war', and the demise of the fence was but the latest round in that war.

Clarissa went off to take a shower in the last remaining ablution block where water still flowed from the pipes. Less than half an hour later she was back, breathless and with her matted hair still covered in shampoo.

"You must come and look at this!" she said, dragging me off rapidly in the direction of the ablution block. "I've just been booted out of that filthy place by one of those behemoths!"

Over at the ablution block a small group of onlookers was watching the novel spectacle of an elephant peeling back a slice of the roof of the building with as much effort as a human being might expend opening a tin of sardines. Every other part of the roof had been similarly treated and the effect was gloriously anarchistic. The elephant, however, knew what it was doing as and it reached down inside the building with its trunk to find water.

"That's one of the showers", chuckled Clarissa. "I was in that very one just a minute ago!"

She went on to explain that the shower had been running for only a few seconds when the cubicle had darkened mysteriously. Then the trunk of an elephant had snaked down from above and she had beaten a hasty retreat.

The Savuti channel, and the marsh that forms at its terminus when the channel flows, has been the stage for many strange events. Many dramas have been played out here – human and animal alike – some of the most interesting of which took place hundreds of years ago. It needs only a little imagination to conjure up the scene as it might have been some two hundred and fifty years ago. Picture a vast green plain dotted with reedbeds and laced by channels of flowing water that reached southwards to its sister marsh at the end of the Khwai. With a little more imagination you can visualize groups of Bayei explorers punting their mekoros southwards into unknown territory, searching for a secure refuge from the scourges of the Lozi invaders from Barotseland.

A hundred years later, David Livingstone, the first white explorer to enter the region, would be travelling in the opposite direction. He was making his way through the fly country on the western side of the Magwikwe sand ridge. On 18 June 1851 Livingstone crossed the Savuti channel, which he called the Sonta, fifteen kilometres

Above
An elephant adds more damage to the last operating ablution block left in the Savuti campsite of the Chobe National Park.

Right
Scenting an unguarded pool of water in front of one of the tents at a safari camp, an elephant manoeuvres its trunk across the ground like a giant snake.

campsite itself), and the hippos moved away northwards to the Linyanti swamps. But the elephant bulls stayed on, deriving their water requirements from the one or two pools left in the channel, as well as the pool in front of Lloyd's camp, and the ablution blocks of the campsite. Then the fresh water that was pumped to the showers and toilets proved much more appealing to them than did the fouled and muddy pans in the nearby bush and so they began to hang around in ever-increasing numbers. Waterpipes were torn up and the walls of buildings pushed over as the fussy elephants tried to get their trunks into the toilet bowls. A battle royal commenced between the game department and the elephants. Special elephant-proof taps

upstream of the campsite, and became the first white man to have seen it. He noted in his diaries that it was three feet deep and thirty yards wide. It was then flowing strongly, but in the following years it ceased to flow: by the end of the 1850s it was completely dry. In the meantime, a tragic drama had been played out on the Mababe, the lonely plains that became the last resting place of a missionary wife called Eliza Price.

When Livingstone had returned to England in 1857, he had promoted the cause of missionary work that needed to be done among the Makololo of the Linyanti. This was taken up by the London Missionary Society and an expedition organized. Headed by two missionaries, Helmore and Price, it would go to Linyanti via the route that Livingstone had pioneered. Plans were made and it was decided that Livingstone would meet them there and a mission station would be built to help the Makololo.

Accompanied by their families, Helmore and Price set forth for the Linyanti in July of 1859 and their journey took them seven months. They had a very tough time of it, their troubles in making any headway made far worse by their lack of experience. Finally, in February 1860 they crossed the Linyanti River and found themselves in the company of Chief Sekeletu. Livingstone, who was supposed to have been there to meet them, was mysteriously absent.

Sekeletu was friendly at first, but after a while grew truculent, and the plans of the missionaries began to go awry. Sekeletu refused to co-operate with any of the ideas put forward for the exact location of a mission station. Then disaster struck! When they had been there a month, they all began to fall ill from a mysterious ailment and one of their staff died. It was not long before they were all laid low with a slow, burning fever and shortly after this, Helmore's son died as well. After another two days the Prices' daughter died, two days later Helmore's daughter passed away and the next day Mrs Helmore died, too. A few days passed before Mr Helmore was laid to rest next

The Chobe National Park is home to tens of thousands of elephants and nowhere are these giants so easily watched or approached than at Savuti. This view is from the hide at Lloyd's Camp. Elephant bulls vie with one another to get close to the tiny waterhole located in the dried-out Savuti riverbed below.

One of Roger Price's wagons broke down & had to be abandoned on the Magwikwe sand ridge.

to his wife. Devastated by the events and barely able to rise from his bed, Roger Price realized that he, his wife and the two surviving Helmore sons had to get away from Linyanti or they would all die there. So, despite being racked by fever, he slowly prepared the wagons for their departure.

For two more months they languished in this weakened state at Linyanti, with Sekeletu making things worse, for he seemed unwilling to let them go.

In the last entry that she made in her diary, Mrs Price wrote: "We have been robbed most fearfully while the packing of the wagon was going on, so that now we have only just enough things to use and scarcely that. As we require the help of the Makololo at the rivers we of course feel much at their mercy. The consequence has been that Roger has had to part with almost everything in his possession, even to our tent . . . I think that none of our friends could know us, we are so reduced. Roger is so thin and pale that he looks more like a dead man than a living man and I am so thin that I am obliged to plaster my bones and have lost the use of my legs."

Finally, in June they managed to get away and across the Linyanti with two of the wagons, travelling during the night at first to avoid the tsetse-fly belts to the south of the river. When they were crossing the Magwikwe sand ridge, however, one of the wagons broke down and had to be abandoned. After this they moved out and onto the Mababe flats and it was here, in July 1860, that Mrs Price died and was buried out on those wide, open plains.

Somehow Roger Price managed to summon up the strength to carry on, but he was a broken man. Nevertheless, they made it to the Khwai River where the guides given to him by Sekeletu turned back and he had to hire some Bushman guides to take him the rest of the way to Toteng. But Sekeletu had not finished with him yet, for, unbeknown to him, his new guides had been ordered by the chief to lead him and his cattle deep into the Khwai tsetse-fly belts to the west. This they did, and having completed their task, they abandoned him in the wilderness. The miracle of this story is that Roger Price and the two Helmore boys survived, but, when they arrived at Toteng, only three out of his original forty-four cattle were still alive. Roger would later find out that Sekeletu had committed one further act of treachery: on the return journey to Linyanti the Makololo guides had disinterred his wife's body from its grave on the Mababe. Cutting off the face, they had taken it back to Linyanti where it was exhibited.

In these and the following years, the flow of the Savuti channel was, in reality, starting to falter and it soon dried up completely. Consequently, the marsh vanished, leaving behind a peaty plain that was to become the favourite haunt of game during the wet seasons. The channel's dry period lasted for the next one hundred years and it was only in 1957 that it started to flow strongly again. In this year a large area was inundated at the terminus of the channel to the west of the Gubatsaa Hills. The acacias that had previously colonized the riverbed and the marsh were drowned, and these skeletal trunks are still today a characteristic part of the Savuti scenery. However, nothing stands still in nature, and the cycle has come full circle: the channel is dry once again and has been so since 1984.

Once the marsh dried out, the vast herds of buffalo for which this place was justifiably famous, abandoned the Mababe as did the elephant breeding herds, leaving behind hardy solitary bulls to squabble over the last remaining pans. This place was also famous for its huge numbers of lions, but when most of the buffalo left, so, too, did the majority of the lions. Nevertheless, a sizeable portion of that previous wildlife glory has remained, and the flat grasslands are ideal for viewing lions, wild dogs and cheetah.

A kilometre away, to the north of the campsite, there is a pan where the game department has been pumping water in an attempt to alleviate the elephant problem of the campsite. At this artificial location, it is possible to park only metres away from a milling mass of up to a hundred bulls. The small pan is literally sucked dry almost before

the water has a chance to wet the clay. There is a pecking order among these elephants that it is strictly adhered to, and easily observed at close quarters. Smaller, more immature bulls back away from the packed confines of the inner circle the moment a larger bull arrives – often in advance of its arrival. There seems to be a hidden communication between all the members of the tightly packed mass: when those lower down in the pecking order fail to yield to seniority, a sharp jab from a tusk does the

job. Occasionally, there is an angry trumpeting and an elephant breaks from the crowd, hotly pursued by another. Then, with the graceful agility of waltzing partners, the seething mass reshuffles itself and the gaps disappear. Yet, out of all of this confusion comes the undeniable fact that every elephant seems finally to drink its fill and then depart serenely into the surrounding forests.

This description does not do justice to how it feels to sit so close to such proceedings. Only metres away, dozens of

At the pumped pan to the north of the campsite and the dry bed of the Savuti channel, elephants monopolize the water to the detriment of most of the other animals. These smaller animals, lions included, must run a gauntlet of legs, trunks, and tusks to get close to the water.

217

dinosaur-sized animals totalling hundreds of tons of living flesh, ignore your presence as though you do not exist – yet their size is ever more obvious because of their closeness. Of course, there are other animals waiting to drink as well and these wait patiently for their chance. Dainty and elegant kudu circle the pan at a distance. So, too, do the impala, baboons and guineafowl. But I must confess that, from an observer's point of view, lions are not my favourite animals. Unless you are lucky enough to see this animal at night or hunting, most sightings during the day are of motionless, comatose lions lying in the deepest shade they can find. Tourists spend more hours in Africa staring at lions, which, to all intents and purposes, may as well be dead, than looking at all the other animals put together. Lions can, however, sometimes be observed doing interesting things at this pan.

On one of the mornings when we were watching this almost prehistoric scene, some lions padded quietly in from the nearby bush. With hardly a moment's hesitation, they strode confidently into the phalanx of elephants, at times almost lost to view amid a forest of legs. One or two of the elephants spread their ears in mock anger, but a snarl and some threatening body language from one of the maned males put a stop to that. Like punctured balloons, the elephants deflated, to stand aside as the lions moved in and drank from the pool.

The Savuti experience has, in the last decade, become a bittersweet affair. On the one hand, it is undeniable that the plains are beautiful and the game plentiful, but on the other, unless you are staying at one of the lodges or have access to one of the commercial operators' campsites, there comes the time to face the return to the campsite – and, frankly, this must be one of the most appalling campsites in southern Africa.

On the afternoon of the second day, after a hot day on the plains, we returned reluctantly to the campsite. Here, the elephants had totally surrounded the one ablution block where the toilets worked and another was hovering over the tap, trying to figure out a way to turn it on. Surrounded by pieces of rubbish and beginning to be offended by the dirty sand, we felt that the hovering presence of so many elephants and the lack of shade during the burning midday hours were starting to get on our nerves. This was not what we had come so far to see and we all agreed that two days had already been enough. Even

Clarissa, who had never been to Savuti before, had become uncharacteristically subdued. Rosemary was more forthright. "This campsite is a ghastly place", she declared after a gust of wind had carried a fluttering bit of toilet paper from behind a nearby bush and deposited it inside the back of the vehicle. "What's the point in staying here?" she demanded, echoing all our sentiments.

North-east of the Mababe there is a place which has managed to weather Botswana's tourist influx with dignity. The road there is hardly ever used by travellers bound for the Chobe, even though it is probably a better track than the traditional route via Kachekabwe. Rarely is another car encountered on this more interesting route (which never leaves the Chobe National Park). It also provides access to the last place in the Chobe National Park where any true feeling of wildness survives – the Ngwezumba River Valley. Higher up the valley, amid the plains and mopane forests of its upper catchment area there are some rocky pools in its bed, and near to these lie a series of large pans. These are rain-dependent waterholes and so the numbers of animals seen here varies tremendously from year to year, according to the rainfall. In one year they might be full enough to last all the way through to the end of the dry season, and when this happens, truly spectacular herds of elephant congregate, as do zebra, eland, giraffe, sable, roan, kudu, and the occasional rhino. The area is also known for its aggressive lions. If the local rains are insufficient, however, it is a different situation altogether. Then the pans will dry up early and by May or June the whole district will be abandoned by the wildlife. Visit this place then and you will see nothing except mud-cracked pans and empty forests. Therein lies the saving grace of this harsh place, for it is this inconsistency that has kept the groping arms of tourist development at bay.

In the late 70s the area of the Ngwezumba pans was truly a wild place. The few tracks that existed had been allowed to deteriorate to the point where they had almost disappeared, and I had spent many months there without seeing or hearing another vehicle. Luckily for me, the pans were consistently full for several seasons in a row and so I was allowed to experience the glory of utter wilderness surrounded by spectacular herds of game. The sights, experiences and adventures of those two or three years would serve to make up most of the fond memories that I would accumulate in a decade and a half as a Botswana

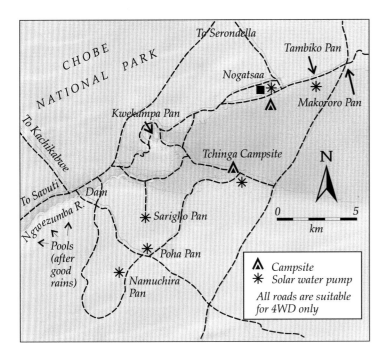

resident. A return visit to this place would indeed be a sentimental journey into the past, and a sort of litmus test of the state of wilderness in this vast region.

The next day we left early, almost eager to be gone from that dustbowl of a campsite. Through long experience of the road ahead, however, I knew that this was not a journey to be hurried. There would be trees across the track and sandy patches to negotiate carefully. Invariably, there would be many stops at the several large pans along the route. I had one small nagging worry. The intermittent fault of the car was now recurring almost daily, and even though I was becoming used to its bad habit and always seemed to be able to get it going again, the nature of the road ahead dictated caution under the circumstances. The heavy sand of that track would have to be negotiated with care in view of the fact that it seemed to be long stretches of sand that now caused the motor to flood, overheat and then cut out. Indeed, twice in the last two weeks it had done so in the midst of sand drifts where stopping meant getting stuck. This had also happened amid a herd of irate elephants in Moremi.

After crossing the channel, I steered eastward to the last of the Gubatsaa Hills, and here I took the small unmarked track leading off, as straight as a die, through the mopane scrub of the Mababe flats. The broad, heavily used tracks of Savuti were left behind and ahead lay the

infinitely more attractive track to the Ngwezumba River. After an hour, the winding route leaves the flat surface of the Mababe and enters the dune country beyond its eastern shore. Heavy coarse sand makes for hard going in places and the track takes one ever deeper into dense forests. Following small valleys, the route occasionally passes attractive pans, and it is at these evocative places that spectacular sightings of game are to be had. The fringes of the pans are littered with dung and broken trees, flocks of guineafowl wander on the grassy fringes, and flies settle in swarms when you stop for a look. At Makapa Pan, the largest of these pans, a walk down to the water's edge revealed the spoor of lion and leopard mixed in among the hoof marks of impala and warthog. In the distance, baboons barked, while in the skies above, Yellowbilled Kites called plaintively. These lonely pans are wilderness personified. Unfortunately, time now always dictates that one must move on, for the days when you could camp out in these parts, before the tourist boom and when the game department never travelled this way, are now long gone.

Of course, this road is now occasionally graded and so it is not nearly as adventurous a journey as it was a decade ago. The attempts at grading the road do, however, make the track worse, for in the process the hard sand in the ruts is obliterated, and the soft sand spread evenly. In spite of these recent attempts to improve the route, this is still a lonely road, and, true to form, it was only several hours later that we encountered another vehicle, which lay stalled in the middle of the road. As we approached, I could see that it was stuck fast in the sand. Labouring away with shovels were several people who now scrambled to their feet. When I stopped to inquire what I could do to help, one of the men came across, a grin of relief on his face – but this quickly faded when he saw me. In the same instant, even as I in turn recognized him, my eyes alighted on a bead-breaker lying among the pile of ropes, jacks and tools that lay heaped nearby – it was *my* bead-breaker!

Such opportunities as this do not come often and I could not resist milking this one to the limit, as I enjoyed extracting my revenge on them for their selfish deed. Since I had last seen the bead-breaker I had had to fix several punctures, and on each occasion had had difficulty in removing the tyre from the rim. Several large blood-blisters on my fingers were mute testimony to this.

"Need any help?" was all I could think of saying, and

219

then, scathingly, ". . . borrowed any bead-breakers lately?"

For the first time that year I almost kissed the bonnet of the car in gratitude that the motor was not up to scratch. I refused to attempt to pull them out, neglecting also to tell them why, and, after retrieving my prized bead-breaker, departed without bothering to inform them that I would in fact alert the game department people stationed at Nogatsaa (still two hours' travel in front of us) of their plight. The sight of their dumbfounded expressions as I drove off was sweet revenge indeed!

By midday we were approaching the familiar open valley where the Ngwezumba riverbed becomes rocky. Here pools form and in the late dry season fantastic views of buffalo and elephant were at one time possible from the small natural ledges that overhang them. The best of these pools lies a couple of hundred metres from the track, and in the distance we could easily see the small clump of trees that indicated where that particular pool lay. I pulled over and stopped. Then, standing on top of the vehicle, I was able to make out the very trees where I had spent so much time many years previously. Looking around, I could see that the place had become a little more overgrown and that the game paths were less defined. There also seemed

to be fewer signs of elephant than I was used to. The temptation to return to a place where so many memories had been made was almost irresistible. Yet I knew that this was a different era: the game department maintained a presence in the area, based at Nogatsaa Pan, and this was now only an hour away.

"Well, what do you think? Shall we go and have a look?" At that moment, however, my mind was made up for me. From around the bend in the road a heavily loaded Landcruiser roared into view and drew up next to us in a billowing cloud of dust. Inside the cab six sets of eyes peered out.

"Thank goodness! I was beginning to think I was lost", shouted the driver over the din of his revving engine. "How far to Savuti, please?"

I pointed up the track and told him. When the sound of their engine had faded into the distance, we moved on, all thoughts of the pool forgotten. I had no wish to create trouble for myself by being caught off-road by the authorities. Indeed things had changed – the days of freedom had gone forever and there was nothing to be gained by antagonizing the bureaucrats. Nevertheless, an hour later, as we approached the camping site at Tchinga I found myself peering hard at the trees surrounding the pan in the hope that there would be no one else there. As we drove down the last stretch of track towards the familiar sight of the little pumphouse, I hoped fervently that we would have the place to ourselves. A short drive around the periphery of the pan revealed the place to be empty – we were in luck! A hundred metres away from the pan I halted under the tree where I had always camped and we started to unload the vehicle. Clarissa, however, had been studying the pan and the several elephants that stood drowsily in the shade nearby.

"Hmm, don't a lot of elephants use this place at night?" she asked.

"Definitely! We'll see some fantastic sights tonight."

As we set up our tent Rosemary wandered off through the trees, enjoying the freshness of the place after the horrors of Savuti. A few seconds later she came tearing back as a large herd of elephants poured out from the nearby forest. Intent solely on reaching the water at the pan, they hurried by in a frantic rush that carried them to within a few yards of our little encampment. Immediately, they scented us and the procession halted in a cloud of

dust. For a second or two they stood swaying from side to side, ears outstretched and trunks raised. Then a large cow stepped forward. The body language of this huge cow spoke volumes about its reaction to us for it managed to make itself look positively vicious. Two red, pig-like eyes glared down at us, as we stood transfixed by the elephants' sudden appearance – and then it stepped forward again. The three of us stepped back as one and our movement brought forth a primeval scream from the cow that would have made a *Tyrannosaurus rex* proud. For the next few seconds there was pure bedlam as the herd wheeled and ran to the accompaniment of more blood-curdling trumpeting. A minute after they had crashed off into the undergrowth, the environs of the pan were silent again. Half an hour later the same thing happened and, when the dust had settled for the second time, I conceded defeat and we relocated our camp to a clump of trees much further away from the pan.

It was obvious that large numbers of elephants were in the area – and that it would be impossible to avoid them

completely. Indeed, the terrain around the pan was criss-crossed by their well-used paths: snapped trees lay all about and the ground was littered with their droppings. Nevertheless, the pan was now two hundred metres away, and I had to admit to myself that we had done the sensible thing.

That evening the sun set early in the hazy, smoke-tinted sky. The unbearable heat of a September day faded and the cool peace of evening settled slowly on the African landscape. In the warm tints of the waning sun the surrounding countryside began to lose its harshness. Far in the distance a lion roared and its faint call carried clearly through the silent forests. Nearby, baboons began to clamber into their night-time roosts in the giant trees encircling Tchinga Pan. Darkness descended and for, a while, the stillness of the cool air was disturbed only by the mournful call of some night-loving bird. The elephants seemed to have vanished!

Later on that night, however, when the moon had

222

risen, they returned in force; it was almost as though the floodgates had been opened. From every direction herds of elephant seemed to converge on the pan. They came rushing silently through the looming forests, following the well-beaten game paths leading down to the water's edge. Forming long trains, the grey ghosts filed past, silent save for the shuffling sounds of their great pads. When they arrived at the edge of the pan, we could hear great splashing and sucking noises as they drank and cavorted in the water. Then symphonies of screams and trumpeting were followed by equally unsettling silences, but the splashes soon started up again, the cycle being repeated endlessly all night long. Lying in our tent, Clarissa and I listened to all this with a mixture of awe and nervousness – awe, at the sheer volume of the prehistoric bellows, and nervousness because of the cracking twigs just outside our tent. Somehow we drifted off into a fitful sleep.

About ten kilometres from Tchinga there is an enormous pan called Kwekampa. If the rains have been good in the previous year, this pan will contain enough

In the mopane scrub of the black-cotton soil near Kwekampa Pan, two Helmeted Guineafowl search for seeds and insects.

water to last through the dry season. When this happens, the stage is set for one of the greatest gatherings of elephant that it is possible to see in the Africa of today.

A couple of days after settling in we set off one morning to see if there was indeed water in Kwekampa. As we approached the forests adjacent to the wide pan, we began to encounter elephants – a sure sign that the pan was full. And so it was. As we broke through the last fringe of trees, a herd of sable cantered away from us, halting on the open flats surrounding the pan. Beyond the suspicious sables, a glittering sheet of blue water stretched for two hundred metres to the opposite shore. There, on the grassy open plain on the other side, were small herds of zebra, buffalo and eland. Vultures were squabbling over an old lion kill under a tree nearby and, as we bumped our way over to a convenient shady tree with a good view of the whole pan, baboons, monkeys and squirrels scampered out of our path.

Most impressive of all were the sheer numbers of

elephants present. They were everywhere! Several large herds loitered on the margins of the water, others were moving down to drink or wistfully dallying before leaving. Lone bulls frolicked in the deeper waters of the pan, and nearby in the shallows, several elephants were rolling blissfully in the mud. There were literally hundreds of elephant in view and Clarissa, who had never seen such an assemblage before, let out a gasp.

Gatherings of wild animals such as this are always stirring sights: this because they are a manifestation of nature's greatness and also because, in our era, they represent an anomaly in the reality of the true situation. This is especially so in Botswana where so much of the country's wildlife has been eliminated in the last decade. The great kilometre-long buffalo herds have now gone from most of the areas. The huge zebra migrations into the Mababe are a thing of the past. Yet in the face of this tragic waste, the elephant populations of northern Botswana continue to grow – some scientists telling us that they now exceed sixty thousand individuals.

It was not always like this. The first written accounts of the elephants of this region are in Livingstone's diaries of his journey to Linyanti in 1851. He mentions their spoor in the area just to the south of the present Chobe National Park. They did not, however, see any of the animals themselves. That honour went to James Chapman and his hunting companions Campbell and Thompson in 1853. James Chapman, a trader, ivory hunter and, later, the first photographer to visit the Victoria Falls, was the first white man to venture into the country to the east of the Mababe Depression. On that trip he had many hair-raising exploits hunting elephants in the area south of the Ngwezumba. On one occasion a breeding herd of five hundred elephants was encountered. Chapman would also be the first man to write about the Ngwezumba, a river he called the Commane. He described it as being populated by many Bushmen, who claimed that their ancestors had once owned cattle. Then, one year, there had been a terrible cold snap and all their children had died. Somehow their 'shamans' had decided that the cattle were the cause of the disaster and so they were all slaughtered. Since that day, they told Chapman, they had lived on the game of the valley.

Large herds of elephants certainly roamed this part of Africa then, but not in the numbers we are used to seeing there today. Also, their movements were fickle, and when Chapman returned to the area in 1855 he found it empty of elephants.

In 1891 the first game laws were promulgated in the newly declared Bechuanaland Protectorate, and in 1893 the first elephant licences were introduced. In 1932 all the wildlife of the Chobe district was proclaimed as protected and this ban on hunting lasted until 1943 when a sudden expansion of the tsetse-fly belts in the Kachekabwe salient (to the west of Ngoma bridge) began to cause concern. Nevertheless, few elephants were hunted or poached during these times. Indeed, the Chobe area was not at that time a place where elephants were ever regularly seen: prior to 1945, elephants were unknown to several generations of Bushmen living in the Ngwezumba Valley. Neither were they common along the Chobe River: one resident lived at the old timber saw-mill, just to the east of Serondella, for three years before he saw his first elephant there in 1949. This was set to change, however, for in the following years the elephant population of the Chobe district began to increase dramatically, possibly as a result of influxes of elephants from the west. This increase in elephant numbers was further helped by the creation of a large game reserve in the Chobe district in 1960, which, seven years later, would become the Chobe National Park.

Soon the inhabitants of the surrounding areas began to confirm the increases and in the Caprivi Strip, there was a dramatic rise in the numbers of elephants being shot while caught marauding crops. All of this was in spite of the fact that five hundred elephants a year were being shot on licence (and many more poached) until hunting was stopped in 1983. Nor did the devastating drought of the 80s seem to have any effect, for elephants continued to flourish, while the other animals with whom they shared the land declined with equal rapidity. Elephants are Botswana's miracle, and to see them as you can at Kwekampa is to experience one of the great wonders of the natural world.

At Tchinga we settled in for a stay that would last a couple of weeks. Inside our tent Clarissa and I arranged our things much as we had at Walvis, Palmwag, Etosha, and in the Okavango. In one corner Clarissa placed her table and spread out all her papers. In the other, next to the light of the window, I stored my easel so that it was always ready for use in the field. The corner where I kept my canvases

was filling up. What with the paintings that I had completed in Damaraland, Okaukuejo, Jau, and Xakanaxa, there was also a large canvas that I was planning to complete at Tchinga. The confines of the tent were starting to feel somewhat cramped. Nonetheless, its position was ideal, for through the window I could see Tchinga Pan and its massive population of elephants.

In the coming days we got very used to the constant presence of these animals – the correct word for our casual behaviour would perhaps be 'blasé'! Indeed, Rosemary took the meaning of this word to new heights as she wandered off on long walks despite the constant comings and goings of the huge beasts. When we needed water we would drive over to the pump, which was situated in a dilapidated shack near the water's edge. This pump would often be left running by the game department, but sometimes it was not, and I would have to start it up myself (a solar pump has since been installed here). In either case there would be elephants hovering expectantly nearby, for they had all learnt that the water directly from the pipe was far more palatable than the stinking, fouled water of the pan. Then, with one wary eye on the elephants, I would proceed to fill the water containers.

As the days passed, the solitude of Tchinga Pan was occasionally disturbed by the arrival of other campers, and then, for a day or two, the atmosphere was different. Sometimes, someone would wander across to say hello and enquire if we had seen anything interesting, but after a couple of days they would pack up and go, and then the magical solitude of the place would settle gently around us once again.

In the meantime, I continued to work hard on the painting which I knew would probably the last I would do on this journey of homage to true wildlife art. I had learned a lot from the experience, much of it not at all relevant to my career as an artist, but, somehow, just the fact that I had done it at all was very satisfying. I was now so organized that I would think nothing of taking my easel and setting it up under a tree. All the experience I had gained during the past months meant that neither wind nor flies, dust nor even inquisitive elephants would disturb me when putting brush to canvas. I had become amazingly tolerant of obstacles such as these, and, also, very adept at working directly in the sun and doing the oil sketches that would form the basis of the more finished painting

Previous pages
Kwekampa Pan during the height of the dry season. During August and September, if this pan has been filled by good rains from the previous wet season, it is host to one of the African continent's greatest gatherings of elephants. Here, granted the right conditions, it is possible to see dozens of elephant herds at a time, each drinking and playing on a different part of this giant pan's extensive shoreline. At its peak in September, upwards of 700 elephants can be seen together at this place.

Painting at Kwekampa was always interesting! The constant passage of herds of nervous cows and calves required careful assessment as to when I should stay put or when a tactical retreat was required.

A buffalo bull pauses to drink from one of the shallow pools in the bed of the Ngwezumba River. Buffalo were once very common in the Nogatsaa area. In the last decade, however, their numbers have been severely depleted by poaching and overhunting.

Opposite
Like Carmines, Whitefronted
Bee-eaters also nest in colonies,
and when they are feeding
they gather on branches
overhanging a stream or river.
In turns or together, they fly out
over the water, and, with
movements too rapid for the
eye to follow, execute aerial
pirouettes in pursuit of insects.
A long glide returns them to
their perch and loudly twittering
companions.

The angry elephant nearly caught up with us. P.A.

I would then complete in the tent. In the process, I had become more of a complete artist than I had ever hoped was possible.

Our long odyssey was, however, in its closing stages. None of us talked about this looming fact, but as the days passed we were all conscious of the need to enjoy every last moment of the experience. Every night-time sound was savoured, every day-time sighting was enthusiastically appreciated – and the time seemed to fly past even faster.

This passage of time was also graphically illustrated by the changes taking place in the skies above. The rains were approaching and in the afternoons the clouds would build up, accompanied by light, fitful breezes blowing from every direction. The herds of elephant were aware of the changes as well, and they became increasingly edgy with the gusts of wind and the scent of the coming rains. Tied as they were to the muddy, stinking pans, they would soon be free to roam wide and far, and they knew it. With the humidity came the heat, and with the heat came the incessant din of the Christmas beetles. Occasionally, on the hottest days, buffalo would visit the muddy fringes of the pan to wallow. Every night, a pride of lions would start to roar, sending the baboons roosting in the trees into paroxysms of nervous barks. These lions, which were very shy during the day, would materialize out of the dusk on most evenings to drink at the pan. Even the lions seemed to sense that a change was coming, as they paced about restlessly among the trees of the pan before melting off into the surrounding mopane forests. In the distance, far over the horizon, low rumbles of thunder sounded through the night.

Kwekampa Pan continued to be at its best and the approach to the pan along the track became quite a nerve-racking ordeal. The skittish elephant herds seemed to be around every corner and sheltering under every tree. One day when we were returning from the pan, a very nervous herd rushed across the road in front of us, with a large cow bringing up the rear. Even as I pulled abreast of them, the cow detached itself from the herd and proceeded to run at us in such a way that I knew immediately that this was not a mock but a real charge. Startled, Clarissa shrank back from the window as she saw the enraged cow thundering onto the track behind us.

"Watch out Paul – it's getting too close!"

We were past it, however, and the track ahead was clear and straight.

"Don't worry, I won't let it catch us!" And with the cow tearing after us, I accelerated the vehicle just enough to keep it at what I thought was a safe distance, all the while watching it carefully in the rear-view mirror. Two hundred metres down the track the enraged elephant gave up, stopped and trumpeted loudly; it was still watching us when we disappeared around the next corner.

When we arrived back at Tchinga, Rosemary swung open the canopy door and literally leapt from the vehicle in a highly agitated state.

"What were you doing? Trying to give me a heart attack?" She then went on to explain that the elephant had been so close behind us, that, for a few tense seconds, its attempt to grab hold of our vehicle had nearly been successful.

"Its outstretched trunk was only centimetres from the roof-rack's ladder", she declared. "I nearly died of fright because you seemed unaware of it being behind us!"

For a moment I was puzzled and then the realization dawned: the rear-view mirror was one of the wide-angle variety, and had the effect of making everything seem much further away than it really was. Rosemary extracted a promise from me that I would never do anything similar again, especially if she was in the vehicle at the time. Luckily, nothing had come of the incident, but sometimes episodes like this can go horribly wrong. It is a strange thing, but all of my close calls with elephant have been in the Tchinga area. The first, many years previously, had taken place fifteen kilometres away at the Ngwezumba pools. A partially demolished Landcruiser was the end result of that encounter with a herd of elephants. The second incident took place in the vicinity of Tchinga and is worth retelling here.

En route to Kasane, I had decided to overnight at Tchinga. When we (Rosemary was with me) had arrived, the pan was dry and the pump broken down. Distressed elephants were hovering about all over the place and so we parked under a group of trees far away from the pan or any of the nearest game paths. Rosemary settled down to sleep in the back of the vehicle and I erected a small dome tent, which I placed at the front of the vehicle next to the bumper. That night the comings and goings of the elephants were a constant source of disturbance and I was woken on several occasions by the sounds of elephants moving about close by. One always feels vulnerable in

Paul Augustinus

227

flimsy tents when these giants of the bush roam close, and for me there is always an overwhelming desire to get up, open the zip and see what is happening outside. Three times I did this only to discover that the elephants had been further away than I thought. Finally, I dozed off into a fitful sleep troubled by vivid dreams.

Then, in the early hours of the morning, I awoke again to the consciousness that yet another elephant was passing close by outside. However, the sounds of its footfalls grew louder and louder and suddenly it let out a deafening trumpet. The next few seconds were moments of pure terror for me. As if in slow motion, I managed to unzip the tent's entrance and, shining my torch through the door, was just in time to see several bizarre events take place. Just centimetres away, the vehicle was rocking madly like a dinghy on a storm-tossed sea. Then, after another blood-curdling trumpet from the unseen elephant, the front of the vehicle rotated smoothly out of sight and away from the tent door! Where there had once been the reassuring solidity of the vehicle's bumper and radiator, there was now just darkness. There was another scream of rage from the animal, and, almost magically it seemed, I found myself next to the vehicle and desperately yanking at the door, which, to my horror, turned out to be locked! (I always locked my photographic equipment in the cab at nights.) Had I not been gibbering with fright, this might all have been very comical to watch, but there I was, standing naked, on the opposite side of a vehicle to an enraged attacking elephant – and I was locked out. To my great relief, the elephant broke off and turned away. With a final defiant trumpeting, it disappeared into the gloom. Inside the canopy, Rosemary was in complete confusion and, while I stumbled around trying to find the keys among my bedding in the tent, my heart was in my mouth that the elephant would return.

Once we had calmed down, I took stock of the situation. It had been my good fortune that the elephant had pushed the vehicle from the side. If it had instead pushed from the rear, the vehicle (whose handbrake was off) would have rolled right over me. As it was, the steel canopy was bent out of shape and the windows had all popped from their frames. Later, when I related this story to Chris MacIntyre, he was almost beside himself with frustration. "You people have all the luck", he declared. "I would pay money to have that happen to me!"

On our sixteenth day at Tchinga, my final painting was completed. Taking it outside, I leant it up against a tree so that we could all look at it. This was no mean occasion, for the completion of the painting also meant that our adventure was coming to an end. It was hard to find anything to say for nobody's thoughts were focused on the glistening paint of the canvas. What we all knew was better left unsaid, and I silently took the painting back inside.

On the last day of October we awoke to a dull, overcast morning and as we started to break camp, the wind picked up. Soon we were grappling with a wildly flapping tent and just as we had let this down, it started to rain. There was a mad rush to get all my paintings safely stored in the back of the canopy. An hour later the downpour stopped as suddenly as it had started, and, as the wind also died down, we set about stowing the sodden gear as best we could for the drive to our last stop before going home – the Chobe River. As we sadly said farewell to the now-familiar environs of Tchinga, the sun came out strongly into a brilliant blue sky, washed clear of the hazes of the previous weeks. The air was fresh, and the bush had come alive with the calls of birds and insects. Puddles of water lay everywhere. The dry season was over.

Five hours later we were cresting the last of the ridges before the track starts its descent to the Chobe River. Here, framed by the splendid trees of the sand ridge, the vast floodplains of the Chobe finally come into view. Below, lay the deep blue meanders of that broad river and beyond were the open expanses of Africa, looking much as they had done in Livingstone's day.

The Chobe River is a place of paradoxes and conflicts – a direct result of the fact that this scenic wonderland with its massive wildlife herds is so close to the Victoria Falls. It is here that the Africa of old can be experienced after a short journey down a tar road from the international airport at Victoria Falls. Crammed into fifty or so kilometres of scenic riverfront, there are vast herds of elephant and buffalo. Lions, sable, hippo, and kudu are common and regularly seen, and the birdlife is spectacular. The proximity to the Victoria Falls has also ensured that this place's destiny is for the type of tourism in which Kenya excels. Even now there are lodges, tented camps and hotels situated here, and some have suggested that the Chobe has already reached saturation point as far as tourism is

I heard the elephant move closer to the vehicle & my tent.   P.A.

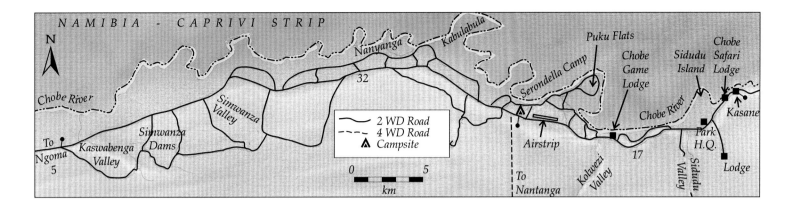

concerned. However, the tracks are such that a four-wheel-drive is necessary and so the atmosphere still has a feeling of wilderness about it.

For a few days we camped in Serondella under the familiar branches of an old acacia tree. The ground beneath that same tree had been my home for years in the early eighties and now it was showing its age. Its canopy was thinner and the branches were sagging. Yet memories lurked everywhere. There was a conflict of feelings here – in returning to a place that had once been a home and yet knowing that the adventure was nearly over.

One afternoon I walked to a small gully leading down to the water's edge. The campsite is perched on a high riverbank on one of the huge meandering loops of the Chobe, and there are several of these gullies within its

boundaries. Elephants often use these convenient places to drink and that afternoon was no different. A large herd was already there, drinking peacefully, and from a vantage-point just above them I was able to watch them in complete safety. In the distance, on the opposite Namibian bank, a herd of cattle grazed and drank in similar fashion. This is one of the startling paradoxes – the sharp delineation between wild and domestic, determined purely by an international boundary. As I watched, a powerboat went past with its cargo of domestic fishermen, and for the next few minutes its bow wave lapped at the shoreline. The elephants below me were undisturbed, however, and after a while they began to wander back up the gully, and through the campsite, eventually disappearing in the forested dunes to the south.

A herd of elephant emerges from the Chobe River in the Chobe National Park, as seen from the campsite at Serondella.

Paul Augustin

That night, lions roared from all quarters, and these calls were mixed in with the bleats and bellows of a large buffalo herd. The next morning, two nearby spirals of circling vultures told a vivid story of the night's events. The kills were visible from the campsite, especially from our own location under the acacia tree, although crowding vehicles soon obscured our view.

In the evening, as we sat around the fire, reflecting on the previous months, it might have been a depressing moment, but it was not, for this was exactly the right time to go home – any longer and we would have started to take our surroundings for granted. I was brimming with ideas for my next series of paintings, and positively looking forward to getting back to my studio. Clarissa, with her thesis well under way, was also content to leave. Rosemary, on the other hand, would have been happy to keep going forever! Nonetheless, as we watched that flickering fire and heard distant thunder echoing over the floodplains, it was very hard not to feel melodramatic: I was once again in the very spot where my fledgling career as an artist had been nurtured and flourished more than twelve years previously. Yet so much had changed, and the frightening realization was that things would continue to change apace.

There is always the tendency to compare the present unfavourably with the past, forgetting all the while that there is no such thing as the good old days. Not any more, for the past months had taught me otherwise – these are the good days! This is so if only because they will certainly be better than tomorrow's world. Our experiences had given me much food for thought. In all our conversations with people we had met along the way there was a single connecting thread – a fatalistic pessimism that lay beneath the surface at all times, a pessimism that development will never stop and that the last areas left to nature will always be under threat and whittled away by successive generations of our species. The human animal is one that is fast evolving away from the natural world. For all of our fine thoughts and hopes of preserving nature, there is also a force at work here that is unstoppable. We have passed the stage where we need skins and meat from wild game. At one time it was so simple: wilderness was the place to be conquered. Now, paradoxically, we are somehow trying to conquer and yet preserve our last wilderness areas at the same time! Soon, we will know everything that there is to know about every place, and then the 'mystery' will be gone forever. Is the planet destined to become a 'museum society', such as Europe is now, where thousands of years of human 'cleverness' are aggressively preserved in buildings, museums and art galleries, yet not a square inch of true wilderness remains? Is it possible that the world's last, semi-wild places are destined to be tamed by scientists, bureaucrats, and the tour operators? Or that, a few decades from now, all that will be left, will be small, carefully 'farmed' reserves, where scientists will have collared, darted and named every lion and elephant? I hope not!

As I sat there on the banks of the Chobe River, listening to the screams of a herd of elephants in the distance and musing on Africa's uncertain future, I thanked my lucky stars that I had been born into the last generation that would so easily be able to enjoy an experience such as we had just had. Indeed, these were truly the good days!

Opposite

Two Lilacbreasted Rollers investigate one of the many large dead trees along the Chobe riverfront. Rollers are especially fond of dead trees because they contain numerous hollows of the kind they prefer for nesting sites.

When the sun sets over the Chobe River, the stage is set for nocturnal visitors such as these. Almost invariably, the strongest memories of any stay at Serondella are of the nights – and of the elephants that venture through the camp on their way down to the river's edge.

BIBLIOGRAPHY

Allen, D. 1988. 'The World's Bustards: A Looming Crisis', *Quagga* 24.

Andersson, C.J. 1856. *Lake Ngami*. Hurst and Blackett, London. Facsimile edition 1987. C. Struik, Cape Town.

Augustinus, P. 1989. *Botswana, A Brush with the Wild*. Acorn Books, Johannesburg.

Axelson, E. 1954. *South African Explorers*. Oxford University Press, London.

Baines, T. 1864. *Explorations in South West Africa*. Longmans, Roberts and Green, London.

Bryden, H. 1883. *With gun and camera in Southern Africa*. Edward Stanford, London.

Bulger, J. 1989. 'Wild Dogs and livestock predation'. *Kalahari Conservation Society Newsletter* 26, Gaborone.

— 1990. 'Wild Dogs in Botswana'. *African Wildlife* 4.

Burrows, R. 1996. 'Harmful handling'. Letters, *BBC Wildlife*, April.

Campbell, A. 1984. 'Great salt pans of central Botswana'. *Marung*, Gaborone.

Carr-Hartley, P. 1995. 'Depletion of wildlife in Botswana'. *Kalahari Conservation Society Newsletter* 47, Gaborone.

Chapman, J. 1868. *Travels in the Interior of South Africa 1849-1863*. Reprint 1971. A.A. Balkema, Cape Town.

Cooke, H.J. 1976. 'The palaeogeography of the middle Kalahari of northern Botswana and adjacent areas'. *Proceedings of the symposium on the Okavango Delta and its future utilisation*. Botswana Society, Gaborone.

Craven, P. & Marais, C. 1992. *Damaraland Flora*. Gamsberg Macmillan, Windhoek.

Crowe, Dr D. 1995. 'Status of wildlife in Botswana'. *Kalahari Conservation Society Newsletter* 47, Gaborone.

Debenham, F. 1953. *Kalahari Sand*. G. Bell & Sons, London.

Galton, F. 1853. *The narrative of an Explorer in Tropical South Africa*. John Murray, London.

Hutchins, D.G., Hutton, S.M. & Jones, C.R. 1976. 'The geology of the Okavango Delta'. *Proceedings of the symposium on the Okavango Delta and its future utilisation*. Botswana Society, Gaborone.

Holt-Biddle, D. 1994. 'A regional survey'. *Vision of Wildlife, Ecotourism and the Environment in Southern Africa. 1995 Annual*. Endangered Wildlife Trust, Johannesburg.

Kay, J. 1962. *Okavango*. Hutchinson, London.

Kriegskarte von Deutsch-Südwestafrika. 1904. Berlin.

Le Roux, S. 1939. *Pioneeers and Sportsmen of South Africa*. S.D. Le Roux, Salisbury (Harare).

Lewis-Williams, D. 1989. *Images of Power*. Southern Book Publishers, Halfway House.

Loutit, B. 1988a. 'The Damaraland Rhino'. *African Wildlife* 2.

— 1988b. 'The Skeleton Coast'. *African Wildlife* 2.

Livingstone, D. 1857. *Missionary Travels and Researches in Southern Africa*. John Murray, London.

McNutt, J. & N. 1990. 'African Wild Dogs – An important research project needs your help'. *Kalahari Conservation Society Newsletter* 29, Gaborone.

Meyers, N. 1972. *The Long African Day*. Macmillan, London.

Oliver, W. & S. 1989. *Visitors' Guide to Namibia*. Southern Book Publishers, Johannesburg.

Orford, R. 1988. 'Culling Lions is not the answer'. *African Wildlife* 2.

Oswell, W.E. 1900. *William Cotton Oswell: Hunter and Explorer*. William Heinemann, London.

Owen-Smith, G. & Jacobsohn, M. 1989. 'Involving a local community in wildlife conservation'. *Quagga* 27.

Patterson, L. 1976. 'An introduction to the ecology and zoogeography of the Okavango Delta'. *Proceedings of the symposium on the Okavango Delta and its future utilisation*. Botswana Society, Gaborone.

Perkins, Dr J.S. 1995. 'Where has all the wildlife gone?' *Kalahari Conservation Society Newsletter* 47, Gaborone.

Potten, D. 1976. 'Etsha: A successful resettlement scheme'. *Botswana Notes and Records* 8, Gaborone.

Schapera, I. (ed.) 1959. *David Livingstone Family Letters, 1841-1856*. Chatto & Windus, London.

— 1960. *Livingstone's Private Journals, 1851-1853*. Chatto & Windus, London.

— 1961. *Livingstone's Private Correspondence, 1841-1856*. Chatto & Windus, London.

— 1963. *Livingstone's African Journal, 1853-1856*. Chatto & Windus, London.

Schoeman, A. 1996. *Skeleton Coast*. Southern Book Publishers, Halfway House.

Shaw, P. 1983. 'Fluctuations in the level of Lake Ngami: the historical evidence'. *Botswana Notes and Records* 15, Gaborone.

Smith, E.W. 1957. *Great Lion of Bechuanaland – The Life and Times of Roger Price*. Independent Press for the London Missionary Society, London.

Spinage, C. 1992. 'Botswana's problem elephants'. *The Rhino and Elephant Journal* 6, Johannesburg.

Swakopmund Municipality. 1987. *Swakopmund – SWA/Namibia's Premier Holiday Resort*.

Tlou, T. 1976. 'The peopling of the Okavango Delta, c. 1750-1906'. *Proceedings of the symposium on the Okavango Delta and its future utilisation*. Botswana Society, Gaborone.

Thomas, D. 1986. 'Ancient deserts revealed'. *The Geographical Magazine*, London.

Viljoen, S. 1988. 'The desert-dwelling elephant'. *African Wildlife* 2.

Wickens, P. 1995. 'Namibian sealing débâcle'. *African Wildlife* 3.

Williams, T. 1988. 'Walvis Bay and other coastal gems'. *African Wildlife* 2.

Winchester-Gould, G.A. 1968. *The Guide to Botswana*. Winchester Press, Johannesburg.

233

INDEX

Sossusvlei – Namib Desert.

Paul Augustinus